"Why has it taken so long for someone to write such
a brilliant and necessary cookbook?"
Stanley Tucci

"With considerable charm and sage words, Angela Clutton
affirms the vital roles of cooking and eating seasonally."
Jeremy Lee

"Angela Clutton's new book *Seasoning* proves once again that she
is one of the most compelling food writers in the UK. Elegant,
exquisite and entertaining, it celebrates the miracles of the seasons
with accessible recipes and gorgeous prose. It deserves a place on
every home cook's bookshelf."
Russell Norman

"Informative, useful, inspirational and so delicious!"
Claudia Roden

"*Seasoning* is so much more than a cookbook; it's a guide to why
certain foods taste better when, and why cooking in concert
with the seasons not only promotes sustainability but leads to
unforgettable meals. Common in-season fare, when placed in
Clutton's hands, becomes uncommonly spectacular."
Bonnie Garmus

SEASONING

For Mum & Dad – without knowing
it, you taught me the joy of seasonal
cooking and living. I think you'd have
liked this one x

Angela Clutton

SEASONING

How to cook and celebrate the seasons

Photography by Patricia Niven / Illustrations by Georgina Luck

murdoch books
London | Sydney

Winter

Spring

Why Does Seasonality Matter in a Modern Kitchen?

That is the question I have kept asking myself throughout the writing of this book. The answers lie at the heart of every vegetable and fruit profile; every recipe, tip, idea and suggestion; and in the choices I have made of which produce to feature and when.

We all know our globalised food system and modern production techniques mean so many of our favourite vegetables and fruits are now around far beyond their traditional seasonality. There is some good in that, for sure. Our world has a lot of people to feed; we have become used to choice; and society feels it has earned the right to have what it wants when it wants it. But there is quite a lot wrong, and damaging, about that approach too.

Producing vast quantities of vegetables and fruits outside their natural season requires significant energy for artificial heating and light. Then yet more energy is needed to store them so they can last as long as possible. And then the chances are that where they have been produced is quite a long way from where they are going to be sold/eaten, so there's all the transportation to factor in – time spent in storage and travelling, which is also never to the benefit of flavour and can often result in food being spoiled and wasted. Choosing to shop, cook and eat more seasonally is a powerful and effective way to make it clear that this is not a basis for a food system that you support.

Beyond even the significant environmental costs (see page 10 for more on climate change, food production and our shifting seasons), food that's produced like this misses out the sheer delicious delight that exists in how the seasonality of land and climate have a unique ability to make things taste the best possible versions of themselves. Winter frosts bring out the sugars of sprouts and parsnips; sunshine doesn't just make summer's peaches sweet but come with depth of flavour too....

The good news is that we are all getting a bit better at knowing all this. There is a growing real-world emphasis on the importance of eating more seasonally, more locally, and moving away from processed or ultra-processed foods. The priorities behind so much of modern cooking – sustainability, simplicity, satisfaction, convenience, cost – share their axis point with the very heart of *Seasoning*. Without doubt, the best way to eat sustainably, healthily, economically and fabulously is to load up on seasonal produce, then be able to keep on reincarnating those through their season.

The motivation behind writing *Seasoning* is to empower the confidence and know-how in being able to do exactly that. To help us all get out of culinary ruts of how we cook – or don't – with certain things. To instead build a culinary arsenal of so many ways to cook, prepare and partner produce that mean we are more likely to want to enjoy it for the duration of its true season.

Taking time to think about why eating seasonally matters so much has made me realise too how important particular times of the year are in connecting food and memory. I think about my mum in a strappy sundress, with her freshly painted toenails drying in the sun while she scrubbed the skins of new potatoes. Standing back watching my dad wield what now seems to me was a very ineffective extendable apple-picker whose claw was reluctant to ever grab the fruit. Podding peas side by side with my mum and sisters for countless school holiday summers and then again years later in the first summer after my dad died. Those memories are all grounded in their seasons.

Even the produce in *Seasoning* that is generally accepted as now being available year-round is here anchored into a particular season or seasons to encourage reconnection with its seasonality. To get back to the arc of the food year that nature gifts us. I don't know about you but I really want to feel the excitement of the first summertime tomatoes and strawberries. There's even a point to the boredom of winter's roots by the end of their season. I want food that fills me with anticipation, surprise, nostalgia, tedium – because that is life. There is joy in not being able to have everything all the time, but in looking forward to something – and then missing it when it is gone.

In writing, researching and cooking for *Seasoning* I've had to really push myself out of my own comfort zone. I hope so much that the result is a book that can be a culinary toolkit and kitchen companion for both less experienced and more knowledgeable cooks alike. A guide for us all on how to maximise the foods and flavours of the seasons. Like adding seasoning to a dish, I want *Seasoning* to make the produce we embrace in our kitchens taste better than ever.

London, 2023

Seasoning in the Kitchen

Seasons

Seasoning is structured by chapters of the four main seasons, while recognising the reality of how these seasons morph and meld into each other. Vegetables and fruits often cross over with the season before or the one just coming. I urge you to embrace that flow of seasonality in your kitchen.

The season(s) marked in bold beneath a produce heading mean that is when the produce is at its prime and most available. Seasons marked in italics refer to when it is still around, just less prime and less available. Where vegetables or fruits also have year-round interest that is marked too.

Vegetables and fruits

Each chapter begins with a reminder of what you might want to look out for either side of the season's main produce that is being featured. Next come profiles of the season's vegetables and fruits:

- **Shop** is about knowing what to look for, and understanding how produce changes through its season and as it ages. It is certainly not about only choosing perfection.
- **Store** mostly means, as a broad brush-stroke, to get things out of any plastic-y packaging asap. Beyond that, each section has detailed tips to prolong produce life.
- **Ways to Use** includes ideas to get us out of always going back to the same tried-and-trusted ways of preparing vegetables and fruits. The more we can mix up what we do with them, the more we can keep on enjoying every last scrap of produce for the length of its season. Also includes tips for using peels, pods, trimmings and more.
- **Flavour Partners** offers inspiration for which flavours to put together. Please think of each bolded ingredient as a nudge to use it with that vegetable or fruit, beyond even whatever particular dish I am urging it towards there. The more confident and comfortable we can all get with putting flavours together, the more intuitive a cook we can all be.
- **Preserve** notes are steers on how to make that vegetable or fruit's flavour presence felt at other times of the year, and also minimise waste.

Meat, fish and dairy

I think their seasonality is too often forgotten or ignored – to the detriment of delight, and the environment. Woven through the season's chapters are thoughts on how these too can be more sustainably incorporated into seasonal cooking.

Recipes and feasts

The tips, suggestions and nudges that make up each produce profile are then brought to life in recipes to suit the culinary mood of the seasons.

These come together into seasonal feasting menu ideas at the conclusion of each chapter. Again, please look to the season before and the next one for ideas of more dishes to put together with what and when. The feasts also include ideas for a seasonal cocktail and simple nature-inspired table decorations.

Ingredients

- Dairy (milk, cream, crème fraîche, yoghurt, etc.) is always full fat.
- A recipe will say whether using salted or unsalted butter particularly matters. Mostly it doesn't as you will be tasting and seasoning a dish as you go along anyway. The butter I use at home is always lightly salted.
- Where no size of egg is specified, again assume that it doesn't particularly matter. I tend to use large eggs, around 60g (2¼oz).
- For sizes of whole vegetables and fruits, I have tried to include weights or dimensions where important to recipe success. Otherwise, go for medium-sized options.

It all builds into what I hope is a cookbook for how we live and eat now, and how we will need to live and eat moving forward: Mindful of seasonality, choosing local produce, seeking balance across the food choices we make, and with absolutely no need at all to compromise on deliciousness.

Shifting Seasons

Seasoning has forced me to really stop and think
– and think, and think – about our perceptions
of seasonality. I suspect I started off with what I
thought was a clear idea of what the seasons were,
and when. Of what they mean for the produce that
is available through the year for us to cook and eat.
What I have discovered is that embracing
seasonality is about understanding the rhythms of
the land and the climate. Even, or especially, as it changes.
Our world is warming and as a consequence our seasons
are shifting. In the UK the weather conventions of our seasons are that winter is
December–February; spring is March–May; summer is June–August; and autumn
September–November[1]. Broadly those still feel right, yet what I feel happening each
year is what the data backs up: Winters are shorter and milder; summers longer and
hotter; springs and autumns shorter[2].

Think about spring, and the joy it is hard not to feel when we get some warmth
earlier than expected. How good it is to have sunshine and to sit outside for the
first time in perhaps months. The trees and flowers may not feel so cheered. Higher
temperatures will make them get a head start on blossoming, thinking that spring
really is here. Except it isn't. Early springs bring very real risk (likelihood?) of frosts,
and an already blossomed tree or flower will be significantly damaged.

Extend that thinking across crops and then understand that in 2017 British apple
growers lost around 25% of their harvest due to frosts after blossoming. In 2018,
carrot and onion crops were hugely damaged by warmer than average temperatures.
In 2012, North America's earliest ever spring was followed by frosts that caused $500m
of damage to fruit and vegetable crops that year in just one state (Michigan)[3].

The problems are about even more than early springs. The shifting seasons mean
that species that are used to having each other to rely on at certain times of year may
not have that any more. There is increased risk of droughts damaging crops. Crop
pests will survive better in milder winters.

If all this sounds rather bleak and depressing, well it's meant to. A global study[2] on shifting seasons and climate change produced a prediction for a seasonal clock in 2100. If patterns continue as they are, that clock shows autumn and winter shrink to being together roughly only three months of the year.

Change lies with power. Meaning governments and money. But we as cooks and consumers are powerful, too. Read this from a report by the European Food Information Council:

"The overall picture that emerges from research, is that the fruit and vegetables with the lowest GHG [greenhouse gas] emissions are those that are grown outside during their natural season without much use of additional energy and consumed in the same country or region. These have environmental benefits because they use less energy for artificial heating or lighting, for refrigeration and storage and avoid losses during storage, which generally helps to produce less GHG emissions, compared to fruit and vegetables that are grown under protection, are imported or stored."[4]

Which is cheering. Not least because it means there are positive food choices we can make. Ones that I think anyone with the privilege of choices has a responsibility to make. Ones that can play a real part in slowing the shifting of our seasons.

[1] https://www.metoffice.gov.uk

[2] *Changing Lengths of the Four Seasons* by Global Warming - Jiamin Wang, Yuping Guan, Lixin Wu, Xiaodan Guan, Wenju Cai, Jianping Huang, Wenjie Dong, Banglin Zhang

[3] https://geographical.co.uk/climate-change/as-the-world-warms-the-seasons-are-shifting

[4] https://www.eufic.org/en/healthy-living/article/are-seasonal-fruit-and-vegetables-better-for-the-environment

Summer

Summer's arrival comes with more than the welcome warmth on our arms. Its smells – like rain at the end of a hot day – evoke the season like no other time of year can. So much of the summer produce here comes with my urgings to smell them. Tomatoes, strawberries, cucumber, peaches, peppers.... To test them for freshness and flavour, yes. But also because the foods that taste of summer are the ones that carry its scent in our memories.

There is a laidback ease to how summer's vegetables and fruits can be prepared and enhanced. Summer cooking works best with dishes that can be made ahead in relative cool and calm; and that are then not just fine to leave until it's time to eat but actually improve that way. Who wants to be dashing about in a hot kitchen on a hot day (especially if you've just got in from a hot journey after work)? Not me. So this is about tomatoes bathing in sunshine, olive oil and salt; cherries with quick-pickled radishes; cooling cucumber soups; roasted strawberries, and many more ways with more of the produce that always tastes best in its true season.

Spring	In Season	Autumn
Asparagus	Aubergines (eggplants)	Beetroot
roccoli – purple and white sprouting, and Calabrese	Lamb, hogget, mutton	Celery
Elderflower and other spring blossoms	Broad (fava) beans and garden peas	Fennel
Lettuces	Courgettes (zucchini) and other summer squash	Leeks
New potatoes	Cucumbers	Hake
Radishes	Mackerel	Maincrop potatoes
oats' and sheep's cheeses	Summer carrots	Pumpkins and other winter squash
Soft herbs	Sweet peppers (capsicums)	Apples, pears and quince
Watercress and baby spinach	Tomatoes	Blackberries and elderberries
Trout	Cherries	Figs
Wild garlic	Raspberries and strawberries	
Gooseberries	Stone fruits – peaches, nectarines, apricots, plums	

Featured Recipes

Aubergines / Lamb

Marinated Poached Aubergines in Garlic and Oregano

Slow-roasted Chermoula Lamb Shoulder with Aubergine Cream

Broad Beans and Garden Peas

Creamed Spinach and Broad Bean Tart

Pea and Tarragon Carnaroli Rice

Courgettes and Summer Squash

Courgette and Cucumber Soup with Courgette Flowers

Patty Pan Squash with Dried Shrimps, Ginger and Lime

Cucumbers / Mackerel

Cucumber, Elderflower and Gin (or Lime) Ice Lollies

Mackerel with Cucumber, Samphire, Tomatoes and Cream

Summer Carrots

Summer Carrots with Little Gem and Salted Almonds

Sweet Peppers

Black Olive, Shallot and Tomato Stuffed Peppers

Tomatoes

Arranque (Tomato, Pepper and Garlic Dip)

The Sweetest Tomato Salad

Cherries

White Bean, Pickled Radish and Cherry Salad

Raspberries and Strawberries

Roasted Strawberry Zabaglione with Cardamom Biscuits

Fluffy Raspberry Pancakes with Raspberry Syrup

Stone Fruits

Apricot and Lavender Choux Buns

Three Summer Fruits, Two Summer Salads:

*Savoury Fruit Salad with Spring Onion,
Lime, Mirin and Chilli*

Sweet Fruit Salad with Mint and Lime

Summer Feasting

Peaches in Champagne

Aubergines

Summer – *Autumn* – *Year Round*

For years it seemed to me that the only way I encountered (and ignored) aubergines (eggplants) was lurking in sad, overcooked, mushy, ratatouille-esque misery. But then their reputation was rescued by mass charring and blitzing. Baba ganoush hit the big time and opened up our culinary minds to just how much you can do with them.

Summer's heat and sun make for the best aubergines. Time spent growing in both results in vegetables (technically fruits, but we think of them as veg) as taut and shiny as a Venice Beach body-builder. Their mix of sizes, shapes and colours brings much potential in the ways to use them even if their flavour is similar across varieties:

Mediterranean/Italian aubergines – The most commonly available aubergines, with skins so deeply richly purple they're almost the glossy black patent of my beloved school shoes. Great for stuffing, roasting, sautéing, baba ganoushing.

Sicilian aubergines – The same shape and size as more mainstream Italian ones, with purple and white striped skin. The colour distinctions sadly disappear on cooking.

Chinese and Japanese aubergines – Long and slender, with skin that is a far paler purple. Thin-skinned and seedless. Think pickling and grilling.

Indian aubergines – These dinky round, plump ones are especially good for stuffing. Often called baby aubergines.

Thai aubergines – Green or white. Round, and small enough to be used whole.

Shop

- Look for shiny skin with gorgeous gloss and vibrancy. No wrinkles, no bruising. Older aubergines are more bitter, and easy to spot as they are losing their shine.
- Hold it and hope it feels hard and heavy.
- Look where the stem meets the skin, and see if its points are sitting down smoothly. If not, the aubergine is already drying out.
- Don't worry too much about dark spots on the skin if everything else checks out – they're often just caused by overly tight packaging.

Store

- Somewhere cool, dry and dark. The fridge is fine but a cool larder even better. Keep them in a cloth or paper bag.
- Don't store aubergines anywhere near potatoes or onions as they'll make the aubergines go off quicker.

Ways to Use

Whatever you do with them, aubergines will absorb fats and flavours like little else can. It's their blessing and their curse.

Salting aubergines to draw out bitter moisture used to be a necessary step in their prep. Less so now as modern aubergines are bred to be not so bitter as their ancestors. (That said, older aubergines – those less shiny ones – will have developed larger seeds inside that do make the flesh bitter, so they might need salting.)

These days, drying aubergines out a little by salting is mostly useful to avoid ending up with over-mushy aubergines when sautéing and frying. It helps achieve the aubergine holy grail of tender flesh inside crispy skin. Simply cut them as per your recipe and put into a colander, scatter over salt, toss, leave to drain for 30 minutes–1 hour, then pat dry in kitchen paper and use. Bear in mind they'll have taken on some salt, so go steady with seasoning the rest of the dish.

Charring gives fabulous smoky depth to aubergines as they cook. The skins blister, then split open, then almost collapse to reveal delicious flesh that can then be blitzed with so many other ingredients and flavours into dips, soups and sauces, or even just spread onto bread that's been rubbed with a garlic clove. There are a few ways to char:
- Over fire, put whole aubergines into a bed of charcoal or the embers at a fire's edge.
- Use a direct gas flame on the hob. Put kitchen foil over the base of the hob to help minimise mess. Sit the aubergine directly on a medium flame and use tongs to rotate it as each side burns and blisters.
- A very hot oven won't give quite the smokiness but still works well. Pierce the aubergine so it doesn't explode, and put into the oven at 220°C fan/475°F/gas 9 or at the highest grill setting. Again, rotate as it chars.

Aubergines work brilliantly when roasted whole, halved, in chunks or slices. Make sure the oven is hot at 200°C fan/425°F/gas 7, and they have oil to enjoy. For roasting whole or halved aubergines: Score the skins, brush with oil, roast until browning and shrivelling. Adding a marinade/sauce partway through the cooking time allows its flavours to really get in there with the ever-absorbent aubergine as it cooks.

To stuff large aubergines: Cut in half, scoop out the centre, chop and cook that inner flesh with whatever other ingredients you want to stuff it with, pile it all back in, and bake. To stuff baby aubergines: Slice through the aubergines as if quartering them lengthways – taking care not to cut through the stem – then open each one up like a flower, stuff and bake.

Aubergines' love of oil lends them well to deep or shallow frying. Salt them and drain as above so they don't become too soggy; then dip batons or slices in a light batter (see the tempura on page 280) or rub the slices with flour, polenta and/or semolina so they take on as little oil as possible. They'll need just a few minutes to cook in hot 185°C/365°F oil. Deep-fried batons are a bit like aubergine fries, and there's a lot to love about those.

Cut long lengths of large aubergines, each slice no more than 1cm (½in) thick, to brush with oil and fry or griddle until tenderly charring. Use the slices to roll up a stuffing or some pesto; or simply dress the slices and serve.

Steaming aubergines lets their truest flavours ring out independently. Steam batons for 5 or so minutes until tender, then drain on kitchen paper, and serve straight away before the colour of their flesh can go a bit murky. Plenty of salt and some hefty dashes of vinegar are simple and brilliant here, or serve with all kinds of oils, sauces and salsas that will be soaked up.

Recipes that say to peel aubergines first will be doing that for a couple of reasons: The skin can be bitter and/or it is easier to remove the skin before cooking than after.

Flavour Partners

The word aubergine comes through French, Catalan, Arabic, Persian and Sanskrit roots. Let those be your culinary inspirations while also remembering that aubergines are such brilliant fat and flavour carriers. Go big and go bold or maybe don't bother – this is not the place for nuance.

Aubergines' baba ganoush bedfellows of **lemon**, **garlic**, **olive oil** and **tahini** are stalwarts for all kinds of aubergine dishes.

Dress griddled slices of aubergines with **capers**, **anchovies**, **basil** and **orange**. Scatter over **mint**, fresh or dried, and roll them around a stuffing that is packed with **feta** and chopped **preserved lemon**.

Fatty meats such as **lamb** and **chorizo** will readily give their flavour to aubergine chunks or slices. Such partnerships are especially good for low and slow cooking of stews or similar, where the flavours really have time to get acquainted.

Paprika, **cumin** and **lime** juice make a fabulous marinade for batons or slices before deep frying; or to pour over aubergines midway through their roasting. As would **miso paste** with **mirin** and **fennel seeds**.

Some **ground ginger** in there would work well, as that flavour so often does with aubergine. Mix ground or grated fresh ginger in a sauce of **sesame oil**, garlic, **sugar** and a little **stock**; then use to toss with steamed aubergine batons once they are cooked, with **sesame seeds** sprinkled over to finish.

Or release in hot oil the flavours of grated **root ginger** plus **cinnamon**, **cardamom**, allspice and chopped **chillies** (perhaps with a chopped and sautéed **onion** or two in the pan as well) before adding cubed aubergines to sauté, or mixing with the silky purée of charred aubergine flesh.

For real depth, reach for spice blends like **garam masala**, **ras-el-hanout**, **chermoula**, **za'atar** or **Chinese five spice**. **Yoghurt** sauces can help calm things down for balance when needed. **Coconut milk** does the same job, as in the aubergine sambol of Sri Lankan cook and food writer Cynthia Shanmugalingam. She roasts aubergines to a char, then mashes their flesh and smoky skins with coconut milk plus sliced **green chillies**, diced **curry leaves** and lime juice. It's a superb dip for bread or roti.

Aubergines love the heat and the sun, so partner them with other produce that feels the same. They'll enjoy being cooked alongside and served with **courgettes** (zucchini), **peppers** (capsicums), and smacked **cucumbers**. **Tomatoes**, too – whether in parmigiana, caponata, moussaka, or the glory of so many Turkish dishes.

More flavour thoughts: **Burrata**; **cashews**; **dates** and **date molasses**; **juniper**; **mozzarella**; **mustard seeds**; **oregano**; **pine nuts**; **pomegranate seeds** and **molasses**; **soy sauces**; **spring onions (scallions)**; **sultanas** (golden raisins); **sumac**; **vinegar** (Chinkiang black, red wine or sherry); **walnuts**.

Preserve

Pickle: Poach baby aubergines in water until tender, drain, make incisions in the skin to stuff with small slivers of garlic or celery, then immerse in pickling brine in a jar.

In oil: Try makdous, baby aubergines stuffed with a mix of walnuts, garlic and chilli, then submerged in oil in a jar and kept for 2 weeks. (See also recipe on page 20.)

In sugar: Turn very small, thin aubergines into sweet preserves. Cut off the end and peel away a few strips of skin. Poach in water until tender. Make a sugar syrup enhanced with cloves, ginger and lemon peel, then submerge the aubergines in the syrup in a jar. In the 'spoon sweets' custom of hospitality across Greece Cyprus and parts of the Middle East these would be served with coffee or simply a glass of water. There's more of a recipe in Claudia Roden's *A New Book of Middle Eastern Food* (and more on page 20 about Claudia's contribution to the aubergine's renaissance).

Marinated Poached Aubergines in Garlic and Oregano

This recipe is inspired – as so much modern aubergine cooking is – by a recipe in Claudia Roden's *A New Book of Middle Eastern Food*. When it first came out in 1968 she was using foods and flavours to make dishes that, at the time, were little heard of outside their own culinary world. Claudia has inspired the work of Yotam Ottolenghi and any of us who seek to bring a little of that flavour sunshine into our home kitchens wherever we are.

Having a jar of these preserved aubergines on hand in the fridge is a terrifically useful way of doing just that. The aubergines all done and ready to serve as part of a mezze, to layer into sandwiches, to top pizzas with, add to a salad....

For 1 x 500ml (17fl oz) jar
1 aubergine (eggplant),
    about 350g (12oz)
250ml (8½fl oz) cider vinegar
2 large garlic cloves

1 tbsp dried oregano
1 tsp salt
around 150ml (5fl oz) extra-virgin
    olive oil

Sterilise a 500ml (17fl oz) glass jar.

Trim and peel the aubergine, then cut into rounds about 1cm (½in) thick. Transfer to a medium saucepan, pour over the vinegar, and then enough water to just about cover. Bring to the boil, then turn the heat down to a low simmer. Partially cover the pan with a lid and cook for 20–30 minutes until translucent. As each slice is ready, lift it out with a slotted spoon onto a plate. Set aside to cool.

Peel and finely slice the garlic cloves. Put a third of the aubergine slices into the jar and top with a third of the garlic, oregano and salt. Do two more layers to use up all the aubergines, garlic, oregano and salt. Now pour over enough olive oil to submerge the aubergines. Seal and put into the fridge.

They are ready to use in 5 days. As long as the aubergines are kept under oil, and the jar is kept in the fridge, they should keep for up to 3 months.

Lamb, Hogget, Mutton

Do you, like me, want the lamb that you buy and eat to be one that's had some time outside, eating lush grass? That has been enjoying the depth of flavour that varied pasture can give its meat, and been moving around enough for its muscles to develop flavour too? Then midsummer onwards is the time to start buying lamb.

While it is true to say that different breeds of sheep can have their lambs at different times of year, for the broad majority of breeds the lambing season is spring and early summer. Which means that when 'new season' lamb is for sale in the spring, we've really got to take a moment and wonder what those are. The suggestion is somehow that they are spring-born lambs. For that to be true they would have been slaughtered while still very young and be milk lamb – a highly prized speciality of lambs that are still at the milk-feeding stage, and have the tenderest young meat. If that is what the butcher is selling, you and your wallet will know it.

No, the widely sold and marketed 'new season' spring lambs aren't that. Mostly they are lambs from sheep that have given birth in winter, out of their usual season. The cold weather means they've been kept indoors, there's precious little grass around for them to feed on, and they'll be quickly matured in order to hit the sales deadlines. That doesn't exactly match the image that supermarkets and butchers want us to literally buy, of spring lambs frolicking in a field. Lamb from midsummer onwards is what gets closer to that image.

As does hogget – a sheep in its second year. By the time they are hoggets these sheep will not just have had the chance to enjoy the kind of longer, more natural life that matters to conscientious meat-eaters, but the kind of life that results in better-tasting meat too. Whenever I give in to the pressure of serving 'lamb' for the family spread in the spring, I make sure it is actually hogget I'm getting. Or even mutton. That is what sheep at over two years old become. Mutton should wear its age with pride. When reared and cooked well, it can be the most delicious version of sheep meat of them all.

Lean into lamb's summer vibes by putting it with light seasonal produce. Use soft herbs liberally. Lamb famously loves rosemary, so give that combination a summery edge by switching it for lavender instead (the two botanicals share flavour profiles). Perhaps some lavender sprigs nestled into a vegetable bed for a joint to roast upon, or dressing an accompanying peach salad with a smattering of pestled lavender buds.

Slow-roasted Chermoula Lamb Shoulder with Aubergine Cream

The delight of this roasted joint is that it starts off with the aubergine rounds making a bed for the meat. There they can take on its fat and juices as the lamb cooks, with the spicy chermoula and sherry vinegar marinade seeping into them too. The lamb then carries on to cook into tenderness, and the aubergines are blitzed to a creamy sauce with garlic and yoghurt. Simple and delicious.

Save any leftover aubergine cream to toss over hot new potatoes, or spread on bread.

Serves 6–8 as a main

6 garlic cloves

1½ tbsp chermoula spice (not paste)

75ml (2½fl oz) olive oil

1½ tbsp sherry vinegar

1.2kg (2lb 11oz) aubergines (eggplants)

about 2.8kg (6lb 4oz) lamb shoulder

225g (8oz) Greek yoghurt

2 tsp lemon juice

handful of mint sprigs

salt and black pepper

Preheat the oven to 220°C fan/475°F/gas 9.

Peel 4 garlic cloves, crush, put into a mortar with a good pinch of salt and pestle to a paste. Mix with the chermoula, oil and vinegar to make a loose paste.

Trim and peel the aubergines, and then slice into rounds, 1cm (½in) thick. Lay them in a large roasting tin, arranging the aubergines to be roughly the same size as the lamb. Sit the lamb skin-side up on top of the aubergines. Pierce its skin several times with the point of a sharp knife. Rub the chermoula paste over the skin. Loosely cover the roasting tin with foil, put into the oven and immediately turn the oven down to 170°C fan/375°F/gas 5.

After 1½ hours, take the tin out and gently lift up the lamb to remove the aubergine slices. Some might be stuck to the base of the joint – be sure to get them all. Put the aubergines slices into a sieve set over a bowl to drain. Pour 200ml (7fl oz) hot water into the roasting tin (but not over the meat), cover it again, return to the oven and turn the temperature down to 140°C fan/300°F/gas 2. Roast for a further 2½ hours, then put the oven back up to 220°C fan/475°F/gas 9, take off the foil, and return to the oven for a final 20 minutes. Carefully lift out the lamb and set aside to rest.

Make the aubergine cream while the lamb rests: Peel and roughly chop the remaining 2 garlic cloves. Blitz the aubergine flesh with the garlic, yoghurt and lemon juice. Season, being particularly generous with the salt. Finely chop the mint leaves from one of the mint sprigs and scatter over. Serve with more mint to garnish.

Broad Beans and Garden Peas

Summer

There's not much better than sitting outside on a warm (can I even hope for hot?) day with a bag of broad (fava) beans or garden peas, and time. Time to enjoy meditatively podding them from their shells. To let the mind wander from thoughts of tasks still to be done... emails to be returned... friends to be reconnected with... and then suddenly find you're thinking of nothing at all. Runners say that pounding the streets achieves that state of zen for them. I say get it from peas.

Would I feel the same way if it was a year-round job? I suspect not. The novelty of the task, and how it coincides with the calm that warm breezy days bring to the kitchen, is undoubtedly part of the charm of podding. It can only be done – and is only worth doing – when they are bang in season, and ideally as soon as possible once the pods have been harvested.

As the pods age the broad beans and peas go from bright, perky and sweetly grassy; to starchy, bland and dull. It's why we all love the frozen bags of these so much – they capture the pea (or bean) at its best. The notes to come can certainly also apply to using frozen garden peas and broad beans, as well as to that particular variety of small, extra-sweet pea we know as petits pois. But get some garden peas and broad beans in their pods in their peak of season, pod them yourself, let your mind wander, and then wonder if their better-than-ever flavour is the result of their freshness, or the satisfaction of having taken a pause in your day to pod.

Shop

- The key is to get pods as recently as possible to them being harvested, as they will start to age and lose flavour as soon as they are picked. Look for pods that are bright green and vibrant.
- Don't worry if there are any slightly blackened tendrils of pea or broad bean shoot at the pods' ends. It's normal for those to wilt quickly.
- Broad beans are the Goldilocks of the bean world: they need to be neither too small, nor too big, but just right. The definition of plump beans should be visible as knuckle bumps in the pods. Lack of any bean definition probably means they are small and under-formed. (It's no good waiting for them to grow/ripen once picked – they won't.) Nor do you want them bulging like an action hero's bicep, as that will mean they have matured too much and started to go starchy.
- As a rough approximation (weights will vary from pod to pod):
  1kg (2lb 4oz) garden peas in their pods = 400g (14oz) podded peas
  1kg (2lb 4oz) broad beans in their pods = 300g (10½oz) podded broad beans

Store

- Peas and broad beans keep best in their pods, but will be deteriorating in freshness all the time. Use them as quickly as you can upon buying. Store in paper bags, in the fridge crisper drawer.

Ways to Use

Fresh from the pod
The youngest garden peas and broad beans can be sweetly tender enough to enjoy straight from their pods. Find out if you can do that with yours by simply having a nibble of one, then toss into a salad.

Or start a late-spring/early-summer meal as the Tuscans would, as described by Italian food writer Anna Del Conte: "... when the broad beans are still young and their skin is tender ... put the unpodded broad beans in a bowl and let everybody get on with it."

As a side, for salads, braised, into rices, pasta and pies

Anything other than very small, young broad beans need to be double-podded of the skins they develop as they age. Pod them, simmer for 3 minutes in well-salted water until tender, drain and refresh under cold water to stop them cooking any further, then slip off the skin on each bean to reveal a gleaming, glistening, bright green broad bean underneath.

Peas just need to be popped out of their pods, blanched and refreshed as above, to be ready to use.

Simply dress pre-cooked broad beans or peas with oil/butter, a few herbs, salt and pepper, and serve. Add a little cream or crème fraîche for richness.

Toss them into a warm or room-temperature salad; or add into a frittata.

Skip the pre-cooking of peas where the dish they are headed into gives enough time in heat to tenderise them:
- Braising with other flavours and stock, wine or cider – as in the recipe for Braised Little Gems with Shallots, Pancetta and Peas on page 293.
- Adding into a risotto or pilaf, or all kinds of pastas.
- Mixing into a pie filling.
- Stir frying.

  (Broad beans will still need to be pre-cooked and double-podded in all these.)

Crushes and purées

Keep things simple by using the back of a fork to crush some cooked peas or broad beans, season, then pile that onto toast. Amp up that basic idea with herbs or spices, a little oil or vinegar. For more of a side dish, cook the crush with a little cream, crème fraîche or yoghurt. Blitz it if you are in the mood for something smoother.

Use roughly crushed/blitzed peas and broad beans for fritters, koftas and pakoras. Crushing is an especially great use for starchier, older broad beans – perhaps as a side, or to make into falafel.

Pods

Podding peas and beans means you will, inevitably, end up with a pile of empty pods. These are absolutely packed with goodness and flavour, and far, far too good to just head straight into the food bin or composter.

Try tossing the empty pea pods in a little seasoned flour and spices, then shallow fry them whole.

Use the pods in the stock for the Pea and Tarragon Carnaroli Rice on page 30. Or add them to a freezer bag for later soup/stock making. Even once they have given their flavour to stock the pea pods are still too good to throw away. They are then tender enough to be blitzed with more or less of the stock for pea-pod soup/pea-pod purée for a dip.

Flavour Partners

The flavour affinity between garden peas and broad beans makes them great to have together, and to use almost interchangeably with other flavour partners.

Leafy salads and the braised lettuce on page 293 will be just as happy with either. Same with other seasonal produce: Try tumbles of roasted new potatoes and summer carrots with peas/broad beans tossed over; young peas and broad beans with radishes; fry off courgettes (zucchini), then add peas/broad beans at the end; sit them on a bed of coarsely grated tomatoes; tear wild garlic leaves through pea and broad bean braises.

When raw, asparagus has a gentle pea-like flavour. Give the cooked spears a little of their pea-ness back by putting them together in salads, risottos, pastas or soups.

All these combinations of peas and broad beans with other seasonal produce will benefit from having some soft seasonal herbs added too. Mint is the classic. Basil is brilliant. The slightly bitter anise notes of tarragon, dill and chervil offer a pleasing counter to the peas' (or beans') innate sweetness, as does sorrel with its lemon notes.

Achieve similar lift with preserved lemon in salads; sherry vinegar for dressings; yoghurt stirred through hot peas/broad beans in the pan.

Peas (and broad beans) have an umami side to them that means they'll enjoy anything else in that line of flavours. Add miso to a dressing with sesame oil and a light soy sauce. Serve scallops on a blitzed pea or broad bean bed. Toss them in towards the end of the cooking time for a one-pot of chicken thighs and stock. Fry off diced pancetta with peas and broad beans. Add them to a smoked fish risotto or kedgeree. Remember that lamb is just coming into the glory of its summer flavours (see page 21) and serve with very simply cooked peas and broad beans.

Scatter fennel seeds over a block of feta, drizzle over honey, bake it and then serve with peas/broad beans and herbs. The Pea and Tarragon Carnaroli Rice on page 30 shows off how much Parmesan loves peas and it is more than okay with broad beans. What I missed out of my earlier Anna Del Conte quote was that in Tuscany they do not just have those young, raw broad beans on their own – there are wedges of pecorino at the table too.

More flavour thoughts: Black mustard seeds; butter; coriander seeds; cream; cucumber; cumin; root ginger; horseradish; nutmeg; saffron; shallots; spring onions (scallions); trout; vermouth.

Preserve

Freeze: There's no need to cook peas first – simply pod and freeze. Broad beans do need to be blanched, refreshed, and double-podded before freezing.

Creamed Spinach and Broad Bean Tart

Much as I love a shortcrust pastry tart – and there are a few dotted through the seasons of this book – summer is not the time for making them. Shortcrust pastry needs a cool kitchen and hands. Summer for me means pre-made puff.

This simple tart is great as part of a larger spread, or on its own with just a few salad leaves alongside.

Serves 4–6 as a main

750g (1lb 10oz) broad (fava) beans, weight in the pods

2 small/medium red onions

300g (10½oz) baby spinach

3 tbsp olive oil, plus a little more for drizzling

2 tbsp sherry vinegar

3 garlic cloves

325g (11oz) ready-rolled puff pastry sheet, defrosted

1 tbsp plain (all-purpose) flour

3–4 tbsp crème fraîche

handful of fresh basil

30g (1oz) any hard cheese

salt and black pepper

WASTE TIPS: Broad bean pods (page 26), Herb stems (see Stocks, page 340; Soft Herbs, page 341), Onion skins (see Stocks, page 340)

Preheat the oven to 200°C fan/425°F/gas 7.

Pod the broad beans and set aside. Peel and thinly slice the onions, then set aside.

Wash and drain the spinach. Sit a large saucepan over a low-medium heat, add the spinach and stir for a couple of minutes until wilted. Tip into a colander. When cool enough to touch, squeeze out the excess liquid. Set aside.

Put the same saucepan back on the heat. Add the oil and, when hot, add the onions and some salt. Cook gently until they're just starting to soften but not colour. Pour in the sherry vinegar and bubble it for a minute or so to reduce. Peel and crush the garlic, add that too, and let it all cook for another 5 minutes.

While the onions are cooking, lightly dust the pastry and a baking tray with flour (or line the tray with baking paper). Lay the pastry on the baking tray, score a border approx 1.5cm (⅔in) inside the pastry edge and prick the inner rectangle with a fork several times. Chill for 15 minutes.

Combine the spinach and the onions in a large mixing bowl. Stir in the crème fraîche, judging how much depending on the moisture still left in the spinach. Season well. Spread evenly over the pastry, taking care not to let it go over the scored border. Bake for 15 minutes.

Meanwhile, bring a pan of salted water to the boil and cook the broad beans for a few minutes until tender. Drain, refresh in cold water and release the bright inner broad beans from their casing. After the tart has had its 15 minutes, scatter over the podded beans and drizzle a little oil over the top. Return to the oven for 5 minutes.

Remove from the oven, tear over the basil, use a vegetable peeler to shave over as much cheese as you want, and finish with plenty of freshly ground black pepper. Serve while still warm, with the cheese slightly melting. (It is fine at room temperature too.)

Pea and Tarragon Carnaroli Rice

This 'not quite' risotto (which if I were Italian I would be calling risi e bisi) uses garden peas, pods and all, and is all the more glorious for it. The pods become the flavour bed of the stock that is stirred into the rice, with the freshly podded peas added towards the end for flavour lift and delicious sweetness. It is a joy to make and eat.

I cook versions of this a lot, right through the year, switching up the produce as the seasons and my mood evolve. Head to page 144 for its autumnal roasted squash and red onion incarnation.

Serves 4 as a main

1kg (2lb 4oz) garden peas in their pods

2 onions

2 bay leaves

2 tbsp olive oil

50g (2oz) butter

70g (2½oz) pancetta lardons (optional)

300g (10½oz) Carnaroli risotto rice

50g (2oz) Parmesan

2 tarragon sprigs

salt and black pepper

Shell the peas and set them aside while you concentrate on making the most of the sweet pods. Cut one of the onions in half. Bring 1 litre (34fl oz) of water to the boil in a large pan, drop in the pea pods, the halved onion and the bay leaves. Simmer for 5 minutes, then strain and discard the solids so you now have a pea-pod stock. (See page 26 for what to do with the now-tender pods.)

Chop the remaining onion. Heat the olive oil and half of the butter in a deep frying pan and cook the onions over a low heat until just softening. Add the pancetta (if using), turn the heat up a little, and sauté until the pancetta is just starting to brown.

Add the rice and stir so that every grain is covered in the juices in the pan. Season with salt and pepper, then add in a couple of ladlefuls of pea-pod stock. Allow the rice to absorb the liquid, then add more ladlefuls of stock. Repeat the process – stirring occasionally, rather than continuously as you would a risotto – until the rice is just about cooked and the dish has the consistency of a thick soup. It will take 15–20 minutes. If you run out of stock, just use some water. Add the podded peas when you get to about halfway with the stock. Find a moment in a pause in stirring to grate half of the Parmesan, and set it aside.

Turn off the heat, stir in the remaining butter and the grated Parmesan. Serve with tarragon leaves torn over, plenty of freshly ground black pepper, and the rest of the Parmesan on the table for people to help themselves to.

WASTE TIPS: Herb stems (see Stocks, page 340; Soft Herbs, page 341), Onion skins (see Stocks, page 340), Parmesan rind (page 341)

Courgettes
(and Other Summer Squash)

Summer – *Autumn*

Courgettes (zucchini) are the summer vegetable whose season I am guiltiest of trying to extend beyond its natural limits. I doubt I'm the only one. They have become something we're a little too used to enjoying all year round, when really courgettes are definitely very much best when in their peak of season: summer through to late autumn.

By 'best' I mean most delicious. Their flavour out of season is almost nondescript. In season, they are bright and fresh-tasting. The first ones of the summer will be tiny, with dense flesh. As the season goes on they'll get a little watery and woollier, and the skins will thicken. They're still fab, we just need to change up what we do with them (much more on that to come).

Courgette varieties run from being Wimbledon green to canary yellow or snow white. They could be long and thin, or look a lot like globes, or a little like a bugle. That's the Italian trombetta variety, which is worth keeping an especial eye out for as it is getting more popular for being seedless, with large flowers and especially sweet flavours.

Note that the courgette isn't the only squash available in summer, it's just the one that's most available. Others include the crookneck squash with its sometimes ridged skin; and my favourite, the dinky late-summer orange/yellow patty pan. All can be kept, used and enjoyed just as you might a courgette. Because when I say courgette, what I really mean is any summer squash.

Shop

- Whatever their colour, shape or size you are looking for courgettes with vibrant skin. When young they'll be glossy, and then that dulls a little as they age.
- Make sure the courgette is firm all the way along. Nothing flabby or soft.

Store

- In the fridge's crisper drawer. Give them a little space to prevent sweating.

Ways to Use

Courgette flowers

All courgettes could come with the female flower they have grown from still attached, but they don't as the flowers wilt so quickly. Very young, very small courgettes might well be sold with the flower, and you should cook/eat them like that too – i.e. still together.

The flowers available to buy separately are the larger male ones. Pull out and discard their stamens, then:
- tear the flowers into salads and as a garnish for soups.
- chop, then cook with lemon and butter; or add into scrambled egg.
- shallow fry whole flowers in a little oil until just about crisping, then serve with a smattering of caster (superfine) sugar over.
- stuff the flower, twist the tops of the petals together to seal the stuffing in, then deep fry for just a couple of minutes; or lay the stuffed flowers in a pan, barely cover them with wine/stock, and poach for 20 minutes.

Now for courgettes proper.

Early and mid-season courgettes

Small, young, tender courgettes really don't need any cooking at all. Just thinly slice, dress and serve.

Even as they get older you can often get away with doing very little to a courgette. All summer long you'll find me, vegetable peeler in hand, slicing courgettes into ribbons. Try these quick-pickled, added to salads, or stirred through freshly cooked new potatoes, pasta or rice whose heat will gently wilt the ribbons. Its seeded core will be left behind – keep it, and chop it to cook with.

Fast cooking helps young courgettes retain some bite about them. To roast courgette chunks, perhaps alongside other summer vegetables, go high and fast with the heat to concentrate flavour while bringing out their inherent sweetness. Or griddle/grill courgette slices and then – when they are warm, tender and therefore most amenable to soaking up flavour – dress them with oils and toss with other flavour partners.

Arrange thin slices on a puff pastry base – with perhaps pesto, or feta beneath – then bake for a very simple, very quick, summery tart.

Deep fry slices, or – if you find yourself with the smallest of youngest, tenderest, cutest courgettes – turn to page 280, find the tempura recipe there and deep fry them whole (ideally with their flower attached).

Later-season courgettes

As courgettes move through their season and their texture loses some crispness, that's the time to move towards low, slow cooking that allows them to collapse into soft tenderness. Any older, woollier-textured courgette is going to be best when its chunks, cubes, slices or dices are slowly, *slowly* stewed with oil, chopped tomatoes and/or wine; with perhaps other seasonal veggies, like new potatoes or peas, added too.

All ages

Stuffed courgettes, of any age, are making a happy comeback. Not that they ever really left my kitchen. Scoop out their insides, chop the seeds and flesh with whatever stuffing mix you fancy, and pack it all back into the shells and bake.

Soups. Hot or cold. See page 36.

Grated courgettes make for wonderful fritters and koftas, cakes and scones. Add into pizza dough (especially lovely with courgette flowers as part of the pizza topping), or use in the stuffing of a pork or lamb joint. Grated courgette becomes a take on tzatziki when run through with yoghurt, garlic, olive oil and salt.

Flavour Partners

Courgettes are so easy going they'll partner with pretty much anything. That, plus the breadth of using options, mean you can really let your flavour mind run free.

Try stuffing fillings that have at least one (but probably no more than two) of a really big flavour like **preserved lemon**, **salt cod**, **prosciutto**, **anchovy**, **capers**, or a strong **sheep's cheese**.

The saltiness of **olives** will enhance the sweetness lurking in courgette flesh.

Nuts are good in a stuffing for the flower or the vegetable, and elsewhere with courgettes. Think **walnuts**, **almonds** and **hazelnuts**. Pound any of those in a pestle and mortar, then mix with grated courgette, grated **onion**, chopped **wild garlic**, and **orange** zest for a gloriously summery stuffing for a **pork loin**. **Pistachios** are a bit spendy to use quite like that, but worth the financial splash where they can star with courgettes more prominently.

Courgettes love hanging out with their seasonal buddies, especially **tomatoes** – whether cooked into something like a parmigiana (instead of, or as well as, the more traditional aubergine/eggplant), or just ripe tomatoes in with a salad. Toss ribbons of courgette with ribbons of **cucumber** for a salad where it is hard to tell from your eyes which is which, but your taste buds will know quickly enough.

When it comes to dressing raw or cooked courgettes you can go a few different ways. Perhaps a **tahini** dressing with some **raisins** or **sultanas (golden raisins)** tossed in there too; or else an **olive oil**-based dressing that is heavy on the **red wine vinegar**; or **yoghurt** run through with **garlic**, **cumin**, **dried mint** and **cardamom**.

It is probably impossible to use too many soft herbs with courgettes. **Mint**, **dill**, **tarragon** and **basil** (and more basil, and more basil...) are my fallbacks. Add any of those herbs to a frittata made from grated courgette and leftover new potatoes.

More flavour thoughts: **Broad (fava) beans**; **brown shrimps**; **burrata**; **caraway**; **fennel**; **feta**; **harissa**; **lime**; **oregano**; **Parmesan**; **peas**; **samphire**; **sesame oil** and **seeds**; **sherry vinegar**; **soy sauce**; **spring onion (scallion)**; **za'atar**.

Preserve

Freeze the flowers: Courgette flowers freeze surprisingly well. Take a little care in the defrosting, laying them between kitchen paper so it can absorb excess moisture. The flowers will emerge a little limp (certainly not sturdy enough to stuff) but better that than wasting them, or not having them. Chop into a salad, for the cucumber soup on page 36, or shallow fry to crispen then serve with a dusting of caster (superfine) sugar.

Confit: Slowly cook down diced courgettes with barely enough water to stop them catching in the pan (plus whatever other flavours you fancy: onions, tomato, garlic, red wine vinegar...) to turn them into a sort of spread/confit. Perfect for spreading on toast or running through pasta. Store the confit under oil in a sterilised jar, in the fridge.

Courgette and Cucumber Soup with Courgette Flowers

This no-cook soup is perfect for a perfect summer's day. It's all about minimal effort and maximum flavour. Note that all the same ingredients, in the same amounts, will work as a lovely salad if you use a vegetable peeler to turn your courgette and cucumber into ribbons.

Please don't worry too much about having the precise weights given here of the cucumber or courgette. Anything roughly around these numbers will be just fine.

Serves 4

about 225g (8oz) cucumber
about 225g (8oz) courgette (zucchini)
1 large garlic clove
1 dill sprig
1 spring onion (scallion)
300g (10½oz) Greek yoghurt

1 lime
6 courgette (zucchini) flowers
½ tsp za'atar
2 tsp oil of your choosing: olive,
   sesame, walnut or hazelnut
salt and black pepper

Trim and discard the ends of the cucumber and courgette. Roughly chop them and put into a blender. Peel and chop the garlic, discarding any green in the middle, and add to the blender along with the dill sprig – its stalk and leaves. Trim the spring onion, slice and add to the blender, whites and greens together. Add the yoghurt and blitz to an almost smooth consistency that will have pleasing flecks of green. (To make this without a blender: Grate the courgette, cucumber and garlic; chop the dill and spring onion as finely as you can; and just mix everything together really well in a bowl.)

Grate the zest of the lime and keep for later. Squeeze the juice of half the lime into the soup, along with 100–150ml (3½–5fl oz) water. How much depends on how watery (or not) your vegetables were and the consistency you are after. Season well with salt. Blitz again briefly to work the liquids in. Now taste – what does it need a bit more of? Salt? Lime? Remember you have the flavour hit of the garnishes to come.

Chill before serving in small bowls. Finish each serving with sliced petals from the courgette flowers, the reserved lime zest, za'atar, oil of your choosing drizzled over and plenty of freshly ground black pepper.

Patty Pan Squash with Dried Shrimps, Ginger and Lime

This is transitional eating with the transitional squash. Just as summer's courgettes are starting to get a bit woolly and dull, and autumn's squashes aren't yet ready, that's when the flying-saucer shape of the patty pan summer squash comes along. It can be used like any yellow courgette to enjoy raw in salads, ribboned, or stewed, but – like a globe courgette, that could be used here instead – I think its shape makes it perfect to be stuffed and roasted.

The stuffing here is vibrant and fresh, with a hefty umami kick from the dried shrimps (available in Chinese groceries).

Serves 2 as a main

- 2 patty pan squash, each about 400–500g (14oz–1lb 2oz) and 12–15cm (5–6in) in diameter
- 2 tbsp olive oil or rapeseed oil
- 120g (4oz) basmati rice
- 40g (1½oz) dried shrimps
- 2 shallots
- 4 tbsp toasted sesame oil
- 5 coriander (cilantro) sprigs
- 2 dill sprigs
- 2 tsp yellow mustard seeds
- 10g (½oz) fresh root ginger
- 1 lime
- 5 mint sprigs
- flaky salt and black pepper
- radicchio or other salad leaves, for serving

WASTE TIPS: Herb stems (see Stocks, page 340; Soft Herbs, page 341), Shallot skins (see Stocks, page 340), Squash seeds (page 341)

Preheat the oven to 190°C fan/400°F/gas 6.

Cut off the top quarter of the squash, and keep the top to use as a lid. Scoop out the seeds in the centre and you will be left with patty pan shells that have a thick border of flesh. Salt inside each one and sit them cut-side down in a baking dish. Drizzle over 2 tablespoons of the oil, scatter over salt flakes and roast for 20 minutes, then set aside.

Rinse the rice and simmer in water or stock until tender. Drain through a sieve when cooked and set aside.

Rinse and drain the dried shrimps.

Peel and chop the shallots. Heat half of the toasted sesame oil in a wok or frying pan, then cook the shallots until softening but not colouring. Cut the stalks off the coriander and dill (keep the leaves near - you'll need them in a minute), finely chop and add to the shallots as they cook. When the shallots are nearly ready, stir in the mustard seeds and grate in the ginger (no need to peel it first). Let them cook for a couple of minutes, then turn off the heat under the pan.

Mix in the cooked and drained rice, the rinsed dried shrimps, the lime's zest and its juice. Chop the coriander and dill leaves along with the mint and add too. Give it a good grinding of pepper and mix well. Now pack the stuffing into the patty pan shells, really cramming it in. Balance the lids back on top, drizzle over the remaining toasted sesame oil and give a final smattering of salt flakes. Turn the oven up to 210°C fan/450°F/gas 8 and roast for 10 minutes.

Serve while still warm or at room temperature. The juices that are in the bottom of the baking dish will be perfect for dressing the salad leaves to serve alongside.

Cucumbers

Summary

The most often-repeated fact about cucumbers is that they are 96% water. It's a fact that seems to suggest they don't really taste of much, and that certainly can be true. Out of season cucumbers are usually beyond bland. But get a good one, in the height of summer when the sun has worked its magic, and that extra 4% packs a hefty flavour punch. Seasonality really counts when it comes to cucumbers.

Given the chance, a long, smoothly slender cucumber in its peak of season wants to taste slightly sweet and come with a floral scent. Whereas the shorter, stubbier, rough-skinned ridge cucumbers have an edge of bitterness (which I mean as a compliment). They also tend to be the ones with the most flavour and character, if only because these ones aren't so often being bred for volume and year-round cucumbering – the factors that inhibit so much of cucumber potential.

Like aubergines and cauliflowers, the cucumber has had an image makeover in recent years. Its slightly buttoned-up elegance (cf. cucumber sandwiches) has got edgier with a rediscovery of the breadth of possibilities in adding them to flavour-packed salads, cooking them, stuffing, smacking, then dousing with spices.... Cucumbers now are like Olivia Newton-John, at the end of *Grease*. Just more convincingly cool.

Shop

- A bland cucumber will smell of hardly anything, a good one will bounce with aroma.
- Make sure the cucumber is firm all the way along its length. Soft spots at the ends are giveaways of it starting to go past its best.
- It's tempting to think that glossy skin equals healthy. That is a slightly misleading sign of vibrancy as cucumbers are often waxed to help them keep in moisture and avoid damage/deterioration when transported and stored.

Store

- Cucumbers need to be kept in the fridge, and will last well in the crisper drawer. They are sensitive to the ethylene gases given off by tomatoes, peppers, peaches and more, so keep the cucumbers away from those – or wrap in kitchen paper to give some protection.
- As they age, cucumbers will start to shrivel a little or even go soft. Refresh them by sitting in iced water.

Ways to Use

- Remove cucumbers from the fridge a short while before using so they can come back to room temperature. Cold cucumbers have dull flavour.
- Give them a wash to remove the wax that most cucumbers come wrapped in.
- Even – no, especially – a mediocre cucumber will benefit from being salted to draw out some of its water and therefore concentrate the cucumber's flavour. Simply cut the cucumber however you want to use it, put into a bowl and toss in salt. You'll see droplets of moisture start to be released almost straight away. Leave them for 30 minutes, tip into a sieve to drain, and use kitchen paper to wipe off the excess moisture.

Peel and seeds
Peel a cucumber only if the recipe really demands it, or you have a nibble of the skin and it is too bitter for your liking. Much of the flavour is in the skin, so removing it can be a shame.

Have a little taste of the seeds and if they are, again, slightly too bitter, then scoop them out with a teaspoon. I should say I hardly ever (i.e. never) bother doing this but then I really like cucumber seeds and peel.

As for the offcuts of prepping/using cucumbers: The very best destiny for cucumber peel is as a garnish to a martini or gin and tonic; or add the peelings to jugs of very cold sparkling water or elderflower cordial. Cucumber peel, seeds and the core that you end up with after ribboning are all good to add to summery stocks, soups, or to blitz for cucumber juice.

Raw
Early-season cucumbers are the crispest, the sweetest. They are the ones most suited to simplicity in how you enjoy them. There's no need to over-complicate a good, young cucumber, and it's hard to beat them in salads. Perhaps delicately diced, or cut into hefty chunks, or – my preferred way – sliced with a vegetable peeler into ribbons so fine you can see the sun shine through them.

When you want to really make sure your cucumber is at one with the rest of the flavours in a salad, give it a whack with a rolling pin to bruise the flesh, open it up, and make it more receptive to taking on board the elements around it. Chop, gently smack, salt as above, then let the pieces loose with dressing or spices.

Dice peeled cucumber into tzatziki/cacik. Grate cucumber to spoon through yoghurt for raita, or to use for a soup. The soup recipe on page 36 blitzes cucumber into a purée that then becomes soup. Similarly blitz/juice cucumbers to use in smoothies, to simply drink the juice (very delicious and refreshing with lots of ice on the hottest summer days), or as the base for a cucumber sorbet.

Perhaps even better than the pickled cucumbers opposite are quick-pickled cucumber ribbons. Not least because they are ready to enjoy in about 30 minutes rather than waiting a week. Follow the principles on page 72.

Cooked

So far, so raw. And so suited to summer days when spending any time cooking over heat feels ludicrous. It's a shame, though, to discount entirely how delicious cooked cucumbers can be. Especially as their season goes on, their texture changes, and they need a bit more of a helping hand.

When cooking them it is best to both peel and de-seed, as otherwise there's a texture battle going on with the flesh. Then dice, slice, or cut into batons to stir fry quickly. Slowly sauté them in butter for a light side dish that can be turned into a sauce with some stock and blitzing. Or stuff cucumbers in the same way as courgettes. Soups are the best friend of older cucumbers.

Flavour Partners

The cool elegance of cucumber allows cooks to go, broadly speaking, in two different flavour directions with it: Either to embrace and enhance those qualities with others that fit similar profiles; or to go the other way and oomph cucumbers up with hits of bold flavour. As ever, it's a flavour partner spectrum.

The cool of **yoghurt** is an easy fit with cucumber. In a soup like the one on page 36 that also brings in **courgettes (zucchini)**; with **garlic** for tzatziki; given **mint** in a raita. All of these needing to be well seasoned with **salt** and **pepper** to bring out the gentle flavours, and given a pep of acidity via a squeeze of **lemon** or **lime**. The seasonality of lush summertime goats' and sheep's milk makes their yoghurts especially good with cucumber (and therefore young **goats'** and **sheep's cheeses**, too).

Partner yoghurt-based cucumber sauces with **lamb**, **duck**, or any **oily fish**. **Salmon** and cucumber have long been a classic partnership for sandwiches and salads. Taking note of the concerns around how salmon is produced (see page 48), perhaps look to **mackerel** or **trout** instead.

Partner cucumber with **strawberrie**s in a sweet salad with a little **rosewater** or **melon**. A savoury pairing would enjoy **shellfish** (prawn cocktail vibes) or **white fish**.

Cucumber's fondness for **gin** is a steer towards using its typical aromatics of **coriander seeds**, **juniper**, **orange** or **lavender**. They all make excellent additions to the quick-pickle brine for cucumber ribbons. The **vinegar** choice there being sweet **moscatel**, or never-fail **sherry**.

Use those also in dressings for the whole family of big-flavour salads – fattoush, tabbouleh, Niçoise, panzanella – that rely on cucumber to bring its cooling edge to the other elements. Cucumber can well handle whatever **herbs** or **spices** might be in any of those, and if the cucumbers have been smacked (see opposite) they'll do an even better job of soaking up the flavours and helping everything meld together seamlessly. Look to **sumac**, **za'atar**, **ground cumin**, **ground cinnamon**. Or add handfuls of torn **basil**, **dill**, **tarragon** to simple oil/vinegar dressings. The **anise** notes of those last two herbs are a signpost to putting cucumber with **fennel** – thinly sliced, together as a salad.

Bang in season cucumbers and bang in season **tomatoes** are perfect together as the classic gazpacho so readily shows. Layer freshly toasted **rye bread** with slices of well-salted tomato and cucumber for a light summery lunch that can only be topped when literally topped with a dollop of freshly made **mayonnaise**. Add **black olives** and **capers** to tomato and cucumber salads – or take those in a different direction with freshly grated **ginger**, **rice wine**, a little **light soy sauce** and a touch of **sugar**.

Punchy, face-puckering **rhubarb** enjoys being calmed by cucumber. Quick-pickle them together into harmony to serve as a side for something simple like **chicken**. Because it is, as ever, all about balance.

More flavour thoughts: **Allspice**; **apple**; **bay leaves**; **black mustard seeds**; **black sesame seeds**; **celery**; **chilli**; **Chinese black Chinkiang vinegar**; **horseradish**; **new potatoes**; **nutmeg**; **orange blossom water**; **radish**; **samphire**; **spring onion (scallion)**.

Preserve

Pickle: I like to try to keep some crunch to my cucumber pickles so choose the youngest, crispest ones for this. For a 500ml (17fl oz) jar: Cut 1 ridge cucumber (about 200g/7oz) into chunks and put half of those into a sterilised jar. Add 2 bay leaves, ½ tsp each of coriander seeds, black mustard seeds, fennel seeds. Crush 2 peeled garlic cloves and add those along with ¼ tsp chilli flakes and 3 dill sprigs and the rest of the cucumber chunks. In a small saucepan, heat 125ml (4fl oz) cider vinegar with 125ml (4fl oz) water and 1½ tbsp fine salt. Once the salt has dissolved, put that into the jar, making sure the cucumber pieces are immersed and adding more vinegar if not. Seal and set aside for at least a week before using. Use in salads, blitz with stock into soup, or – and this is best of all – coat in breadcrumbs and deep fry.

Cucumber, Elderflower and Gin (or Lime) Ice Lollies

Make these once and I promise they will become a summertime staple. That's not a promise I make lightly. There are few better – or more refreshing – cucumber experiences that when its juice is concentrated, sweetened with elderflower, and frozen for the nostalgia kick of an ice lolly. I couldn't tell you if I prefer the lime or gin options. The answer is always whichever is in the freezer.

Makes 6 or 8 ice lollies, depending
on size of mould
1 cucumber, about 350g (12oz)

200ml (7fl oz) elderflower cordial
2 limes or 50ml (1¾fl oz) gin

ice lolly moulds and wooden sticks

Peel the cucumber. Cut away a 30g (1oz) piece and set that aside. Blitz the rest of the cucumber and then push the purée through a sieve to get as much juice out of it as possible, around 125–150ml (4–5fl oz). Discard the dry cucumber pulp. Add the elderflower cordial to the cucumber juice, with 200ml (7fl oz) water. If using limes, add their juice; otherwise add the gin. Mix.

Cut the reserved piece of cucumber into thin rounds, and then each round into quarters. Scatter those into the lolly moulds. Put the sticks into the moulds, then fill to halfway with the cucumber juice mix. Freeze for an hour, then fill with the rest of the cucumber juice mix. Freeze overnight before unmoulding to serve.

WASTE TIPS: Cucumber peel (see pages 41 and 340), Lime rind (see Citrus, page 338)

Mackerel with Cucumber, Samphire, Tomatoes and Cream

Mackerel is my summer fish go-to (see page 48 for why). It needs just a few minutes to pan fry but inevitably always leaves a little of its flesh and flavour behind in the pan. Make the most of that by turning it into a light sauce. Any danger of richness that suggests is here perfectly counter-balanced by sitting the mackerel atop a light cucumber and raw samphire salad. The end result is a glory of bright flavours, textures and colours.

This recipe suits laidback cooking for a group as the salad elements of samphire, cucumber and tomato can all be done and plated ahead, ready and waiting for the mackerel to be cooked and served.

Serves 4 as a main	1 tsp black mustard seeds
300g (10½oz) cucumber	3 tbsp extra-virgin olive oil
180g (6½oz) samphire	200g (7oz) small tomatoes
4 tsp sherry vinegar	300ml (10fl oz) double (heavy) cream
4 mackerel fillets	salt and black pepper

Use a vegetable peeler to slice the cucumber into ribbons, and arrange on a serving dish or individual plates. Add the samphire and gently toss. Pour the vinegar over and toss, then set aside.

Dry the mackerel on kitchen paper, then season the skins with salt. Set a large frying pan over a low–medium heat and dry-fry the mustard seeds until they pop. Spoon those over the samphire and cucumber. Set the same pan over a high heat, add the oil and get it hot, put the tomatoes into the pan and quickly cook them for a couple of minutes until their skins are splitting. Use a slotted spoon to lift the tomatoes out of the pan and onto the samphire and cucumber.

Turn the heat down to medium and lay the mackerel fillets into the oil skin-side down. Let them cook for a couple of minutes until the flesh on the uppermost side starts to turn opaque and the fish can easily lift off the base of the pan without leaving the skin behind. At that point turn the fillets over, finish cooking them for another minute and then lift them onto the samphire, cucumber and tomatoes. Return the pan to the heat, pour in the cream and let it bubble for a minute to reduce, rubbing at the base of the pan with a wooden spoon to lift off any bits of mackerel left behind. Pour the cream sauce over the mackerel and samphire, grind over some black pepper, and serve while still hot.

Mackerel

Mackerel are seriously fast fish. In an hour they can swim through roughly 6 miles (10km) of sea in the pursuit of the warm waters they love and which are why summer is the ideal time for mackerel fishing and eating.

The pace and migratory instincts of mackerel are its joy in appearing in various parts of the world as the waters dictate, but these instincts also pose a challenge for the sustainable maintenance of mackerel stocks. As mackerel move quickly, and are going increasingly further, there are disagreements between nations on stock levels and quite whose mackerel are whose. These have started to cast shade on how acclaimed mackerel has been in recent years as a (perhaps even 'the') sustainable fish option.

While mackerel quotas are being quarrelled over, what can or should we as consumers do? I think the answer lies in reconnecting with mackerel as a seasonal fish from local waters. It is too easy for our collective heads to be turned by how cheap mackerel is, how quick and easy to cook, and how healthy it is with those fabulous fish oils we know do our joints and brains such good. Too easy to then want – or even expect – to have it all year round. And that is where the trouble can lie.

Its fellow oily fish, salmon, can perhaps be a cautionary tale/tail. Wild Atlantic salmon stocks are almost gone (and rightly tightly protected where they are still around) and so have been replaced by Atlantic salmon farms. Extensive breeding has bred extensive popularity that is being satisfied at a considerable cost to the environment and the welfare of the fish.

I'm talking about farmed salmon escaping into the sea and causing problems by breeding with wild salmon and changing their genetic make-up. They also compete with them for food, putting wild stocks at further risk of surviving. Farmed salmon are so tightly packed into cages they become the perfect home for sea lice, and the pesticides used to control them can damage other sea life. I could go on, but you get the picture. We have to make our own food choices and one of mine is to not buy farmed Atlantic salmon (and fresh Pacific salmon only occasionally because it has a long way to come to reach me in London).

And so, my summertime kitchen might well miss salmon's ease and delicate depth of flavour, were it not for mackerel. All summer long I am mackerel-tastic. Pickling, pâté-ing, barbecuing, grilling, roasting, salad-ing and feasting. That wanes through the autumn as the mackerel move on to other coastlines; stops in the winter; and then come the spring I'll look forward to the mackerel's return all over again.

Summer Carrots

Summer

It's midsummer and my parents-in-law are round for lunch. It's also the first Sunday lunch we've done since moving flat and so the excitement is revved up several notches. My mother-in-law asks what I've done to make the carrots taste so good. I cannot for the life of me think *what* I did with them, until it dawns that the answer is 'hardly anything'. They were scrubbed, steamed, given the lightest dusting of salt and served. What made those carrots taste so good is that they actually tasted of something in their own right. Which given this was summer meant they were naturally sweet, slightly fragrant, and with a lovely delicate flavour.

Quite a world away in terms of size, flavour and texture – as well as in how we want to cook and eat them – from winter's carrots of page 197. Summer carrots are simply winter carrots picked while younger. They are shorter, thinner, often (hopefully) with perky green fronds still attached. Whereas mature winter carrots can seem heavy and flat in flavour, these have a lightness that can lift the season they are harvested in.

Shop

- The perkiness of the carrots' tops is a good indicator of the freshness of the carrots. If the fronds are a little sad and tired, the carrots might be too.
- Carrots and tops should smell sweetly earthy.
- Carrots that are at all limp or bendy are starting to dry out. Although they can be revived with a spell in very cold water.

Store

- You need to take the tops off to help the carrots keep fresh for longer. Otherwise the tops will, in a bid for their own survival, drain moisture out of the actual carrots. Cut the tops off (leave a little stalk attached to the carrots), soak in cold water for 10 minutes to remove any grit, then wrap in kitchen paper and keep in the fridge.
- The carrots themselves don't need washing, especially if they have any soil still on them. The earth will help them keep fresh. Wrap in paper/a paper bag and store in the fridge, or a cool cupboard/larder.

Ways to Use

Summer carrots absolutely and definitely
do not need peeling. Their skin is still so
thin. Just give them a nice wash. When
I'm cooking whole summer carrots
I usually leave a few centimetres of the
stalk attached, mainly for attractiveness.

Raw

I love a quick-pickle of a summer carrot. Slice into fine
ribbons using a mandoline or vegetable peeler, then sit
in a 50/50 mix of water and vinegar (perhaps a nice
muscatel vinegar) with salt, sugar and a few spices.
The acidity will help the carrots relax. See page 72
for more on quick-pickling.

Ribbons and very finely sliced matchsticks are great in
summer salads or slaws. The longer they have in an acidic (citrus or
vinegar) dressing, the more relaxed (i.e. less crunchy) they'll become.

Cooked

A simple steam can be all summer carrots need to let their flavour really come through.
When young and small enough to steam whole they'll only need 10–20 minutes
depending on size. They will taste sweetly carroty, with a simplicity that can be best
appreciated when part of a meal with a lot else going on flavour-wise.

Roasting until tender and charred brings out the carrots' sugars and caramelises
them. Roast them whole unless thicker than your middle finger, at which point halve
them through their length or try slicing into long, thin diagonals. They need little more
than oil and salt as roasting companions – sliced shallot and thyme are good additions.
Roast them in the dish that a joint of meat has cooked in and they'll soak up all the
umami left behind. Blitz roast carrot leftovers into a dip, make into soup, or toss into a
summer stir fry.

Shallow fry thin lengths of summer carrots – perhaps having dipped the carrots in
beaten egg, a spice mix of your choosing, and then breadcrumbs to lightly coat before
they hit the hot oil.

Stew summer carrot lengths in oil and/or butter, then dress with red wine vinegar
and plenty of herbs to serve.

Carrot tops

Soak in cold water for 10 minutes to remove grit. Dry with kitchen paper before using.

Tear or chop the tops to use as a bitter herb. Bitter enough to need compensating for
with sweet or salty elements.

Flavour Partners

Carrots are umbellifers, which means they are part of the family of aromatic plants known for their slightly frothy, ethereal-looking leaves and flowers. They enjoy time with the rest of the family, so that means **parsley**, **parsnips** (seek out young summer parsnips for the same reasons we're loving young summer carrots here), **coriander** (**cilantro**), **chervil**, **dill**, **fennel** and **lovage**.

Cumin, too. It's another umbellifer and worth special mention for what it can do when added to carrots before roasting them. It brings out the carrots' earthiness that marries so well with the caramelisation of the sugars achieved in the roasting. Try also using it to fragrance summer carrot lengths stewed in oil and/or butter.

Carrots are often described as being 'nutty'. Enhance those attributes by partnering with **walnuts** and **hazelnuts** especially – toasting them first to maximise their flavours. Toast and toss over cooked carrots, or pestle into a dressing.

Juxtapose the sweetness of summer carrots with sour flavours for fabulous balance. Most obviously **lemon** – especially when married with **chillies** and **coriander** (**seeds** or **leaf**). **Lime** for quick-pickling, or for zesting over roasted, stewed or raw carrots in a salad. Also – and perhaps especially – **orange**. Squeeze the juice into dressings, grate the zest over pretty much anything. **Orange flower water** is a joy for finishing cooked carrots and, again, adding to salad dressings. **Apples** bring their own hit of sweet and sour that works well for summer carrot salads and slaws.

Vinegars are essential for dressing carrots. Go for a light white wine vinegar (champagne or muscatel) or in the opposite direction with something big and heavy like a red wine vinegar or sherry vinegar. Those are especially good for dressing summer carrots that have steamed alongside some small summer **beetroots**; or adding to summer carrots as they roast along with some **new potatoes**.

Summer carrots welcome strong salty, umami flavours. For the **cheeses** that could mean **feta**, **Gruyère**, **ricotta** or **Parmesan**. Perhaps salty black **olives** tossed in for the last few minutes of roasting, or along for the ride in a salad.

More flavour thoughts: **Anise**; **broad (fava) beans**; **cardamom**; **cayenne**; **celery**; **cinnamon**; **cucumber**; **garden peas**; **garlic**; **ginger**; **honey**; **lamb**; **mustard seeds**; **pork**; **sesame seeds** and **oil**; **shallots**; **soy sauce**; **spring onions (scallions)**; **sultanas (golden raisins)**; **tahini**; **yoghurt**; **za'atar**.

Preserve

Ferment: Small summer carrots are the perfect size to ferment whole. Use a brine that is 3% salt to water, and leave to ferment for at least 4 days before trying. Wonderful in summer salads.

Summer Carrots with Little Gem and Salted Almonds

The earthy glory of cumin and za'atar bring depth of flavour to summer carrots, which is then enhanced by mixing with lime, and salt via the nuts. While salted almonds are my preference, other salted nuts that you might have in your cupboard can be easily swapped in – salted peanuts and cashews especially.

Any leftovers can be blitzed with stock into a fabulous soup.

Serves 2 as a large side
350g (12oz) summer carrots with tops
100ml (3½fl oz) olive oil
1 tsp ground cumin
1 tsp za'atar
150g (5oz) little gem lettuce
  (1 or 2, size depending)

2 tbsp sherry vinegar
40g (1½oz) salted almonds
  (toasted or not)
½ lime
salt

Trim the carrots, leaving an inch or so of stalk on top. Keep the fronds for garnish if they're nicely green and perky. Wash the carrots, but don't peel them. If your carrots are much thicker than your middle finger, then slice in half lengthways at an angle.

Heat half of the oil in a large frying over a medium-high heat and sit the carrots in the pan, in a single layer if you can. Toss in the cumin and za'atar. Give a smattering of salt and cook, uncovered, for 20 minutes until tender. Move them round 3 or 4 times so they all get a chance to cook evenly and take on colour.

While the carrots cook, remove any outer leaves from the little gem(s) only if they are very sad and wilting. Slice the lettuce into quarters (or halves if using two small ones) through the root.

When the carrots have had their 20 minutes, nestle the little gem pieces among the carrots. Pour over the sherry vinegar and the rest of the oil. Turn the heat up high and cook for another 10 minutes so the little gem can char and tenderise. Use that time to slice your almonds into long slivers and chop 2 tablespoons of the carrot tops.

Add the almonds to the pan. Gently toss. Scatter over the chopped carrot tops, squeeze over the lime half and give it some more salt. Serve soon.

WASTE TIPS: Lime rind (see Citrus, page 338)

Sweet Peppers

Summer – *Year Round*

My favourite pepper (capsicum) fact is one that came to me very late: green and red (or yellow, or orange) peppers are just peppers picked at differing stages of ripeness. That blew my mind a little on first finding out.

I always knew the green ones were my least favourite of the family. Now I know that was most likely because the green pepper is picked before it is fully ripe, before its natural sugars have had chance to develop. Once it has become red (or yellow, or orange) the pepper has become its own sweetly true self.

All members of the pepper family share a measure of capsaicin – the chemical that gives them spicy heat. My focus here is on the sweet peppers, which have little of that, rather than the hot ones like paprika, habaneros and jalapeños. Bell peppers are the most common of the sweet varieties, with the longer, thinner Romano peppers offering rather more flavour but still going gently on the heat. Baby peppers are sweet peppers that have been bred to be smaller.

Shop

- Look for peppers with glossy firm skin, without any wrinkles.
- Dark spots around the outer folds of the pepper could be a sign that it has gone a little mouldy inside.
- Hold the pepper, literally weighing it up, and know that heavier ones are likely to be 'meatier' for want of a much better word.
- Give it a smell and hope you get a distinct note of paprika (paprika being made from dried and ground peppers). If the pepper doesn't smell of much, it may not taste of much either.

Store

- Wash your peppers if you must, but be sure to dry them thoroughly to avoid mould developing
- Store out of the fridge if using soon, in the fridge otherwise.
- When in the fridge, remember peppers are sensitive to smells so don't put them near anything else that is a bit smelly.
- Don't pack your peppers together too tightly – give them space to breathe.

Ways to Use

As popular as raw peppers are for salads or crudités, I think a pepper needs to be cooked to let its full flavour through.

Roasting and grilling will release and enhance the peppers' natural sweetness. Roast chunks of pepper alongside other summer vegetables (courgettes/zucchini, aubergines/eggplants, tomatoes...), with garlic cloves nestled around and plenty of oil and salt over. Or to roast/grill them for using the peppers in a dip, sauce or salad: Get the oven on a high heat (220°C fan/475°F/gas 9) or its highest grill setting. Sit the peppers in a dish, uncovered, and roast/grill until charring and blistering all over – you'll need to give them a few turns for even cooking. Go lightly with the charring to use them skin-on, but if you will be removing the skin let them get properly black all over before allowing to cool out of the oven and then simply pull the skin away. (The skin will be bitter now – good to eat, not so good for stocks.)

A halved bell pepper with its core removed is the perfect shell to stuff and carry all kinds of flavour. Depending how long your stuffing needs to cook in the oven once inside the pepper, you might need to quickly blanch the peppers shells for a few minutes first to get them on their way to tenderising. Baby peppers can be fun (but fiddly) to stuff.

Slowly cooking down sliced or chopped peppers in a pan is another great way to get their flavours out and add other flavours too. The longer they cook the softer they will become and all the more delicious, too. Think piperade or peperonata (see overleaf) – two ways of turning peppers into a sauce that is fabulous with sausages, pasta, as a base for a shakshuka, or perhaps just piled on toast.

Note that any pepper trimmings you cut away – seeds, core, top – are a great addition to stocks. Pop them into your freezer stock bag of veg odds and ends.

Flavour Partners

The Mediterranean is famous for the peppers it produces and so the flavours of Italy, Spain, Greece, Cyprus and more provide a wealth of ways to embrace cooking and serving. The staple Med flavours of **garlic**, **capers**, **anchovies**, **lemon**, **onion** or **shallot**, **tomato** and **basil** all work abundant wonders with peppers.

To go in the direction of Basque piperade it's about sautéing chopped pepper and onion, plus garlic, and then stewing with tinned (or skinned, de-seeded and chopped) tomatoes and sweet paprika. For Italian peperonata lose the paprika, and perhaps add some herbs like **thyme**, **rosemary**, **bay** or **sage**. Both dishes will benefit from a little sugar to round out the acidity of the tomatoes, and some vinegar for depth and, again, balance. **Red wine vinegar** and **sherry vinegar** are especially good with peppers – good to know when prepping a salad dressing for a pepper-laden dish.

Any leftover piperades, peperonatas and other versions of sautéed, sweated and stewed peppers can be blitzed for dips or to spread on toast. Just taste and see what they might need more of: A few blitzed **beans**, **nuts** or **breadcrumbs** to thicken? **Vinegar** or capers to sharpen? Basil, **coriander (cilantro)** or **parsley** to lift? And perhaps some finely chopped **spring onion (scallion)** to finish.

The collapsed, tender flesh of charred and skinned peppers become a great addition to big summer salads/platters. They'll play happily with lots of other elements: chunks of nearly stale **bread** that are reviving themselves in pools of **olive oil**, hard-boiled **eggs**, essentially ripe and simply sliced tomatoes, simply cooked **fish**, **buttery new potatoes** and **proper mayonnaise**.

Roasted and skinned peppers (ones you have just done or jarred ones) are delicious blended/crushed with **nuts**, **oils** and **spices** into dishes like romesco and muhammara. To be enjoyed in their own right as a dip, sauce, condiment for topping flatbreads before baking, or even turned into a soup. Similarly, try blitzing roasted peppers with **roasted aubergines (eggplants)**, garlic, olive oil, vinegar and **chilli flakes**.

For stuffing peppers you need to think about how the flavours work together of what you are stuffing with, and then how the stuffing works in terms of flavour with the peppers. The nuttiness of cooked **black rice** mixed with **crab** or a medley of cooked-down summer vegetables – think **courgettes (zucchini)** and/or **aubergines** – with plenty of **herbs** and **spices** is always a winner. On page 58 is another of my favourite and most-cooked ways.

More flavour thoughts: **Caraway seeds**; **chillies**; **chorizo**; **coriander seeds**; **cumin** (**seeds** and **ground**); **feta**; **fino sherry**; **honey**; **lime**; **mackerel**; **mustard seeds**; **nigella seeds**; **olives**; **paprika**; **preserved lemons**; **salt cod**; **tahini**.

Preserve

Freeze: Peppers are very freezer friendly. Wash and dry, then freeze chopped or whole.

Pickle: Baby peppers can be pickled whole; larger ones will need de-seeding and slicing/chopping first.

Ferment: Seek out Olia Hercules' *Summer Kitchens f*or a superb recipe where peppers are stuffed with cabbage and chillies, then fermented along with dill, celery, carrot, tomatoes....

In oil: Slice charred and skinned peppers (or leave them whole) before putting into a jar and submerging in olive oil. Add in other flavours of garlic, herbs, capers or anchovies as you wish.

Dry: This is, without any doubt, the most pleasing, smug-inducing way to preserve peppers. To dry them in an oven: Lay them on baking paper on a baking tray in a cool 50°C fan/125°F/gas ¼ oven, with the oven door slightly ajar and turn them occasionally. They are done when completely dry, even brittle, to the touch. How long they take to get to that point depends on their size and thickness – it could be a few hours, or up to 12. If the weather where you are is very *very* hot, you could try tying string to their stalks (or threaded through their tops) and then hang by the sunniest window. Less romantic – but certainly efficient – is to use a dehydrator. Store dried peppers in sterilised jars, then rehydrate in water/stock to use in your cooking.

Black Olive, Shallot and Tomato Stuffed Peppers

Many of the core flavour partners for peppers are here literally stuffed inside them as they bake. Serve them warm, with bread to dunk into the broth juices that bake around the peppers.

The tomato vine will give extra flavour depth to the broth, so include it if you have it, but don't worry if not.

Serves 4 as a main or 8 as a small sharing plate
4 bell peppers (capsicums), about 225g (8oz) each
150g (5oz) shallots
150ml (5fl oz) extra-virgin olive oil
500ml (17fl oz) vegetable or chicken stock
250ml (8½fl oz) dry white wine
350g (12oz) small tomatoes (optionally on the vine)
2 garlic cloves
70g (2½oz) pitted black olives
1½ tbsp sherry vinegar
8 basil leaves
salt

Halve each pepper lengthways, then cut out the core and seeds. Bring a large pan of salted water to the boil. Put the pepper halves into the water, cook for 2 minutes, then drain and make sure all the water is out of the peppers. Sit the peppers cut-side up in a large baking dish.

Preheat the oven to 190°C fan/400°F/gas 6.

Peel the shallots, halve lengthways and cut into long slim lengths. Heat 100ml (3½fl oz) of the oil in a large saucepan over a low–medium heat, add the shallots and gently cook until softening and turning translucent. Pour in the stock and wine, season with salt, add the vines from the tomatoes (if using), bring to the boil and then turn down to a low simmer for 10 minutes. Discard the tomato vines (if using).

Peel and finely chop the garlic, then sprinkle among the peppers. Use a slotted spoon to lift the shallots out of the broth, and divide those among the peppers too. Chop the olives and do the same, then follow with the sherry vinegar. Tuck in the tomatoes, cutting any up as needed to help them fit inside the peppers. Season with salt and pour over the remaining 50 ml (1½fl oz) oil.

Pour the broth around (not over) the peppers. Put the dish into the oven and roast for 45 minutes.

Tear the basil leaves, and tuck around the tomatoes in the peppers. Serve.

WASTE TIPS: Herb stems (see Stocks, page 340; Soft Herbs, page 341), Pepper trimmings and shallot skins (see Stocks, page 340)

Tomatoes

Summer

This is how my lunch rolls at least a couple of times a week during the summer: A thick slice of good bread, toasted, topped with sliced tomatoes, olive oil and salt, anchovies and lots of cracked pepper. The oil and salty tomato juices roll down my chin as I eat it and I am in heaven. When the tomato season passes, that is the dish I miss the most.

Seven-year-old me would not have believed it – and, worse, would think I've really let her down. But no-one had told the dinner ladies at my school that all the tomatoes on the lunchtime 'salad bar' needed to make them taste at least better was a little olive oil and salt. That bit of info could have saved me – and them – no end of strife as I kicked up a fuss at being made to eat the hard tomatoes forced onto my plate.

They tasted of barely anything but to any extent they did, they were bitter not sweet, as I now know tomatoes can so easily and rightly be. Ripe in-season tomatoes pack all the core flavour profiles to lesser or greater degrees, and excel with umami – the taste of savoury deliciousness.

Much marketing fanfare is made of vine-ripened tomatoes. The implicit suggestion is that letting them ripen while still attached to the vine is more natural and results in better-tasting tomatoes. The reality is more confusing than that. There comes a point in the life of a growing tomato where its cells seal the stem of the tomato off from the vine and there's no longer a flow of flavour going from vine to tomato. But the vines do look so lovely, don't they? And if we eat with our eyes then perhaps the vine does indeed give extra flavour. (It is also tasty in its own right. See Ways to Use on page 63 and the recipe on page 58.)

What matters more to tomato flavour is speed of ripening, how long the tomatoes are stored, and the temperatures they are growing in/being stored at on their journey from harvesting to your kitchen. The optimum temperature for tomato growing is 21–24°C (70–75°F). Hello balmy days of summer. Once fully ripe, tomatoes cannot be stored for too long without deteriorating. Keeping them cool helps slow the deterioration, but cool temperatures also damage the fruits. Tomatoes are often packaged while immature and ripened as they travel from wherever they are being grown to wherever they are being sold, with temperatures carefully controlled to try to get the ripening times just right.

It all comes down to the best-tasting tomatoes being ones that have grown in gentle heat, picked at the perfect moment of ripeness, and without far to travel once harvested. Translation: local and seasonal.

Shop

- They should feel heavy, with a little give in response to a (gentle) squeeze, and should smell of tomato.

Store

- Tomatoes like temperatures of 10–12°C (50–54°F), but that range is hard to achieve on summer days. I keep mine out of the fridge at night but accept that keeping them in the fridge is inevitable in the daytime even if I know it is too cold really. Ripe tomatoes will be okay in there for a few days, but much longer and their colour, flavour and smell all start to deteriorate. Try to limit their storing time.

Ways to Use

Tomatoes stored in the fridge have their flavour style cramped by the cold. They need to be brought back to room temperature before using. Better still, sit them in a spot of sunshine and let its warmth bring them back to flavour life.

Salads

You don't need me to tell you that tomatoes can be sliced, chopped or chunked into all kinds of salads all summer long. On page 66, you'll see how I make The Sweetest Tomato Salad, and here are a few other tips and favourite ways:

- Larger tomatoes are often watery. Draw out that excess juice before using – and simultaneously concentrate their flavour – by tossing cut pieces in salt, setting them aside for 15 minutes, then drain, pat dry and use. Remember when it comes to seasoning that the tomatoes are already well salted.
- Don't do that for a bread salad like panzanella, where chunks of slightly stale bread relish tomatoes' reviving juices. You want as much juice as possible to soak into the bread. (Fresh bread becomes overwhelmed and soggy.)
- To use cherry tomatoes in a salad, give them a quick roast first (see overleaf) or a few minutes in a very hot pan with a little oil. Either way allows their skins to burst, and the exposed flesh is more amenable for melding with other salad flavours and the dressing. They'll give up their own juice more freely too. The oil the tomatoes quickly cooked in will also have taken on a little tomato-ness – use it in your dressing.
- Most importantly: tomatoes in their delicious peak of season deserve minimal messing about.

Grated

Grate large, firm-yet-ripe tomatoes to use as the salad bed for other ingredients such as double-podded broad (fava) beans, or burrata.

Roasted

Roasting tomatoes brings out their flavour and sweetness. Do it in an oven no less than 200°C fan/425°F/gas 7, as lower temperatures make for watery roasted tomatoes. For the same reason, don't cover them or pack too closely – steam needs to be able to escape or they'll just become soggy. Drizzle with oil and vinegar before roasting, then be sure to treasure the flavour-packed juices left behind in the roasting dish. Roast tomatoes on the vine for prettiness of serving.

Soup

Roasted tomatoes make for glorious soups. All the intensity of flavour that the roasting has achieved needs just a simple blitz with stock and you are there. If bits of blitzed roasted tomato skin will bother you, run it through a sieve before serving.

Tomato soups made with raw tomatoes haven't had the benefit of intense heat to get extra flavour into and out of the skins, and so it is always a good idea to strain the soup before serving. Just don't be tempted to skin or de-seed the tomatoes before making the soup – the soup needs the flavour they will give it as it cooks.

Cold tomato soups like gazpacho need to be enjoyed exactly like that: cold. Hot tomato soup is equally divine, especially with an old-school swirl of cream. Room-temperature tomato soup is grim.

For toppings: tarts, pizzas, bread

The only trouble with topping tarts and pizzas with slices of raw tomato is that, as they cook, they can leach excess juice into the dough base and make it soggy. Nobody wants that. Salt them as under 'Salads' to extract excess moisture for anything other than small tomatoes. Layer them onto puff pastry for a quick tart; or try a tomato tart tatin.

Rub a halved tomato over toasted bread (that has already been rubbed with a garlic clove and olive oil) to really get tomato flesh and flavour deep into the bread. Give that plenty of salt and, on those rare summers' days that I resist my go-to of sliced tomato + anchovy on toast for lunch, it is mainly because this was my breakfast.

Pile up tomato dices onto thick toast for bruschetta. Tuck small tomatoes into the dimples of a focaccia before baking.

Stuffed

The best tomatoes for stuffing are large ones of around 200g (7oz) each (anything small is too fiddly); and a little under-ripe so they won't collapse when prepped and cooked.

Slice off their tops and keep for lids. Scoop out the insides, taking care not to break the tomato 'walls'. The insides should then be chopped up and added to whatever you intend you stuff your tomatoes with. Perhaps cooked rice, couscous or quinoa with herbs aplenty, spring onion (scallion), goats' cheese.... Spoon the stuffing back in, pop the lids on, sit them in an oiled baking dish, drizzle a little oil over the tomatoes and bake in a 200°C fan/425°F/gas 7 oven for 30–40 minutes. Serve straight away or at room temperature; or make them ahead and chill, then reheat in a hot oven.

Stews and sauces

Amidst so many year-round, world-round ways of using tomatoes in stews and sauces, I think these are especially suited to summer cooking and eating.

- Chop and add to a parcel of fish, white wine and herbs to bake in the oven.
- Chop them even smaller to include in a summery sofrito/mirepoix.
- For a fish stew (like the Zarzuela on page 120), add the tomatoes just before the wine/ stock and let the tomatoes collapse into the juices.
- Include them in a medley of other summer vegetables, such as aubergines (eggplant), courgettes (zucchini), peppers (capsicums), long beans, in a slow-cooked stew.

Most stews and sauces are best made with larger tomatoes that have been peeled and de-seeded, so you don't end up with those floating around in your finished dish.

Skins, seeds and vines

To skin a tomato: Use the point of a sharp knife to cut a cross in the base. Sit it in just-boiled water for 1 minute, then lift out and the skin should peel away easily. If not, pop it back into the water for a further minute. Use the skins in stocks (or dehydrate them in a 60°C fan/150°C/gas ¼ oven until completely dry and grind into tomato powder). Under-ripe tomatoes are very hard to peel.

Tomato seeds and surrounding pulp are also deliciously good to keep for stocks.

The vines carry enough flavour to make them worth adding to a stock or sauce (as on page 58).

Flavour Partners

The fundamentals are **extra-virgin olive oil** and **salt**. Then, almost as essential as those, are **anchovies**, **capers**, **black olives**, **garlic**, **basil**, **mint**, **salty cheeses** (like **feta**, **mozzarella**, **Manchego** and **Parmesan**), and pretty much any **vinegar**. Any of these, in any combination, in any way, will make tomatoes shine.

Tomatoes can even take them all: Lay salted and drained tomato slices onto puff pastry and top them with anchovies, capers, sliced garlic and black olives. Pour over olive oil and then comes the cheese. Bake, then serve with basil and mint leaves torn over, and a gentle drizzle of **red wine vinegar**.

I say gentle but I mean vital. The vinegar brings a sour, acidic hit to play with the natural sweet-and-sourness of tomatoes. That's also why **tamarind** works well – perhaps added to a softening of tomato chunks in a pan with spices, or into a soup. **Lime** is the best citrus squeeze for tomatoes.

The spicy bitterness of basil equally serves to bring out tomato sweetness. As does the pinch of **sugar** all my tomato cooking and salad-ing gets, often accompanied by a pinch of **ground cinnamon**. Its warmth – and that of **cloves**, **sumac**, **allspice** and **cumin** – suits tomatoes. A mix of them brings depth to a tomato-laden tabbouleh, or go simpler with just one of those into the dressing for a tomato salad.

When tomatoes are being gently cooked down into a warm salad or side, or featuring in a **white fish** or **shellfish** stew, that's the time to reach for grated **root ginger**, crushed **coriander seeds**, **turmeric**, **cardamom**, and **mustard seeds**.

Those are all also the kind of flavours that are useful in bridging tomatoes' partnership with other seasonal produce. **Cucumber** is a famously classic partner with tomato, and perhaps most famously of all in gazpacho, but that is insipid without its **sherry vinegar** hit to bring things together. Same with a kachumber salad that has as its basis diced cucumber, onion and tomato but needs, well, more, for it to work. Sometimes that more is **spices**, sometimes it is **herbs**, sometimes it is **citrus**, and often a combination. Take the same approach with summer's **courgettes (zucchini)**, **peppers (capsicums)**, **long beans**, **broad (fava) beans**, **new potatoes**. All are good with tomatoes so long as there are other punchy flavours knocking around to elevate.

Remembering that tomatoes are fruits, add **peaches**, **strawberries**, **watermelon** or **plums** to a tomato salad and relish their mutually summery vibes.

More flavour thoughts: **Bacon**; **beef**; **clams**; **chillies**; **curry leaves**; **dill**; **elderflower**; **fennel**; **girolles**; **grapefruit**; **harissa**; **horseradish**; **lamb**; **lemongrass**; **mackerel**; **nasturtium**; **nutmeg**; **oregano**; **pancetta**; **prosciutto**; **saffron**; **shallot**; **shellfish**; **spring onion (scallion)**; **tahini**; **vanilla**.

Preserve

The store cupboard mainstays of tomato ketchup, jam, purée and harissa are all eminently do-able at home, but possibly most satisfying and useful of all is:

Sauce: A true abundance of really good tomatoes is definitely worth making into tomato sauce or passata. As simple as cooking down tomatoes with onions and garlic, stock, essentials of vinegar and sugar, then working through a mouli or sieve.

Arranque
(Tomato, Pepper and Garlic Dip)

A green pepper in my fridge means pretty much just one thing is coming soon: arranque. The word translates from Spanish as both 'beginning' and 'burst', making this dip aptly named for its burst of flavour at the beginning of a meal.

I first encountered it in the small coastal village of Rota in Cadiz, Andalusia, I can't say for certain if it is a particular Roteñian speciality, particular to that locality, but it's not a dish I've seen elsewhere. And so I swiftly learnt to make it, with thanks to the locals' eagerness and generosity in sharing how it is done.

The Andalusians do, of course, know a thing or two about making the most of tomatoes, garlic, olive oil and salt. This time it's blitzing them with green pepper for kick, and bread to thicken. The result is typically served with small breadsticks, crusty bread, or perhaps another green pepper sliced into lengths and used as a spoon.

Serves 4 as a dip
450g (1lb) ripe tomatoes
1 green bell pepper (capsicum)
2 garlic cloves
50–75ml (1¾–2½fl oz) extra-virgin
   olive oil
75–100g (2½–3½oz) fresh
   breadcrumbs
salt

Use the point of a sharp knife to score a cross into the base of each tomato. Sit the tomatoes in a bowl, cover with boiling water and set aside for 1 minute. Lift the tomatoes out and peel away the skins. Roughly chop the tomatoes and put – seeds and all – into a blender. Remove the stalk, core and seeds from the pepper. Roughly chop and add to the blender. Peel and roughly chop the garlic cloves and add those too. Pour in 25ml (scant 1fl oz) of the olive oil, add salt, then blitz until almost but not entirely smooth.

Spoon the mix into a bowl and salt generously. Work in the breadcrumbs, using 50g (2oz) initially and then adding more – and more olive oil – as needed. The amounts will depend on how juicy (or not) the tomatoes were. The aim is for it to be creamy and thick enough to scoop up with a breadstick. Keep tasting as you go and adding salt as needed.

WASTE TIPS: Bread (page 338), Pepper trimmings (see Stocks, page 340),
Tomato skins (pages 63 and 340)

The Sweetest Tomato Salad

Achieving the sweetest tomato salad depends upon having the sweetest tomatoes. Ones that are perfectly ripe and perfectly in season; somehow sweet and floral and musky and deeply umami all at the same time. (That said, among the 'flavour boosts' are a few handy cheats for if the tomatoes you happen to have are at all lacking.)

Tomatoes
Ripe and flavoursome. At room temperature, please. Sliced or chopped as you wish.

Dressing
Use the best extra-virgin olive oil you can get, with red wine vinegar in the ratio 2:1. Which means (this is perhaps painfully clear, but also the kind of clarity I benefit from) that for 50ml (1¾fl oz) of oil you'd use 25ml (scant 1fl oz) vinegar. Make too much and just keep it for next time; make too little and it's the work of seconds for more.

Timing
Make the salad ahead of time, let it sit in the sun's benevolent gaze for a while, and its heat will warm and deepen the flavours, helping them meld together. Gently toss occasionally so all the tomatoes get equal bathing/basking.

Salt
Always and lots. I double-salt. Straight onto the tomatoes before the dressing, and then a little extra on top shortly before serving so it floats majestically on top.

Black pepper
Personal choice – I go gently.

Basil
Plenty and always. Torn shortly before serving and scattered over.

Mint or (not *and*) tarragon
Often. Torn and added with the basil.

Parsley
Leaves never, stalks often. Very finely chop and scatter over.

Shallot

This is a classic addition, but the endeavour to benefit ratio is not high enough for me. If you fancy it, use one shallot per large tomato (or two or three smaller ones). Peel, finely chop and scatter over the tomatoes before the dressing.

Flavour boosts

Cheats, should your tomatoes need them. Don't do all of these; pick one or two at most.
- A pinch or two of ground cinnamon to bring out the tomatoes' natural sweetness.
- A pinch or two of caster (superfine) sugar, or a little elderflower cordial, into your dressing for extra sweetness.
- A pinch or two of ground cumin into your dressing for muskiness.
- Lay a few tinned anchovies over the top to oomph up the umami.
- Finish with a squeeze of lime juice for general lift.
- Rinse, chop and add a teaspoon or two of capers for extra flavour (but then hold back a little on the salt).
- Use balsamic vinegar instead of red wine vinegar for extra depth of flavour; swap for muscatel vinegar for its gentle sweetness.

Other good things to add to a tomato salad (pick just one!)

Figs, blanched long beans, steamed samphire, torn mozzarella, sliced celery stalks and leaves, charred courgette (zucchini) chunks.

And then...

At the bottom of the bowl, when it is all finished, will be a puddle of deliciousness. It's not just from the dressing but from the tomatoes, too, as the salt has gently drawn some of their juices out. Decant and keep in the fridge to use in other dressings or for cooking with over the next few days. Or tear yourself a piece of bread and dunk away.

Cherries

Summary

When I was little, cherries for me were mainly about squabbling with my sisters as we ate them on the grass on the first hot days of the school holidays. We'd dangle cherries on their stalks from our ears as makeshift earrings, and eat so many our fingers and tongues bore the fruity, juicy stains for a good while afterwards.

These days cherries are no less intrinsically linked in my heart with the arrival of proper summer – but now I take my time with them, wondering what I will be able to do with them in the kitchen, revelling in their depth of flavour, the range of colours, and the breadth of varieties. From the deep red colour and sweetness of a Stella, Sasha or Venus cherry; through to the pale Rainier or Napoleon cherries; or the Waterloo cherry that some think is the finest of all – there are so many interesting, delicious types to look out for as the season progresses.

Some are heritage varieties, some are new breeds or strains. All will taste their best when eaten as locally as possible to where they grew – cherries just don't travel well. The joy of a cherry is in the shimmer of its skin, the plumpness of its flesh, its musky scent and juice a complicated tangle of flavour layers. Those attributes can't help but be dimmed by thousands – sometimes tens of thousands – of miles of travel. I urge you to enjoy your cherries as locally as you can, when you can. That is happily easier to do for me here in the UK than it would have been a little while ago thanks to a heartening revival of cherry orchards, which needs the purchase-power of shopper support if it is going to have real momentum.

Cherries broadly break down into three styles:
- Sweet cherries, which is what all the lighter-coloured varieties are.
- Sour cherries, often called Morellos, which are for cooking with.
- Hybrids between sweet and sour, sometimes known as 'dukes', which have dark skins.

Beyond those groupings it's a cherry smorgasbord of delights to discover.

Shop

- Look for ones with green stalks. As those turn brown it means they are aging and drying out.
- The skin of the fruit should be tight and glossy.

Store

- Store in the fridge, with the stalks still on. Don't wash the cherries until using them.

Ways to Use

To pit or not to pit:
- Pitting cherry stones is essential whenever having to keep picking them out
  as you eat would be pretty unappealing to watch someone do; and/or where the
  stones will get in the way of enjoying whatever it might be. Pit them with a little
  care for cherries can still look whole once pitted if that is the look you are after.
  For a tart, perhaps.
- A cherry-pitter tool makes removing the stones barely any faff at all. (Also, very
  useful for pitting olives.)
- A pitting exception is when making your way through a bowl or bag of cherries.
  Those are times when taking out the stones can be a useful pause in just eating one
  cherry after another at speed.

With many fruits the fridge suppresses their flavours and they need to be brought back
to room temperature to be most enjoyed. Not so with cherries. The cold makes them
even more refreshing and means that often the very best thing to do with cherries is
hardly anything at all. Just pit them, chill, and serve on ice cubes with torn basil leaves
strewn over. What could be better – or easier – on a hot day?

Only marginally more effort is to sit pitted cherries for a couple of hours in alcohol
and spices (the section on Flavour Partners has more on choices for both). Done
like that they make for a fine fool by lightly puréeing the cherries and stirring them
through a 50/50 mix of Greek yoghurt and whipped cream. Or you could layer up the
macerated cherries with cream, ice cream and chocolate sauce for a sundae. Or maybe
heat them and use as a topping for a sweetly indulgent pain perdu.

Switch the macerating alcohol for vinegar and they become quick-pickled cherries.
For using in a salad, piling onto toast with labneh, or serving with cheese.

Cherry pies and tarts are always welcome in summer. As is the clafoutis that no
matter how hard cooks might try to better by switching out the classic cherries for
other fruits, somehow it's the cherries we come back to.

Sour Morello cherries are the more usual choice when it comes to savoury cooking
but don't discount sweet or semi-sweet cherries for savoury dishes. Especially at the
beginning of their season when they will be firmer, less juicy, and not so sweet as later
in the summer when the heat has developed their sugars. Try throwing a handful
of cherries in at the end of pan frying meat to serve as a side, or make into a sauce if
quickly cooked down with a dash of vinegar or red wine.

The longer you cook the cherries the more of a compôte they'll become. Keep that simple by just halving, pitting, and letting them gently simmer in a pan with wine or vinegar or just water, with sugar, honey, spices or other flavours as suits the sweet or savoury direction you intend. As the ratio of liquid goes up it becomes more like poaching, making for a looser end result, and meaning the choice of alcohol matters even more.

For more depth of flavour, roast halved and pitted cherries for 15–20 minutes in a 180°C fan/400°F/gas 6 oven, so they can collapse and just begin to caramelise.

Flavour Partners

Rich, smooth, cool **dairy** is a calm base for the bouncy flavours of cherries to play on. Perhaps in a cheesecake; cherry ice cream; or heat fresh cherries just enough to soften, then use with black cherry jam in a lushly creamy and custardy trifle. Think, too, about cherries with seasonal **young goats' cheeses** or **labneh**.

I'd use either of those as a flavour bridge to putting cherries with **mackerel**, a long-established partnership and an idea worth extending to other **oily fish**. That includes **anchovies**, whose umami hit always brings out the best in savoury cherry dishes.

Reach for almost any wine or spirit with your cherries and they'll be happy. For a quick compôte to serve with vanilla ice cream or alongside a simple loaf cake: Poach pitted cherries in **red wine**, **white wine**, **limoncello**, **vermouth** or **brandy** along with a little **sugar**, **orange zest** and some **cinnamon**; chill until needed.

Try giving a squeeze of **orange** juice or zesting its skin into sweet or savoury dishes that feature cherries. **Grapefruit** is the next-in-line citrus for cherry affinity. Lemons and limes not so much.

This for anyone who remembers cherry liquorice wheels as a kid (love them or hate them they were a smart flavour partnership): A little **liquorice** paste or syrup will give the same idea – with rather more sophistication – to sweet cherry recipes. Go steady, a little is plenty, when adding to a cherry tart, pie or crumble.

Cherries' fragrant, floral notes can be balanced with spices such as **ground ginger** and **cinnamon**; strengthened with **lavender**, **rose**, **vanilla** or **hibiscus**. As I work my way through my fridge's stash of **elderflower** cordial from spring (see page 285), I'll use it liberally with cherries and especially together in jam.

More flavour thoughts: **Almonds**; **bay leaves**; **black pepper**; **chocolate**; **coffee**; **harissa**; **hazelnuts**; **lamb**; **mace**; **maple syrup**; **nutmeg**; **pork**; **raspberry**; **rosemary**; **sage**; **tarragon**; **thyme**; **walnuts**.

Preserve

Cherry season is painfully short. That makes it all the more appealing/essential to find ways of extending how we can enjoy them.

Jam: For scones, spooning into the middle layer of a Victoria sponge, and also as a sauce for game meats, beef or duck if you heat it through with a tablespoon or so of sherry vinegar or red wine vinegar. Use sour Morello or sweet cherries.

Syrup: To drizzle over a sponge cake, add to glasses of not-so-great champagne, or mixed with sparkling water for a glamorous take on gloriously childish cherry-ade.

Freeze: Remove the stalks, then freeze with or without stones pitted. To avoid them becoming one huge clump of frozen cherry, lay them on a tray in the freezer, without the cherries touching. Once frozen, transfer to the freezer container you want to store them in.

'Cocktail Cherries': Bottle cherries in maraschino, brandy and spices for year-round garnishing of Negronis, Manhattans or Old-Fashioneds. Also for an excellent emergency pudding with ice cream and some of the boozy/fruity juice poured over the top.

White Bean, Pickled Radish and Cherry Salad

This salad fully embraces sweet and sour elements – not least because cherries are typically packed with both. Quick-pickled radishes bring more punch, add in peppery watercress and some herby hits, and the result is a salad that is as easy as it is delicious – very. Unlike many summer salads that need dressing shortly before serving so as not to over-wilt the leaves, this one will happily sit once made, enjoying the benefit of more time for its flavours to get acquainted.

Take note of the basic principles here of quick-pickling that can be applied to pretty much anything else you might want to do that way: cucumber ribbons, red onion slices, long beans, cherries.... The choice of vinegar and spices/herbs can be switched up, but the core quantities and method will be the same.

Serves 4 as a main

150g (5oz) radishes, without leaves

5 dill sprigs

½ tsp coriander seeds

100ml (3½fl oz) rice vinegar

1 tbsp caster (superfine) sugar

3 tbsp extra-virgin olive oil

10 cherries

2 handfuls of watercress

1 x 400g (14oz) tin white cannellini
   beans

2 mint sprigs

fine salt

Top and tail the radishes, slice them thinly and put into a bowl with two of the dill sprigs. Lightly crush the coriander seeds, then toast for 30 seconds in a small saucepan over a low heat to release their flavour. Pour the vinegar into the pan with 50ml (1¾fl oz) water, 1 teaspoon salt and the sugar. Heat until the salt and sugar have dissolved, then pour the liquid over the radishes and dill. Set aside for 1 hour.

Drain the radishes out of the pickling liquid. Keep the liquid but throw away the dill. Make the salad dressing by combining 3 tablespoons of the reserved pickling liquid with the olive oil and a good pinch of salt. Halve the cherries, remove their stones and put into a large bowl with the pickled radishes and watercress.

Drain the beans, rinse them, add to the radishes, then toss in the dressing. Tear over the leaves from the mint and remaining dill sprigs. Check the seasoning – radishes love salt so you might want to add a little more. Serve.

Keep the rest of the pickling liquor to use in salad dressings.

WASTE TIPS: Herb stems (see Stocks, page 340; Soft Herbs, page 341)

Raspberries and Strawberries

Summer

Summers mean strawberries; and strawberries mean summer. They just do. Much as we might try to kid ourselves into fancying strawberries out of season, the two are intrinsically linked in our minds and stomachs – and not just by memories and emotions, but by cold hard fact: Strawberries share a chemical compound with cut grass, which means there are similarities in the way our brain responds to both those smells. Thanks to (Z)-3-hexenal, we literally cannot help associating summer days of mowing the lawn with eating a bowl of sweetly ripe strawberries.

Such sweetness is best achieved when the strawberries have not been rushed into ripening. Yet the time their sugars need to develop clashes with the pressure on producers to rush strawberries out early for their natural season, to fulfil the eagerness we consumers have for them and the promise of summer they bring. More practically – but just as profit-driven a motive – strawberries harvested before being completely ripe are firmer and therefore easier to pick, handle, transport and store. The problem is, though, that strawberries won't ripen further after harvesting. When picked a little under-ripe, they will stay a little under-ripe, and fail to ever fully deliver on their promise.

All of which makes me feel a little sad for strawberries. When they are such a treat they surely deserve to be a triumph. If that means their season is shorter than really we might all like, then perhaps what we need to do is fully embrace that. To roll with the reality of its seasonality.

Raspberries are more reliably ripe as these fruits won't easily let go of their branch until ready. Remember that when out picking any wild ones, and don't try to tug too hard at an unwilling fruit. When it is ripe it will easily be freed. (And will leave its core behind on the branch, which is how you know a black raspberry is just that, rather than a blackberry.)

Black raspberries share a balance of sweet and sour with the classic pink ones; whereas golden raspberries are sweeter, almost melon-y or pineapple-y. Using a mix of raspberry varieties is a really lovely way to discover how a fruit whose flavours feel so familiar to us, is actually much more nuanced than we might think.

Shop

- A good, ripe strawberry will smell distinctly of strawberry. Insipid smell will mean insipid taste. Same with colour – go for ones that are deeply, glossily red.
- Raspberries should also be bright and look full of plump juicy life. Avoid any with their hull still attached as that means they were picked before being fully ripe. Or just use them knowing those ones will be less sweet.
- Raspberries are delicate and prone to crushing if stored for a while. Check the bottom of a raspberry punnet and if it's over-juicy that probably means the ones at the bottom have got a bit mushed.

Store

- Don't wash raspberries or strawberries until it's time to use them.
- Keep them in the fridge, uncovered or just with kitchen paper lying over single layers of the fruit. Neither strawberries nor raspberries will last long or well in the fridge.

Ways to Use

- Bring raspberries and strawberries back to room temperature before using so their flavours that have been suppressed by the cold of the fridge can bounce back.
- Wash strawberries before twisting out their hull otherwise water will get into the fruit through the hole the hull leaves. (Which is also why hull-free raspberries should only be washed shortly before using.)

For the simplest of sweet servings, sprinkle caster (superfine) sugar over the fruits and let them sit for a while. The sugar will draw excess juice out of the berries, intensifying their flavour while at the same time creating a sweet strawberry/raspberry sauce. Add a little alcohol by way of wine, vermouth or other fortified wine for extra deliciousness.

Macerated or not (although I pretty much always would), these berries are fabulous to fold into ice creams and syllabubs. Make a fool, taking the lead from the one on page 163. Layer them into trifles or sundaes. Sit them in the middle of a Victoria sponge, nestled among the cream or custard filling. Pile macerated raspberries and strawberries into the British classic of summer pudding, and give a satisfied sigh as you turn it out and see that all the lovely juices have not just turned into a sauce, but stained with crimson fruity flavour the slices of white loaf that felt so unpromising when first going into the dish.

Use the berries just as they are (i.e. un-macerated) for crumbles, pies, tarts. Add them into fluffy pancakes as on page 81. A raspberry clafoutis is a very good thing, a strawberry one less so.

Blitz the berries with a little sugar or honey (and perhaps other flavours) for the most useful of purées/sauces, where they fall on that spectrum being dependent on how much liquid is added to thin them out. After blitzing do be sure to run them through a sieve to remove seeds. Use those as ripples for ice creams, sauces for desserts, or to whisk into a salad dressing.

Cook down the berries with sugar and just a little water for a speedy compôte.

Roasting does little for a raspberry, but can lift a strawberry from mediocre into heavenly deliciousness. Slice or chop, give them a little sugar or vinegar as their destiny dictates, lay in a single layer, and roast at 190°C fan/400°F/gas 6 until gorgeously jammy (see page 79 for more). Use in sweet dishes pretty much just as with raw/macerated ones, knowing they are now softer.

A roasted strawberry is a surprisingly welcome addition to a savoury summer salad. As are the raw fruits of either of these berries for their fruity acidic hit.

Flavour Partners

There's good reason Wimbledon sells tennis-court loads of strawberries and **cream** each year: these fruits love all things **dairy**. So why not include strawberries and raspberries on a summer's cheeseboard. Look to partnering them with **yoghurts** or **young goats' cheeses** that bring a tangy lactic hit; with sharp **mascarpone** or **crème fraîche**; and with the indulgent all-in richness of whipped creams and **custards**.

A dash of macerating alcohol can help temper the balance when putting berries with these sweeter dairies. Go for **brandy**; **gin**; darkly fruity **kirsch** or **maraschino**; or **orange liqueurs**. **Amaretto** is another top choice, specifically for raspberries that love its **almond** notes. For the same reason tuck raspberries into an almond frangipane tart, or drizzle a raspberry sauce over almond milk panna cotta.

Sticking with the nuts: **walnuts** and **hazelnuts** are excellent with these fruits. Pestle walnuts into a dressing where they appear in a salad; or make a simple sundae of soaking sliced strawberries in your choice of tipple and a little sugar, then layering those up with whipped cream and toasted hazelnuts.

Some people might add **white or dark chocolate** to that by way of a grating or a ripple. Not me, because the excitement of a chocolate-dipped strawberry is one I'll never share. But I accept I am in the minority there.

I'd far rather take a strawberry laced with **vinegar**. **Balsamic** is the classic, but I think **red wine or sherry vinegars** are equally good. Just a few drops on a bowlful of berries can lift their flavour no end. Drizzle vinegar onto strawberries before roasting. Make sure raspberry and strawberry salad dressings are nicely vinegar-ed.

Or, if not vinegar-ed then citrus-ed. It's the same idea of acidic lift. **Orange** is good with these, **lime** is best of all. Finish raspberry and strawberry dishes with a grating of lime zest; squeeze its juice into sweet or savoury salad dressings.

Add chopped **chillies** to the dressing of a savoury raspberry/strawberry salad that might also feature **cherry tomatoes**, **cucumber** and **broad (fava) beans**; or fruits such as **apricot**, **peach** or **plum**. I'd also add some **spices** there, and really anywhere sweet or savoury that feature these berries. Any (or any mix of) crushed and toasted **coriander seeds**, **cardamom**, or **sumac**. Ground **cloves**, **anise** and **cinnamon** help strawberries evoke the warm spiciness more evident in wild strawberries than our cultivated ones.

Try this iced wine punch for a really refreshing summer drink that brings together raspberries' love of both booze and spices: Put ½ teaspoon of ground cloves and a dozen bruised cardamom pods into 150ml (5fl oz) brandy. Chill for 3 hours, then strain. Add to the brandy a bottle of red wine, the juice from 1 lemon and 2 oranges, 1 tbsp sugar, 1 tbsp rosewater and 300g (10½oz) raspberries. Chill again until ready to serve. Finish with 500–750ml (17–25fl oz) sparkling water (amount to taste), some sprigs of soft herbs, and cucumber slices. Serve over ice, with your shoes off and feet up.

More flavour thoughts: **Basil**; **blackberry**; **cherry**; **coconut**; **elderflower**; **figs**; **honey**; **lamb**; **lavender**; **Madeira**; **mint**; **mustard seeds**; **orange blossom water**; **pineapple**; **red wine**; **rosewater**; **sumac**; **sweet vermouth**; **tarragon**; **trout**; **watermelon**.

Preserve

Vinegar: This is far simpler than double-fermenting raspberries into a true raspberry vinegar but does (nearly) as well in a salad dressing, with goats' cheese, figs or lamb. Put 400g (14oz) raspberries into a bowl and lightly crush with a fork. Pour over 400ml (13fl oz) white wine vinegar, stir, cover the bowl with a cloth and leave somewhere cool and dark for 3 days, stirring occasionally. Strain the liquid into a medium saucepan, add 200g (7oz) caster (superfine) sugar, and bring to the boil. Turn the heat down and gently simmer for 5 minutes, skimming away any foam that comes to the surface. Pour into a sterilised bottle and set aside for 2 weeks before using. It'll keep for up to 6 months.

Freeze: Raspberries freeze far better than strawberries. Freeze them in a single layer before transferring to bags. They'll be very soft when you defrost them – best for ice creams or other things where that doesn't texture loss doesn't matter, like the pancakes on page 81. Use straight from the freezer for smoothies.

Jam: Of course.

Fluffy Raspberry Pancakes with Raspberry Syrup

The ideal forkful of pancake stack needs to have in perfect balance: fruitiness, sweetness, and lightly fluffy sweet pancake-ness. That nirvana is achieved here by cooking raspberries into the pancake batter, with then more raspberries as a syrup to spoon between the pancake layers.

They're a delight for breakfast or brunch – and in my house a Boxing Day late-morning tradition. For that I use frozen fruits, which are just as good here.

Serves 2 with a stack of 5 or 6 pancakes, size depending

15g (½oz) butter, plus extra for frying

110g (3¾oz) plain (all-purpose) flour

1½ tsp baking powder

2 tsp caster (superfine) sugar

1 egg

150ml (5fl oz) whole milk

pinch of salt

250g (9oz) raspberries

1 tbsp honey, plus more to taste

2 tsp icing (confectioners') sugar

Gently melt the 15g (½oz) butter in a small saucepan and set aside to cool.

Put the flour, baking powder, sugar, egg and milk into a mixing bowl. Add a pinch of salt and the cooled melted butter, and whisk together well. Set aside for 20 minutes, using that time to make the raspberry syrup.

For the syrup: Blend 175g (6oz) of the raspberries with 2 teaspoons water and the honey. Push through a sieve to get rid of the seeds. Taste the syrup and decide whether or not to stir in more honey to taste – it will depend how sweet or not the raspberries were, and how sweet you want the syrup.

Only make the pancakes right before eating them. Use a fork to gently crush all but a few of the remaining raspberries. Spoon those lightly crushed ones through the batter. Set a large frying pan over a medium heat. Add a small piece of extra butter, let it melt, then ladle in mixture for pancakes about 10cm (4in) wide, with space between them. Leave the pancakes alone to cook until bubbles start to blister on the surface – that's the time to turn them over and give them just another minute on the other side. Lift out onto plates, stacking them up with raspberry syrup between each pancake. Repeat with the rest of the batter, adding more butter as the pan needs.

Ideally the pancake stacks will be served straight from the pan but if you need to keep some warm until they are all done, put them onto plates and into an 80°C fan/ 175°F/gas ¼ oven.

Serve while hot, with the icing sugar, remaining raspberries and syrup over the top.

Stone Fruits – Peaches, Nectarines, Apricots, Plums

Summer – *Autumn*

Feeling peachy? I hope so. If not, take a moment, get a juicily ripe, sweet peach and let it bring you joy. For that is the power of this wonderful, happy-making fruit. Nectarines too, although somehow the phrase 'feeling nectariney' feels less likely to catch on.

Only one gene separates these two close relations. It's the gene that determines the texture of their respective skins. Whereas a peach has gentle fluffy down, a nectarine is smooth. Both fruits can be white, yellow or red fleshed.

There is little to choose in terms of flavour between both fruits' flat varieties and the ones that look like tennis balls. Round ones do seem to offer sweeter jeopardy – their shape makes the odds that bit higher of juice bursting out when a whole one is bitten into, and of it being deliciously awkward to eat without getting into a peachy mess. And surely that is what we all want from a peach/nectarine: succulent flesh so filled with nectar it can barely be contained.

As ever, the likelihood of getting ripe peaches, nectarines, apricots or plums is increased by choosing ones that have been produced nearest to where you are. The further they've had to travel, the earlier they will have had to be harvested, and the longer packaged, stored and travelled. None of these fruits will much ripen once harvested. They will soften, yes. That is just not quite the same thing as ripening. It matters for flavour as much for how easily their flesh will come away from the stone. They will part ways easily when ripe.

In their peak of life in high summer, peaches/nectarines will taste creamily fruity; apricots have something more floral going on. Plums start to get that bit more darkly spicy as befits the autumn season they are the presagers of.

Shop

- Each of these stone fruits will, when ripe, clearly smell of itself.
- If you can, cradle the fruit in your hand and give the gentlest of squeezes. There should be a little give.
- Any sign of wrinkles, or blemishes, or baggy skin means older fruits.
- Plums sometimes have a cloudy, chalky look to their skin. That is perfectly natural.

Store

- Remove packaging and let air circulate around the fruits – which also means avoiding them touching each other.
- Keep them out of the fridge if they need some warmth to soften them up a little. Otherwise, keep them in the fridge where they will be fine for a few days.

Ways to Use

Raw

Perfectly ripe stone fruits are hard to beat just as they are. Fridge-cold for refreshment in the case of peaches and nectarines; at room temperature for apricots and plums so their musky flavours that the fridge can dampen have time to bounce back. Enjoy them naked (the fruit, not you, although...); with ice cream, or a gentle pour of thick double (heavy) cream draped over.

Barely any more effort: Let slices of these fruits macerate for an hour or so in a sprinkling of sugar or honey drizzle, possibly plus something boozy by way of champagne, brandy or vermouth.

Switch the alcohol for vinegar and you are on your way to a quick-pickle. Steer towards the lighter ones (white wine, cider, rice) for peaches and nectarines; red wine vinegar for apricots; sherry vinegar for plums. Half an hour is enough time for the sliced fruits to sit in the vinegar with an equal measure of water, plus some salt, sugar, and herbs/spices. Then use in sandwiches or salads, as a condiment or side.

All these stone fruits will enjoy being part of a sweet or savoury salad.

Cooked

Under-ripe stone fruits need heat to bring the tenderness they are missing. Over-ripe, or older, stone fruits need cooking to save them from being wasted.

Poaching is my go-to for its ease and transformative powers on slightly lacklustre fruits. Use wine (red, white, sweet or fortified) and/or water; with a little sugar or honey. Look to the Flavour Partners to come for ideas of what else to put into the pot but go steady so as not to overwhelm with extra flavour. Make sure the fruit is submerged and let them gently simmer until tender. Once the fruits are out, bubble the poaching liquor over a high heat into a syrup to serve alongside.

Nectarines and peaches are glorious to poach whole, then slip off their skins, slice and serve. Or halve and stone them before poaching as with apricots and plums – noting these smaller fruits will poach quickly. Serve warm or chilled. Put them on top of your porridge or under cream/yoghurt. Use as a side for roasted meats. Or as a starting point for making them into ice cream.

Blitz poached fruit with some of the un-reduced poaching liquor for a purée, using more liquor to take it into being a syrup.

A compôte needs less liquid in the cooking pan – just enough to stop the fruits catching on the base – with the fruits cooked through to collapsing.

Make an upside-down cake by arranging fruit slices/halves in the base of a well-greased cake tin, then pour over cake batter and bake. Bake a stone fruit medley into a crumble.

For even simpler baked fruits: Sit them halved or sliced into a baking dish, pour over a little liquid (alcoholic or not), give them honey/sugar and any other flavours you fancy, then bake at about 175°C fan/375°F/gas 5 until tender.

Fry slices of peach or nectarine in a little butter in a frying pan to then take in sweet or savoury directions depending on how you use them and what you put them with.

A summer's tagine or casserole will be given fruity lightness and depth by adding in halved plums or apricots for the last 20 minutes or so of its cooking time.

Flavour Partners

These fruits are often described as being variously sweet, floral, fruity, musky, spicy. Make those the core flavour partners to lean on for stone fruits that taste the best possible versions of themselves.

Dust slices of any of these fruits with **caster (superfine) sugar** to create a delicate film of sweet lightness that the Sugar Plum Fairy would be proud of. **Honey**, **maple syrup**, **light brown sugar** or **demerara** bring richer toffee notes. A mix of white and brown sugars is especially lovely when making meringue to go with stone fruits.

Deliver more sweetness by way of alcohol: Turn to **mirin** for a savoury salad; or **sweet vermouth**, **white or dark rum**, **muscat wine**, **champagne** or **white sangria** for sweet dishes. That last option reminds me how much these stone fruits enjoy

other fruits. Put them with **tomatoes**, **cherries**, **raspberries**, **strawberries** and/
or **watermelon**. Late-summer stone fruits can enjoy a partnership with early
blackberries in which sweet or savoury serving options abound – nestle them together
into a crumble; quick-pickle the blackberries for a stone fruit savoury salad; drizzle
blackberry syrup over poached stone fruits (peaches and nectarines especially).

The blackberries work because they bring gently floral, musky spiciness. Same
with **figs** whether by way of a vinegar, syrup or the fruits. Bake halves of figs and
nectarines together, with sweet **Pedro Ximenez sherry** poured over, and sprigs of
lavender or **rosemary** tucked into the dish. **Vanilla** would be a little overpowering
in that combination but is broadly so very useful with the stone fruits to bring out
their sweetness.

More core spices to reach for with these stone fruits (this can only be the tip of
a starting point as the options are myriad): **Cardamom**, **cloves**, **cinnamon**, **cumin**,
ginger, **saffron**. Add a balance of those flavours into a poaching liquor or compôte,
whisk into a salad dressing, tuck into a pie or crumble.

The crumble topping on page 333 will do service with any stone fruit crumble,
not least because it features **nuts**. All the stone fruits are great with nuts. Use ground
hazelnuts or **almonds** instead of some of the flour in pastry for a stone fruit tart; or
toast those and toss over a sweet or savoury stone fruit salad. Churn a vanilla ice
cream with **walnuts** and finish with a stone fruit syrup ripple. Scatter **pistachios** over
a sweet salad.

These stone fruits are triumphant in savoury dishes where there is a salty element
for them to bring sweet (and slightly sour) balance to. That means **fish sauce** and
soy sauces in dressings. Salty cheeses like **gorgonzola** or **burrata**; and the wealth of
seasonal **sheep's and goats' cheeses** that start with **feta** and carry on. Pair griddled or
pan-fried stone fruits with **prosciutto**.

More flavour thoughts: **Anise**; **basil**; **bay leaves**; **coffee**; **cream**; **elderflower**; **fennel**;
game meat; **juniper berries**; **lime**; **liquorice**; **mint**; **orange**; **radicchio**; **rose**; **sesame**;
tamarind; **tarragon**; **thyme**; **yoghurt**.

Preserve

Jam: Take account of their different pectin levels: Plums are high in pectin so will make
firm jams. The others here are low in pectin so will either need some added, or just
enjoy them as softer-set conserves.

Apricot and Lavender Choux Buns

The reaction to just seeing a plate of these choux buns tends to be one of slight incredulity at how ridiculously decadent, elegant and fabulously camp they are. Tell people what they are – choux pastry cases filled with lavender-suffused crème pâtissière and apricot purée – and those reactions turn to haste to have a taste of one. They never disappoint. All the elements of purée, crème pâtissière and choux pastry cases can be made ahead. Then to serve it is just a case of building them.

Serves 8

For the apricot purée

250g (9oz) ripe apricots

1 tbsp honey (lavender honcy ideally)

For the choux buns

40g (1½oz) unsalted butter

2 tsp caster (superfine) sugar

pinch of salt

80g (3oz) plain (all-purpose) flour

2 large eggs

2 tbsp icing (confectioners') sugar,
  to finish

For the lavender crème pâtissière

500ml (17fl oz) whole milk

1 tbsp lavender flowers

100g (3½oz) caster (superfine) sugar

5 egg yolks

20g (¾oz) cornflour (cornstarch)

20g (¾oz) plain (all-purpose) flour

pinch of salt

1 tsp vanilla extract

For the apricot purée: Quarter the apricots, discarding the stones. Blitz with the honey until smooth. Chill until needed. This can be made up to 2 days ahead.

For the crème pâtissière: Heat the milk in a saucepan until gently bubbling. Add the lavender, take off the heat, set aside for 30 minutes, then strain out the lavender. Add half of the sugar to the milk and heat until again gently bubbling. Turn the heat off.

Whisk the egg yolks in a heatproof mixing bowl with the rest of the sugar, both flours and a pinch of salt, then very slowly and gradually pour in the sweetened milk, adding it little by little and mixing well after each addition. Once all mixed, pour the mixture into a clean pan. Simmer very gently and keep stirring until the custard becomes very thick. Take it off the heat, stir in the vanilla, and spoon into a bowl. Cover its surface with clingfilm (plastic wrap), then let it cool. Put into the fridge until needed – be sure to chill it for at least an hour to help it firm up even more. The crème pâtissière can be made up to 2 days ahead.

For the choux buns: Cut the butter into small pieces and add to a saucepan with the sugar, 125ml (4fl oz) water and a pinch of salt. Bring to the boil, then immediately remove from the heat and tip in the flour. Beat with a wooden spoon to a smooth paste that comes away from the pan sides. Spread the paste over a plate to cool.

WASTE TIPS: Egg whites (page 338)

Beat the eggs. Turn the cooled choux paste into a mixing bowl and slowly add the beaten eggs bit by bit. Beat after each addition and keep adding egg just until the choux mix is smooth, glossy, and will only slowly and reluctantly drop off a spoon. Chill the choux dough for 30 minutes before carrying on.

Preheat the oven to 200°C fan/425°F/gas 7. Line a baking sheet with baking paper.

Spoon the choux out into 8 equal blobs on the baking sheet. Bake for 5 minutes, then turn the oven temperature down to 180°C fan/400°F/gas 6 and bake for a further 25–30 minutes until the buns are risen and richly golden. Work quickly to stab a hole in the side of each and cool on a wire rack. The choux buns will be crispest when fresh but can be stored for up to 2 days in an airtight container.

To serve: Cut the top halves off the cooled choux buns. Put a spoonful of apricot purée onto each base, spoon over some crème pâtissière, and then another spoonful of apricot purée. Gently sit the lids back on, and finish with a dusting of icing sugar.

Three Summer Fruits, Two Summer Salads

Take the same summer fruits, give them just a few variations of ingredients, and enjoy how deliciously and refreshingly different each version can be. Choosing which salad to make when is all about connecting mood and food.

The sweet salad here is about no more than sitting ripe fruits in a simple syrup that is given a lift from lime and a pinch of salt. Serve it fridge-cold for maximum refreshment.

The savoury salad has a few more elements at play to balance the sweet acidity of the fruits.

Savoury Fruit Salad with Spring Onion, Lime, Mirin and Chilli

Serves 2 as a main

3 ripe plums

2 ripe peaches or nectarines

100g (3½oz) ripe strawberries or
  cherry tomatoes (or a mix)

2 spring onions (scallions)

1 lime

2 tbsp mirin

2 tsp toasted sesame oil

2 tsp extra-virgin olive oil

1 tsp light soy sauce or tamari

¼ tsp chilli flakes

salt

Halve the plums and peaches/nectarines, and discard the stones. Hull the strawberries/tomatoes. Slice all the fruits around 3mm (⅛in) thick and put into a serving dish or onto individual plates. Trim the spring onions and slice into long, very thin lengths. Toss with the fruits.

Finely grate the zest of the lime and set aside. Squeeze its juice and mix with the mirin, oils, soy sauce/tamari and chilli flakes. Add salt to taste. Toss with the fruits and set aside for 30 minutes, at room temperature.

Serve with the lime zest sprinkled over and another pinch of salt.

Sweet Fruit Salad with Mint and Lime

Serves 4

3 ripe plums

2 ripe peaches or nectarines

100g (3½oz) ripe strawberries

2 mint sprigs

1 lime

2 tbsp caster (superfine) sugar

salt

Halve the plums and peaches/nectarines, and discard the stones. Hull the strawberries. Slice all the fruits around 3mm (⅛in) thick and put into a serving dish or divide among individual bowls. Snap the mint sprigs in half and tuck in.

Finely grate the zest of the lime and set aside. Squeeze its juice into a small pan, add 1 tablespoon water, the sugar and a pinch of salt, and heat until the sugar dissolves. Cool to room temperature, then pour over the fruits. Toss and chill for at least 2 hours, giving an occasional toss.

Serve fridge-cold with the lime zest sprinkled over and another small pinch of salt.

A few feasting menu ideas

As courses or to mix and match for smaller sharing plates

———————

Black Olive, Shallot and Tomato Stuffed Peppers

Slow-roasted Chermoula Lamb Shoulder with Aubergine Cream;
Summer Carrots with Little Gem and Salted Almonds

Cucumber, Elderflower and Gin (or Lime) Ice Lollies

———————

Courgette and Cucumber Soup with Courgette Flowers

Creamed Spinach and Broad Bean Tart; The Sweetest Tomato Salad

Fennel and Lime Bundt with Mascarpone (from Autumn chapter)

———————

Savoury Fruit Salad with Spring Onion, Lime, Mirin and Chilli

Mackerel with Cucumber, Samphire, Tomatoes and Cream

Roasted Strawberry Zabaglione with Cardamom Biscuits

———————

Arranque; Marinated Poached Aubergines in Garlic and Oregano

Pea and Tarragon Carnaroli Rice

Sweet Fruit Salad with Mint and Lime

———————

White Bean, Pickled Radish and Cherry Salad

Patty Pan Squash with Dried Shrimps, Ginger and Lime

Apricot and Lavender Choux Buns

To drink

For the table

Peaches in Champagne

For 6

1 ripe peach

1 chilled bottle of champagne (or other
   sparkling wine)

Halve the peach, discard the stone, and cut
each half into 6 slices. Put 2 slices into a
champagne glass, and top with champagne.
As the 1970s food writer Margaret Costa
(whose recipe this nearly is) says:
"Look at it. Drink it. Eat the peach."

Repeat as desired.

- Lay sprigs of lavender or ornamental grasses
  along the table. Similarly, lengths of larkspur,
  dahlias, sunflowers, dandelions or roses.

- Arrange hydrangeas, peonies, sweet peas,
  or ox-eye daisies in low vases.

- Float the heads of roses in shallow bowls.

- Freeze edible flower petals/flower heads
  in ice cubes and use to serve with drinks.
  Rose petals, pansies and violets work
  especially well.

- Reap the benefit of having frozen slices of
  winter's citrus (page 242), and use them now
  in summer drinks/a punch bowl.

Autumn

The summer holidays are over. Whether the sigh that causes is one of relief or wistfulness, the first chilly airs of an early evening mean there is no denying autumn is around the corner. It's time to put away my lightest, flounciest dresses and let thoughts turn to cashmere sweaters with huge collars, lipsticks the colour of red autumn leaves – and the magnificence of vegetables and fruits that always arrive with perfect timing just I am getting twitchy to get back into the kitchen for some 'proper' cooking.

In the autumn you will hardly get me out of it. Playing with apples and pears; beetroots; leeks; figs; blackberries; game meats... and best of all, pumpkins and squashes. They are the true sign that autumn has landed, signalling a return to roastings and mashings; gratins and braises. My liquorice, cinnamon, cloves and star anise are drawn again to the front of the spice shelf. The glass of red wine I drink as I dance around the kitchen while cooking finds its way too into these more robust dishes and flavours. Every evening feels like my own mini version of a harvest festival – cooking as a way of giving thanks to nature for the bounty bestowed.

Summer	In Season	Winter
Aubergines (eggplants)	**Beetroot**	Brussels sprouts, kales and more dark winter greens
Lamb, hogget, mutton	**Celery**	
Broad (fava) beans and garden peas	**Fennel**	Cabbages
	Leeks	Carrots, parsnips and salsify
Courgettes (zucchini) and summer squash	**Hake**	Scallops
Cucumbers	**Maincrop potatoes**	Cauliflower
Mackerel	**Pumpkins and other winter squash**	Celeriac and swede
Summer carrots		Chard – Swiss, rainbow and ruby
Sweet peppers (capsicums)	**Apples, pears and quince**	Kohlrabi
Tomatoes	**Blackberries and elderberries**	Waterfowl – duck and goose
Cherries	**Figs**	Oranges – Seville, blood, bergamot and mandarins
Raspberries and strawberries		Venison
Stone fruits – peaches, nectarines, apricots, plums		Rhubarb

Featured Recipes

Beetroot

*Baked Za'atar Meatballs with Tomato Sauce
and Beetroot Tops*

Sloe Gin Baked Beetroot, Mackerel and Watercress

Puy Lentil, Beetroot and Baked Feta

Celery

Celery and Hazelnut Gratin

Braised Beef Short Ribs with Honeyed Figs

Fennel / Hake

Zarzuela (Fennel and Fish Stew)

Fennel and Lime Bundt with Mascarpone

Leeks / Hake

*Pulled Pot-roasted Pheasant with Leek
and Celery Couscous*

Leek and Bean Broth with Grilled Hake

Maincrop Potatoes

The Crunchiest Roast Potatoes

The Fluffiest Mash

Pumpkins and Other Winter Squash

Roasted Squash, Red Onion and Carnaroli Rice

*Pumpkin Soda Bread with Rosemary
and Caraway*

Apples, Pears and Quince

Deep-fried Apple Rings with Cinnamon Sugar

Pears in Red Wine with Bay and Thyme

Blackberries and Elderberries

*Autumn Salad: Beetroot, Fig, Blackberry,
Radicchio and Hazelnut*

Blackberry and Cassis Custard Fool

Figs

Fig, Chocolate and Pecan Frangipane Tart

Fig and Bourbon Ratafia

Autumn Feasting

*Fig and Bourbon Ratafia
Champagne Cocktail*

Beetroot

Summer - Autumn - *Winter*

Like many a child of the 1970s/80s, the beetroot of my formative years was mainly crinkle-cut and pickled. And I loathed everything about it: from the inevitable staining of fingers and favourite dresses, to its smell and, most of all, its taste. It would be years before I realised that beetroot came in anything other than a Marks & Spencer jar, and saw for the first time a true beetroot.

One with actual roots and leaves attached; its rough skin just waiting to reveal the glistening, sweet flesh beneath. Ideally, if we're lucky, there's a little soil still on there, too. Soil that is somehow redolent of the deep earthiness of flavour that beetroots carry, and that came as a taste revelation to me. These days I can't imagine not having beetroots in my cooking life, and whenever I use them I always try to bear in mind that they are best prepared in ways that protect and embrace that earthy flavour.

Along with the classic garnet-red beetroots, keep an eye out for golden beetroots with their thin skins; white beetroots that bring all the earthiness you'd expect of beetroot but are a little milder and less stain-ful; or the chioggia, a.k.a. 'candy-stripe' variety, so-called certainly because of their colouring (although the striping sadly disappears on cooking), but I think also a nod to the inherent sweetness of all beetroots.

Shop

- Beetroots should feel firm. You don't want any wrinkling or withering – both signs of getting older and losing moisture.
- Try to buy beetroots with some soil still on them. It's a good sign they haven't been out of the ground for too long.
- Similarly, try to buy beetroots with leaves attached. Not just because they are delicious, but if they are nicely glossy with edges that aren't wilting, it's a good sign of healthy, fresh beetroots.

Store

- Leave any soil on – it acts as a protective cover. Only wash off when it's time to use.
- Soil-on beetroots can be stored out of the fridge, somewhere cool and dark. Soil-less beetroots are best kept in the fridge.
- Beetroots with leaves attached will need them removing to help the roots stay fresh longer; otherwise, the leaves will just try to draw moisture out of the roots. Take the leaves off as soon as you can and keep them separately in the fridge, wrapped in damp kitchen paper or a cloth.

Ways to Use

Raw beetroot brings lots of potential. Finely chop/shred for a remoulade. Or go for 'carpaccio' beetroot salad by simply shaving raw peeled beetroots as thinly as your fingers or a mandoline will allow, and styling the circles on a platter – a beauty of a dish that's at its most show-offable with a mix of beetroot varieties to give you a medley of colours.

Once you've got the knack of slicing them so thinly, how about beetroot crisps: Peel, slice thinly on a mandoline, toss in oil, then bake for an hour or so at 150°C fan/325°F/ gas 3 until dry and crisp. Season with za'atar and plenty of salt, then serve.

Grate raw beetroots for salads and slaws; to add to meatballs or koftas; for latkes (instead of the more traditional potato); or to add to a flatbread dough.

The cooking time for whole beetroots can sometimes be a bit of mystery. If they take longer than a recipe says, take some heart in knowing that it's not your fault, the recipe's fault, nor the beetroot's fault. Give yourself (and your beetroots) time – or cook them well ahead of time.

Roasting achieves the deepest intensity of flavour that I think holds most true to what a beetroot wants to taste like. Wrap each one loosely in foil or put them together into a covered dish with a little water, wine or vinegar to stop them drying out. Add in your pick from the Flavour Partners to come. Maximum corralling of flavour is achieved by roasting with the skins left on. Once cooked and cooled, the skins will slide off with the barest rub of your thumb and you can use those beetroots in salads, etc. But when you are cooking them alongside other elements you'll be serving them with (for example, if you are roasting beetroots and carrots together to serve together), peel the beetroots *before* roasting.

Try beetroots hasselbacked, then served with a flavoured butter that can settle into its every delicious groove.

Beetroots can be boiled or steamed, too, of course. Leave on a few centimetres of the roots and tops to limit the extent the beets' colour – and therefore flavour – will bleed out into the water.

The sweetness of beetroots should really make them useful in sweet cooking. I say it *should*. Other than with chocolate in cakes or brownies, I don't know if I can ever fully escape that feeling and flavour of the earth, which I so love about beetroots but which I don't necessarily want for dessert. Even beetroot ice cream is a thing. (Just not *my* thing – it might be yours, though.)

Having asked you to buy beetroots with leaves attached: A few of them, rinsed in ice-cold water to perk them up, are a great addition to salads – let them sit a while in the dressing to soften and lose any excessive bitterness. Stir leaves into pots of dal or lentil stews shortly before serving. Think of them as you would spinach – knowing the leaves will shrink like spinach, too. You can also stir fry like you would Swiss chard (silverbeet) – beetroot's botanical cousin.

The beetroot stalks that connect the bulb to the leaves are lovely when finely chopped and used to add to fried-off onions in the base of a dish (like you might celery); or simmered and blitzed into a soup.

Flavour Partners

Autumn's **blackberries**, **plums** or **figs** are in season at the same time as beetroot and make perfect partners. Summer's **cherries** do something similar for the young beetroot available in the warmer months, especially if the cherries are quick-pickled (see page 72).

Oranges act as a foil for beetroot's sweetness in all kinds of savoury dishes. Roast peeled beetroot with a good squeeze of orange juice, its shells thrown into the roasting tin, too. Other aromatics for adding to beetroots when roasting: Sprigs of **woody herbs**, whole **garlic** cloves, and you won't go wrong with a hefty pour of **sloe gin** or **dry white vermouth**.

Go heavy on the **vinegar** for roasting or dressing beetroots: **Red wine**, **sherry** or **dark fruit vinegars**, such as blackberry or fig, are especially good. Serving cooked beetroot with a **pickle** will give the same balance of acid to sweet. Beetroot is fabulous with **soused herring** or **mackerel**.

Beetroot's influence on culinary cultures is evident in its spread from Germany (where some accounts say it originated) into recipes across Scandinavia, the Middle East, the Caucasus and into Eastern Europe. Look to all of those cultures for beetroot inspiration and, while you're there, explore the heritage borschts of different regions and seasons. Some are chilled, or not. Light, or rib-sticking. Vegetarian, or made with meat stocks, or with chunks of **pork**. Sometimes blended smooth, or with the elements left whole and distinctive. **Dill** and **horseradish** are borscht's most usual flavour-fellows and well worth remembering whenever doing anything in the beetroot line of things.

Mix either (or both) of those through the silky **dairy** that so often makes an indulgent bed for the depth of beetroot to recline upon. Think about **crème fraîche**, **labneh**, **yoghurt** or **soured cream**.

Liquorice is completely, intensely, maybe even surprisingly, lovely with beetroot. Break liquorice sticks into the water in which you are about to boil beetroots, add to a jar of pickling beetroot, or include a little liquorice paste in a dressing for roasted beetroots.

Nuts are a double-win with beetroots, as they share not just seasonality but also deeply earthy flavours. Pound **walnuts** into a sherry vinegar and olive oil dressing. Look to **hazelnuts** and **pecans** with beetroots, too.

More flavour thoughts: **Anchovies**; **capers**; **caraway**; **coconut**; **coffee**; **cumin**; **duck**; **grapefruit**; **lemon**; **lime**; **miso**; **mushrooms**; **mustard**; **oregano**; **rosemary**; **soy sauce**; **tahini**; **watercress**; **za'atar**.

Preserve

Pickle: My childhood/childish prejudices aside, pickled beetroot can be very delicious. Use a red wine vinegar.

Freeze: Cook and peel your beetroot first, then freeze whole or sliced.

Dry: Make beetroot powder to use as an alternative to less-than-natural pink food colouring for red velvet cakes and to bring sweetness and colour to smoothies. Peel the beetroots, slice as thinly as you can, and spread in a single layer in a baking tray. Put into a 50°C fan/125°F/gas ¼ oven until completely dried out. Store in an airtight container and grind them to a powder as needed.

Ferment: The sweetness of beetroot lends itself to home fermentation for beetroot wine. Marvellous in itself, or taken a fermentation further and turned into beetroot vinegar.

Baked Za'atar Meatballs with Tomato Sauce and Beetroot Tops

This is not just a terrific dinner, but shows off just how beetroot stalks and leaves are delicious and useful in their own right, too. This dish would certainly be nice enough without the beetroot stalks cooked into the base of the dish, or indeed the beetroot leaves added for the finish – but not nearly so good as with them.

Serve with plenty of couscous, stirred through with lots of chopped herbs, salt and a squeeze of lemon.

Serves 4 as a main

For the sauce

2 red onions

3 tbsp olive oil

4 garlic cloves

stalks and leaves from 6 beetroots

5 anchovy fillets, drained of oil

1 x 400g (14oz) tin chopped tomatoes

2 tbsp grated fresh horseradish

2 tbsp crème fraîche

salt and black pepper

For the meatballs

1 red onion

2 garlic cloves

400g (14oz) minced beef or lamb

1 tbsp za'atar

80g (3oz) breadcrumbs

1 egg

2 tbsp olive oil

salt and black pepper

Make the sauce first: Peel and chop the onions. Heat the olive oil in a large deep frying pan and cook the onions over a gentle heat until starting to tenderise and taking on a little colour. Peel and finely chop the garlic cloves, and add those too.

While they are cooking, separate the beetroot leaves from the stalks. Sit the leaves in very cold water to keep them perky. Finely chop the stalks, and add to the frying pan. Let them cook down for 5 minutes, stirring, then add the anchovies and chopped tomatoes. Rinse out the tomato tin with water and add that to the pan too. Season. Simmer for 20 minutes. Set aside while you make the meatballs.

WASTE TIPS: Anchovies (page 338), Horseradish (page 339), Onion skins (see Stocks, page 340)

For the meatballs: Preheat the oven to 210°C fan/450°F/gas 8.

Peel and grate the onion and garlic into a bowl, add the minced meat, za'atar and breadcrumbs, and season well. Beat the egg and add, then use your hands to bring the mixture together. Divide into 20 equal pieces, rolling them into balls as you go. Sit the meatballs on a baking tray, drizzle over the oil and bake in the oven for 15 minutes.

For the last 5 minutes of the meatballs' baking time, put the sauce back on the heat and stir in the horseradish. Lift the beetroot leaves out of the water and sit on kitchen paper to dry, then just before the meatballs are ready, stir the crème fraîche and beetroot leaves through the sauce. Remove the meatballs from the oven and sit them on top of the sauce. Pour over any oil left behind in the baking tray, grind over plenty of black pepper and serve straight away.

Sloe Gin Baked Beetroot, Mackerel and Watercress

This is the kind of thing I typically feel like eating on those transitional weeks where summer is becoming autumn. It is that bit heartier than the food the hotter weather put me in the mood to cook/eat, but there is still a lightness to it that appeals when I haven't given up on summer *quite* yet....

Serves 4 as a main

750g (1lb 10oz) raw beetroots

75ml (2½fl oz) sloe gin

3 thyme sprigs

3 garlic cloves

150g (5oz) watercress

75ml (2½fl oz) extra-virgin olive oil

2 tsp Dijon mustard

½ lemon

4 hot-smoked mackerel fillets

2 dill sprigs

salt and black pepper

Preheat the oven to 200°C fan/425°F/gas 7.

Wash and trim the beetroots, leaving a few centimetres of root and stalk attached. Put into a baking dish, pour over the sloe gin and 75ml (2½fl oz) water, then add the thyme, unpeeled whole garlic cloves and season. Cover with a lid/kitchen foil and bake for 1 hour, or until the beetroots are tender. (Check part way through the roasting to make sure the dish isn't becoming dry. Add more gin/water if needed.) Set the beetroots aside to cool, then rub the skins off them and cut into chunks. Discard the thyme but keep back the roasted garlic cloves and any juices left in the dish.

Arrange the watercress on a serving dish or individual plates and tuck the beetroot chunks among the leaves. Pour over any reserved roasting juices.

Whisk together the olive oil, mustard and a squeeze of lemon. Squeeze the flesh out of the tender garlic cloves, crush with the back of a spoon, and mix into the dressing. Season well, adding more lemon to taste.

Remove the skin from the mackerel, break the flesh into chunks and toss in around two-thirds of the dressing. Add to the beetroot and watercress. Pour over the rest of the dressing and finish the dish with the dill leaves scattered over, a smattering of salt flakes and a few grindings of pepper.

WASTE TIPS: Herb stems (see Stocks, page 340; Soft Herbs, page 341),
Lemon rind (see Citrus, page 338)

Puy Lentil, Beetroot and Baked Feta

Feta and red onions are baked together to become gorgeously tender in this fresh, punchy salad that can be enjoyed just as much served hot as at room temperature. Some warmed flatbreads alongside work well.

Serves 4 as a main; 6–8 as a starter or sharing plate

2 large beetroots

3 red onions

1½ tbsp fennel seeds

5 tbsp olive oil

1 tbsp red wine vinegar

300g (10½oz) feta cheese

300g (10½oz) Puy lentils

large handful of mint leaves

large handful of flat-leaf parsley leaves

1 tbsp apple balsamic or other balsamic vinegar

salt and black pepper

Steam the whole beetroots until tender (40 minutes–1 hour, depending on the size and age of the beetroots) and set aside to cool.

Preheat the oven to 190°C fan/400°F/gas 6.

Peel the onions and slice thinly into rounds. Break the rings up, put into a large mixing bowl, and mix with the fennel seeds, 3 tablespoons of the olive oil, the red wine vinegar and some seasoning. Spread a large piece of kitchen foil over a baking tray. Pile half of the onion mixture into the middle of it, break up the feta and scatter it over, then pile the rest of the onions on top. Bring the foil over the top and seal the edges to form a loose parcel. Bake in the oven for 25 minutes.

Meanwhile, rinse the lentils, put into a medium saucepan, cover with plenty of water, and bring to the boil. Simmer for 15–20 minutes until just tender but still with some bite. Drain.

Spread the lentils over a serving dish. Chop the mint and parsley leaves and stir through with some seasoning, the remaining 2 tablespoons of olive oil and the balsamic vinegar. Cover to keep warm. Peel the beetroots and cut into chunks. Arrange those over the lentils, then pile over the now softly baked contents of the foil parcel. Eat straight away, or allow to cool before serving.

WASTE TIPS: Feta brine (page 339), Herb stems (see Stocks, page 340; Soft Herbs, page 341), Onion skins (see Stocks, page 340)

Celery

Autumn - Winter - *Year Round*

Celery is one of those vegetables whose seasonality has, I feel, got a little lost along the way. Perhaps that doesn't really matter for year-round chopping of celery into the base of so many dishes. Because that is frankly how most celery ends up (in my kitchen, anyway) – sautéed off with onions, garlic and carrots for sofritos/mirepoix. That, or as celery batons for awkward balancing of dips. It does matter though, in so much as it is part of our general disconnection with the land and what it produces and when.

If this book is about feeling the rhythms of nature resonate in your kitchen (and it is about that, in case you were wondering), then I am going to stand up for reconnecting with celery as a cool-weather crop. Before commercial farming made it not only easier to grow celery, but prolonged its season and availability, celery was prized as an autumn/winter luxury. Upper- and middle-class Victorians even had a vogue for glass celery vases to show it off (and therefore their wealth) at the dinner table.

Part of its allure was that celery was hard to grow. It needs the high water content of rich, peaty land to flourish, which is why in Britain areas such as the Cambridgeshire Fens became famous for it. That fame endures with PGI-accredited Fenland Celery with its traditional seasonality running 8 weeks from October to December. It is a type of white celery, its colour the result of being grown with the soil banked around to protect it from the cold and, inevitably, from the light. It's a similar idea to white asparagus. The resulting white celery is definitely worth seeking out in its season and revelling in its sweeter and nuttier flavour.

Not that what I am going to go on to talk about here is only for white celery – white and green alike need to be broken free from their sofrito/crudité shackles.

Shop

- Yes, you can buy celery hearts with the tougher outer ribs removed. And yes, you can also buy loose celery stalks free of their connecting base. But I'm not quite sure why you would want to buy either. They're more expensive than buying a whole celery (it's the price you pay for their pre-preparedness), and you are going to lose out on those other bits of the vegetable that are so fabulous. Better to buy the whole thing, prepare it yourself, and just use all the bits in different ways.

- Look for celery that is holding itself together tightly, and nice and firm. It should look crisp, not be going soft anywhere, and no yellowing or browning on the stalks.
- Same with the leaves – look for them to be bright and crisp.
- Pale celery (see white celery, left) has a milder flavour. The greener it is, the stronger the flavour.

Store

- Celery bought at its perky best keeps well – easily for up to a fortnight in the fridge, as long as it's not in its coldest part. Celery's high water content means it can freeze, even in the fridge, and it then goes all mushy when you try to use it.
- Wrap in a damp towel or kitchen paper in the fridge to keep fresh longest. Or just place in a bag with air holes.
- Try storing under water in the fridge.
- Keep the celery connected to its base until you need to separate the stalks for using.
- Celery that is starting to go a bit sad can be cheered up by standing it in some water.

Ways to Use

Get to know your celery:
- The outer stalks are the toughest, and they're also darker in colour, which shows they'll be packing the strongest flavour. If stringy, just pull the strings out.
- The celery heart is its inner stalks. More tender of texture and sweeter in flavour.
- The bases of all the stalks are especially aromatic.
- The leaves of the outer stalks are larger and more bitter than the delicate leaves of the heart.

When celery stalks are cooked, their natural bitterness evolves into something more bittersweet. That's what makes them so great for mirepoix/sofrito. But note that if celery colours too much when fried off, it can go the other way and become more bitter. Keep the heat low, go slow, and you'll round out its flavours to their best.

The bittersweetness is what makes all celery trimmings such a great addition to stocks. Add to the pot, too, when poaching a chicken or ham. Same when poaching fish, but go steady so as not to overwhelm with celery flavour.

Celery soups are always a win. Where it is the flavour lead you will benefit from using all different parts of the celery, so it can naturally complement itself. Where it is more of a base for other soup flavours to build on, consider whether those flavours are strong enough to contend with the heft of outer celery stalks, or need a more delicate celery hit.

Smaller celery leaves are a perfect garnish for celery soups, in a salad, or chopped up as a herb.

Roast the tender stalks of celery hearts as you would any other vegetable and often alongside them, too.

Bake, braise or stew the hearts by giving them a first few minutes in a pan with butter and/or oil over a medium heat, then add stock, wine, dry vermouth or cider (plus whatever other flavour partners you fancy) and cook through until tender. Or skip the initial browning and simply poach in any of those same stocks, etc.

With a richly meaty slow braise, it can be lovely to add larger chunks of celery only for the last 20–30 minutes of the cooking time. That way, they retain more of their crunch and bitterness, making a pleasing contrast to ultra-tender meat. See the Braised Beef Short Ribs with Honeyed Figs on page 114.

Celery's crunch and peppery bitterness can work brilliantly in stir fries, but blanch first for just 30 seconds in boiling water to take the edge off, refresh in cold water, then drain and dry.

Quick-pickle hearts for a salad, or perhaps a cheeseboard.

Thinly slice raw celery hearts for a remoulade. Slice even thinner still for a slaw.

Flavour Partners

Celery's bitterness, especially as it evolves into bittersweetness, enhances and complements the sweetness of **meats** and **fish**. Take that central point and use it in different ways:

Criss-cross celery stalks as a bed for roasting a joint of **beef** or **lamb**, with **garlic cloves** and **woody herbs** tucked in too. It becomes a meltingly tender side and gives the juices incredible flavour.

Add chunks of celery, earlier or later in the cooking process (see above), to a **venison** casserole that is packed with other flavours, such as **bay leaves**, **garlic**, **juniper berries** and **horseradish**, all of which celery will enjoy playing with.

Celery has long been a traditional partner to **chicken**. Try it in a stuffing or in chicken soup. And while we're on birds: all kinds of **game birds** will benefit from celery. That could be stalks braising along in the pot; as a side dish; or cold game, such as **pheasant** or **pigeon**, with raw or quick-pickled celery hearts as a salad.

Celery remoulade is a great accompaniment to **game terrines**, likewise **mackerel** or **smoked fish**, or perhaps into/alongside a **prawn** or **lobster** roll.

That remoulade would be good with some **apple** in there. Some **walnuts** would be terrific, too, given celery and walnuts share aroma profiles. **Chestnuts** work well for similar reasons.

The richness of **cheeses** make a fine partner to celery and I think perhaps it is with cooked celery that cheese excels. It could be a cheese sauce over the stalks as they bake; or simply some grated **Parmesan** browning under the grill atop a celery gratin.

Blue cheese and celery soups are a classic, and the appealing saltiness of a **feta**, **Roquefort** or **Stichelton** reminds me how much peppery celery loves a salty partner – which means also just some sensational **salted butter** on a celery heart stalk; **anchovy mayonnaise**; **anchovy fillets** laid over raw or braised hearts; or **samphire**, perhaps quick-pickled with finely sliced celery.

More flavour thoughts: **Almond**; **bottarga**; **chervil**; **cider**; **coriander seeds**; **dill**; **fennel**; **ginger** (**ground** and **root**); **mustard** and **mustard seeds**; **nutmeg**; **orange**; **oysters**; **parsley**; **pear**; **pork**; **soy sauce**; **tahini**; **tarragon**; **tofu**; **truffle**.

Preserve

Celery is another vegetable that is really at its best used fresh, to make the most of its best qualities: that crisp flavour and texture. If you really have too much celery and can't think what to do with it, dehydrating is your best bet (although I am not sure worth the fuss).

Celery and Hazelnut Gratin

This dish is all about celebrating the luscious simplicity of celery. It is, like celery itself, somehow rustic yet elegant all at the same time. It makes an excellent side dish for meat or fish, but can be just as good as the main event of a meal. You'd just need some peppery leaves alongside, and maybe chunks of bread to mop up the baking juices.

Serves 6–8 as a side; 4–6 as a main

1 whole head of celery, about
   650–700g (1lb 7–9oz)
2 bay leaves
300ml (10fl oz) double (heavy) cream
250ml (8½fl oz) chicken or
   vegetable stock

75g (2½oz) shelled hazelnuts
75g (2½oz) breadcrumbs
30g (1oz) Parmesan
salt and black pepper

Preheat the oven to 180°C fan/400°F/gas 6.

Pull all the celery stalks away from the base, trimming away only the very toughest ends. Wash thoroughly. Pull away and keep all the leaves. Cut all the stalks into roughly 5cm (2in) lengths – if they seem stringy, just pull the strings off. Tumble the celery pieces and the celery leaves into a gratin or baking dish, tuck in the bay leaves and season well with salt and pepper.

Mix the double cream with the stock and pour over the celery. Cover with foil and bake for 1–1½ hours until the celery is properly tender.

Make the gratin topping as the celery bakes. Roughly crush or grind the hazelnuts, then mix with the breadcrumbs in a bowl. Grate in the Parmesan and mix again, adding some salt and pepper too.

When the celery is ready, turn on the grill. Scatter the gratin topping over the dish and put under the grill (uncovered now, obviously) for 5–10 minutes until gorgeously browned.

Serve while hot, but a few minutes away from the heat for the celery juices to calm down and thicken is no bad thing.

WASTE TIPS: Celery trimmings (see Stocks, page 340)

Braised Beef Short Ribs with Honeyed Figs

Short ribs need the kind of low and slow cooking that is going to make the meat pretty much fall off the bone with tenderness. And that's just what they get here.

When you're making this it might seem counter-intuitive not to just follow the usual routine and chop the celery up and add towards the beginning, sofrito-style, with the onion. But the point here is not to cook the celery down so it almost disappears, but to cook it just long enough to tenderise a little, while leaving it with a strength of flavour that will help cut through the richness of the rib's braise.

Some kind of potato or root veg mash is terrific alongside.

Serves 4 as a main

2 red onions

3 tbsp rapeseed or olive oil

50g (2oz) butter

4 beef short ribs

1 garlic bulb

1 tbsp juniper berries

3 bay leaves

2 tarragon sprigs

5cm (2in) piece of fresh root ginger

6 large carrots

2 tbsp plain (all-purpose) flour

½ bottle of red wine

4 celery stalks

150g (5oz) cavolo nero

salt and black pepper

For the honeyed figs

4 ripe figs

1 tbsp sherry vinegar

1 tbsp honey

¼ tsp ground cinnamon

WASTE TIPS: *Carrot peelings (see Stocks, page 340), Cavolo nero ribs (page 341), Ginger (see Horseradish, page 339), Onion skins (see Stocks, page 340)*

Peel the onions and slice into thin half-moons. Set aside.

Choose a large casserole dish that can go in the oven and on the hob and set it over a medium heat. Add the oil and butter and, once they're good and hot, brown the ribs all over (doing it in batches if you need to). Remove the ribs to a plate and set aside.

Preheat the oven to 150°C fan/325°F/gas 3.

Put the prepared onions into the same dish, turn the heat down and gently cook, adding a little more oil if it looks at all dry. Meanwhile, pull the garlic cloves off the bulb, peel and chop. When the onions are softening but have not taken on any colour, add the chopped garlic. Crush the juniper berries in a pestle and mortar and add those too, along with the bay leaves and tarragon sprigs. Grate the ginger straight in (there's no need to peel it). Stir round, season with salt, and let it gently cook while you prepare the carrots. Only peel them if very gnarly, otherwise just scrub and cut into chunks. Add the carrots to the dish, then return the beef ribs along with any of their juices. Dust over the flour and toss everything round for a minute so the flour disappears into the mix. Pour over the wine and however much water you need to add to just about cover it all. Season, bring to a simmer, then cover with the lid and place in the oven for 2 hours.

After 2 hours, trim the celery stalks, slice into chunks and add to the casserole. Return to the oven for 20 minutes.

Pull the cavolo nero leaves from their ribs, and tear them into the casserole. Stir it all together and give it another 10 minutes in the oven for the leaves to wilt.

Check the seasoning. Now try hard not to serve the ribs straight away. They will benefit from sitting for 10–15 minutes out of the oven to rest a little. Keep the lid on and they won't go cold, they'll just get extra tender.

Use that time to make the figs: Turn the oven up to 190°C fan/400°F/gas 6. Cut the tops off the figs and cut a cross into the top of each one. Give them a squeeze to open them up, then sit them snugly, cut-sides up, in a large piece of kitchen foil inside a baking dish. Mix together the vinegar, honey and cinnamon in a bowl. Spoon the mixture over the figs, pushing it into the cuts you just made. Bundle the foil, loosely but securely, to seal. Bake for 5 minutes, then open up the foil and bake for another 5 minutes, or until squeezably tender. Serve alongside the braise.

Fennel

Summer - Autumn - *Winter*

To paraphrase Richard Gere in *Pretty Woman: People's reactions to fennel are very dramatic; they either love it or they hate it. If they love it, they will always love it. If they don't, they may learn to appreciate it, but it will never become part of their soul.*

Or that's how the conversation between Gere and Julia Roberts could easily have gone if only their date had been at a farmer's market not an opera house.

Fennel is a vegetable I adore. My husband, on the other hand, is not naturally drawn to it. I like to think that over the years he has come to appreciate it – some dishes, like the Zarzuela (Fennel and Fish Stew) on page 120, are close to being part of his culinary soul. But as Gere very nearly said, it really is a love-it-or-hate-it kind of vegetable and that is due to its whack of anise flavour. Those same profiles are subtler when they appear in celery, dill, tarragon, chervil, even celeriac. With fennel they are square on, and so the cook's challenge is to either embrace, harness and celebrate that – or find ways to mellow it out. You'll find plenty of both approaches here.

Note that I am really talking here about the Florence fennel bulb (a.k.a. finocchio), rather than the sweet herb fennel grown for its leaves and seeds. But for that the same flavour partners would apply.

Shop

- Look for bulbs that are firm and crisp. As they get older they'll lose moisture and look a bit tired. Slimy patches or browned bits can be signs that the fennel has been in cold storage too long.
- At the risk of sounding contradictory, don't worry too much about perfection, though. Sometimes a pristine 'perfect' fennel can actually be lacking in flavour. Ideally, you'll be able to see colour gradations through the bulb from white to creams to all the greens. It should look full of flavour life.
- Round bulbs tend to be sweeter than the flatter ones.

Store

- In the crisper drawer of the fridge, but not for too long as its flavour will diminish.
- Pick off the fronds and store separately, wrapped in damp kitchen paper or cloth and in the fridge.
- Resurrect a tired fennel bulb by cutting off any bruises, slicing it and sitting in ice-cold water for up to 1 hour before using. Don't be tempted to do that for longer, though. All you'll achieve is it losing fennel flavour to the water.

Ways to Use

Get to grips with your bulb:
- First, remove the fronds and save to use as a herb.
- Trim away the stalks that are coming out of the main bulb. Use for flavouring stocks and soups, but not too much else as they're pretty tough.
- Cut/pull away the outer layer of the bulb if it is a little too damaged for your recipe, and, again, use for stocks and soups.
- As soon as you start cutting into your fennel bulb it will want to start oxidising and discolouring. Chop and use quickly, or pop the pieces into a bowl of water with lemon squeezed into it.

A mandoline is your friend for shaving/slicing fennel to use raw in sauerkrauts and salads. Slice following the grain of the bulb. Sometimes you want the crisp flavour and texture of fennel just as it is, but to soften up the slices a little you could give them a nice massage in the juices of an orange so its acidity can get to work relaxing the fennel. Use that orange juice in your salad dressing so the flavours carry through.

The intense flavours of fennel calm down a bit when it is cooked. That can be a good thing for salads: Simmer fennel (more on that below), drain, toss in oil while it's still warm enough to take it on board, then chill before using in your salad.

Nestle fennel slices or wedges around a joint of meat or game birds when pot-roasting. Bake fish (fillets or whole) on a bed of fennel slices.

Roast fennel with other seasonal vegetables. Or roast it alone, then perhaps blitz to a dip with oil and other flavour partners.

Simmer/poach fennel slices or wedges until tender (how long that takes depends, fairly obviously, on their size) and from there you can take the fennel in a few different directions. What you simmer them in is also worth taking a moment or two over: stock; water with some herbs or spices added; milk; white wine or vermouth; or Pernod for we real anise-heads. Then:
- Lay the fennel into a buttered dish, top with grated Parmesan and bake until golden and bubbling.

- Cook pasta in whatever the fennel simmered in (for a glorious through-line of flavour), then toss the pasta with the tender fennel, add salt and oil, and serve.
- For a fennel sauce: Simmer the fennel in milk with a knob of butter added, then blitz the fennel to a purée with as much of the milk as needed to achieve the consistency you want. So good with pasta, possibly plus Parmesan, definitely plus lots of black pepper.
- Serve the tender fennel just as a side, with the cooking liquor reduced down.
- Dress the simmered fennel while still warm, but serve cold or at room temperature, on its own or as part of a salad.

To deep fry fennel wedges: You could just dip them in beaten egg and breadcrumbs before they go into the hot oil, or go for a tempura batter (see page 280). Either way, tenderise first by blanching for a few minutes in boiling water, refresh in cold water, then drain and dry.

Grate fennel for using in cakes. Really. It's very very good. Head to page 122.

Flavour Partners

The flavour challenge/opportunity with fennel is always that you are either trying to balance out its hefty anise-ness with other big flavours that can stand up to the challenge; or you go for giving fennel a more neutral flavour bed that lifts up and celebrates all the fennel is bringing. Whenever you use it, you just need to decide where on the spectrum you want to land.

Let's go for boldly balancing first:

Anything **citrus** is going to work really well. **Orange** or **grapefruit** segments for a fennel salad. **Orange**, **lime**, **lemon** or **yuzu** (zest and juice) for using with raw or cooked fennel.

Talk of fennel and acidity makes **vinegar** the next flavour stop. With fennel I find myself especially reaching for **sherry vinegar** (although, when isn't that the case...), **rice vinegar** and – rarer for me – a good **balsamic**.

Fennel can seem bitter when raw but perversely less so if you put it with other elements that are also bitter. That could be sliced **radicchio** or some massaged raw **kale**. Together their mutual and complementary bitter notes will need just some good **olive oil** and a smattering of **salt flakes** for harmony to be achieved. But you might like to try adding a touch of sweetness, too, by way of grated or mandolined **apple**, some **honey** or **maple syrup**.

The bold, salty flavours of **black olives**, **capers** and **anchovies** are fine partners for raw or cooked fennel. Try any of those added at the end of roasting some fennel wedges, when the fennel has caramelised a little and its sweetness craves a salty lick.

I often find myself drawn to the warming notes of **harissa** and also to its component spices, such as **caraway seeds**, **cinnamon**, **cumin** – whatever works in harissa will work with fennel.

Try infusing the water, wine or stock you are poaching fennel in with a little **saffron**. It also brings a little mellowing warmth, and starts to veer towards that calmer end of the fennel flavour partner spectrum. There, I'll also find **cucumber** and **kohlrabi; potatoes** to be sliced and baked with fennel slices; **leeks**; and **white fish** that roasts on top of fennel or cooks in with it for a broth/stew like page 120's Zarzuela (Fennel and Fish Stew).

Cheese, **butter** and **cream** will also temper fennel's mood.

More flavour thoughts: **Bay leaves**; **black pepper**; **cauliflower**; **cider**; cloves; **coconut**; **damsons**; **garlic**; **juniper berries**; **lamb**; **Madeira**; **Marsala**; **nuts**; **oysters**; **parsnip**; **pears**; **pesto**; **poppy seeds**; **pork**; **scallops**.

Preserve

Pickle: A muscatel vinegar is the best call for pickling fennel, thanks to the edge of slight sweetness it brings. Pick a few of the flavour partners above to pack in there too – not too many different ones, or the flavours will get a bit confused. Orange peel + cinnamon stick + juniper berries would be a great combo. With maybe a bay leaf for good measure.

Zarzuela (Fennel and Fish Stew)

This is a go-to dish in my house. Most often on Saturday night rotation, when I want to cook and eat something I can prepare in advance or that needs very little finishing after our Saturday-night ritual of a cocktail (or two).

Its marriage of fennel and aromatics hits the sweet spot of the fennel flavour spectrum: there is just enough going on to balance out fennel's dominance, yet somehow also let it shine. Hake is my preferred choice of white fish (see page 131 for why), but do switch that up for whatever is fresh and seasonal. The essential accompaniment is good bread for mopping up the juices.

Serves 4–6 as a main

2 onions

3 tbsp olive oil

3 garlic cloves

1 fennel bulb

2 bay leaves

2 thyme sprigs

1 tsp smoked paprika

250ml (8½fl oz) white wine or dry vermouth

800g (1lb 12oz) filleted skinless loin of hake or other white fish

2 prepared squid, including wings and tentacles

8 raw king prawns

salt and black pepper

Peel the onions, cut in half and slice into thin half-moons. Heat the oil in a large deep frying pan or casserole, then add the onions and cook gently with a lid on, so they soften but do not colour. Check the onions regularly to make sure they aren't catching on the bottom of the pan.

Meanwhile, peel and crush the garlic cloves. Prepare the fennel: Remove and set aside the fronds, trim off the upper stalks and keep for stock, then thinly slice the fennel bulb into rounds. When the onions are nearly tender, add the garlic and fennel to the pan. Mix, season with salt, put the lid back on and sweat the vegetables for about 5 minutes, or until the fennel is softening. Stir in the bay, thyme and paprika, pour in the wine/vermouth and let it bubble for a minute, then add 500ml (17fl oz) water. Season and gently simmer with a partial lid on for 20 minutes.

Remove the herbs and either carry straight on or set the sauce aside if making ahead of time. Reheat, if it has cooled.

Cut the hake into chunks and stir into the sauce. Cut the squid into rings and add those too. Turn the heat up and cook for 5 minutes. Sit the squid wings on top, cut each set of tentacles in half and add to the pan, and lastly sit the prawns on top. Cover and leave for 5 minutes for all the fish to cook through. It's ready when the prawns are pink.

Scatter over the fennel fronds, give it plenty of black pepper and serve straight away.

WASTE TIPS: Onion skins and fennel trimmings (see Stocks, page 340)

Fennel and Lime Bundt with Mascarpone

This is a cake that can multitask from mid-afternoon through to after-dinner, its inherent va-va-voom helped along by the glamour of the bundt tin shape. It's not just for the fennel fiends in the same way as carrot cake isn't limited in its appeal to people who absolutely adore carrots; and I love (some) banana cakes but can't bear raw bananas. It's a cake with broad appeal, is what I mean.

Serves 10–12

200ml (7fl oz) rapeseed oil, plus 1 tbsp
   extra for greasing

320g (11oz) self-raising flour, plus
   1 tbsp extra for dusting

400g (14oz) fennel

280g (10oz) light soft brown sugar

4 large eggs

3 limes

½ tsp salt

280g (10oz) icing (confectioners') sugar

1 tbsp fennel seeds

500g (1lb 2oz) mascarpone (or other
   full-fat cream cheese)

½ tsp vanilla extract

2.4-litre (10-cup) bundt tin

Preheat the oven to 175°C fan/375°F/gas 5. Use a pastry brush to brush 1 tablespoon of oil over every bit of the inside of the bundt tin, then sift over 1 tablespoon of flour, making sure it is even across the tin. Turn the tin upside down so any excess can fall away.

Trim the tops and bottom of the fennel (you are aiming for about 250g/9oz trimmed weight), then coarsely grate the bulb into a large mixing bowl. Add the oil, brown sugar and eggs, and mix well. Grate in the zest of just two of the limes, sift in the flour and salt, and fold to mix together well.

Spoon the batter into the bundt tin and ensure it is evenly distributed. Bake for about 50 minutes until the cake is risen and with a gentle bounce to it when you touch the sponge. If you notice that the top is browning too quickly, cover loosely with foil.

Take the bundt out of the oven and leave it to cool in its tin for 20 minutes, then use a knife to loosen the edges of the cake and carefully turn it out.

Only ice the cake once it is thoroughly cooled. Squeeze the two limes whose zest you grated. Sift 180g (6½oz) of the icing sugar into a bowl and mix with enough lime juice to make a thick just-about-pourable icing. If you need more juice, there's another lime waiting. Pour the icing over the bundt and grate over the zest of the third lime. Quickly toast the fennel seeds in a dry frying pan and scatter them over.

To serve: Beat together the mascarpone with the remaining icing sugar, vanilla extract, and a squeeze of lime juice. Serve in a bowl alongside the cake, for people to help themselves to.

WASTE TIPS: Fennel trimmings (see Stocks, page 340), Lime juice (see Citrus, page 338)

Leeks

Autumn - Winter - *Spring* - *Summer*

As I have just named all four seasons, perhaps 'year-round' would be a truer accolade to award the luscious leek? Maybe yes, but also definitely no. For an autumn/winter leek is quite a different kitchen proposition to a spring or summer one.

Spring and summer leeks are the dinky small ones. All young and tender and slim. They are sweet enough to be eaten raw, need little more than a gentle steam, take well to charring, and can even make a decent sub for Spanish calçots. Absolutely lovely yet quite distinct from the large, earthy leeks they mature into.

Leeks are a crop that don't mind the cold, that can weather frosts well, and be stored for long periods in the ground or out of it. All of which adds up to them being at their best in the autumn/winter. Which is handily also exactly when their versatility and sweet warmth of deep savoury flavour is the most welcome.

Shop

- Look for leeks with strength of colour across their length of white to green. Avoid any that are turning yellow, or looking dried out.
- Soil or grit between the layers is a good thing: it helps the leek stay fresh and (hopefully...) means they've been stored underground rather than just in cold storage. Again, a win for freshness and flavour.

Store

- Store unwashed and only wash them for using. Keep in a cool larder or in the fridge, loosely wrapped.

Ways to Use

First job is to make sure all the dirt is out of all the crevices of your leeks. To start cooking and then find bits of grit floating free is to become suddenly less proud of having bought leeks with the earth still on them.

- Begin by trimming off the roots at the white end, and then the coarse green leaves at the point where the outer layer of leek is splitting.
- Don't throw any of the trimmings away – once washed they are sensational for stocks or for stuffing into the cavity of a chicken before roasting.
- Then, just cut the leek as you need it to be for whatever you're cooking, and immerse the pieces in cold water for their grit to drift away.
- Change the water a few times, as needed, and help things along by using your hands to move the leeks about a bit. Drain and dry before using.

Leeks will give their best flavour when allowed to cook gently. Go too fast or too far and you will end up with acrid, burnt leeks. A crisped onion is lovely, but crisped leeks are tough and bitter (it's the small, spring leeks that you want for charring). If cooking off some leeks in butter and/or oil, a little water in there too can help avoid the burn.

The gentle flavour of leeks makes them a terrific addition to poaching chicken, ham or fish. And it's that same gentle succulence that will round out flavours in leek soups. Keep the pieces whole for a broth (perhaps with pieces of poached chicken and potato for a cock-a-leekie) or blitz for something altogether smoother and more lustrous.

Poaching leeks is perhaps the best and most versatile of ways where their contribution to a meal is more than just being sweated down into the base of a dish. Poach in water, wine, vermouth, cider or stock, with aromatics added. And then consider your options:

- Serve as a side with the poaching liquor (especially if more than 'just' water) reduced down into a sauce.
- Maybe follow the same method, but serve cold.
- Use the poaching time to make a dressing you can wrap the leeks in while they are still warm.
- Lift the leeks into a baking dish, top with butter/cream/cheese/breadcrumbs, and bake for a gratin.
- Poached leeks can also become the lead feature of a pie filling, or be elegantly arranged on a pastry base for leek tatin.

For stuffed leeks: Poach the whole length of the trimmed leek, then cut along its length without cutting all the way through, so the leaves fall free into rectangular wholes. Whatever filling you want goes into the centre, they get rolled up nice and tightly, then gently cooked in a pan with a little oil and some water (or wine, etc.) to stop them catching.

Layer up leeks (pre-poached or not) in a bake, making sure there is enough liquid in there, so that the leeks don't dry out and scorch while cooking.

Steaming leeks protects their delicate flavour and enhances their sweetness.

Flavour Partners

Leeks go with pretty much anything. Like onions, they are the enhancer and harmoniser of so many other flavours. So let me here just pick out a few classic leek combos and then leave you to it.

Let's think first of flavour partners that build upon the laidback luxe of leeks. That roll with its silk-dressing-gown vibes.

Smooth **dairy** first and foremost. Meaning **butter** and **buttery sauces** (hello **hollandaise** for poached leeks). Spoonfuls of **cream** or **crème fraîche** will lush-up chopped leeks cooked in butter, with **pancetta** and **garlic** in there too, and then tossed through **pasta**.

Cheese and onion is a classic that takes on a more elegant twist with leeks. Try salty **mature sheep's cheeses** or **blues** for leek soups, or to top a gratin. Chopped **hazelnuts** or **walnuts** would be great scattered over.

Blitz poached leeks with some of their poaching liquor as a bed for seared or grilled **scallops**.

Look to **eggs** for a leek soufflé or adding leeks to scrambled eggs or an omelette. For leeks mimosa, dress poached leeks with chopped hard-boiled egg and some of the punchier flavour partners that are coming up.

Potatoes are best known with leeks for soups. Or stir some garlic sautéed leeks through a buttery mash (plus cheese too? or is that too much?). Add sliced leeks into a boulangère (see page 134).

Leeks love anything in the pork line of things. **Bacon** added into soups or pies, **black pudding** into leek and potato patties, or crisped up to garnish a leek and potato soup.

The **anise** family is a go-to flavour bridge for leek in pork dishes, and also with **chicken** or **fish**. Think **tarragon**, **chervil** or **dill**. Where a recipe suggests potato with leek, take a moment and wonder if **celeriac** would work just as well or even better with the leek than the potato would – I reckon it might.

And now we're at the puncher end of things:

Go heavy with the **vinegar** (especially red wine vinegar and sherry vinegar) for dressing leeks.

Fry off **capers** to add to leeks mimosa with a **mustard**-heavy vinaigrette and chopped **shallots** and **gherkins** in there too.

Gently cook leeks with **girolles** (or other **seasonal mushrooms**) in a pan with plenty of garlic and a good pour of **Marsala** or **Madeira**. Gratings of **horseradish** to finish and that's a fine lunch piled on toast, or as a side to **roast beef.**

More flavour thoughts: **Anchovies**; **bay leaves**; **chicken**; **cinnamon**; **coriander seeds**; **crab**; **grapefruit**; **juniper**; **lemon**; **mackerel**; **mint**; **mussels**; **nutmeg**; **orange**; **oregano**; **Parmesan**; **parsley**; **tahini**; **tamarind**; **thyme**.

Preserve

Freeze: Chopped and sweated leeks can be frozen in portions. Poached leeks can be frozen too, and leek soups will freeze well. The message being that a cooked leek will freeze better than a raw one. They can go bitter if frozen uncooked.

Pulled Pot-roasted Pheasant with Leek and Celery Couscous

Pot-roasting the pheasants like this ensures the flesh is very tender and can be pulled off the bones to get as much meat as possible from them. Serve on a bed of couscous run through with the vegetables that have taken on so many lovely flavours in the pot.

Serves 4 as a main

3 leeks

400g (14oz) carrots

4 celery stalks

large bunch of flat-leaf parsley

2 large fennel bulbs

2 pheasants

4 tbsp olive oil

25g (1oz) butter

1½ tsp coriander seeds

1 star anise

2 bay leaves

6 whole garlic cloves

120g (4oz) raisins

200ml (7fl oz) fino sherry

240g (9oz) couscous

salt and black pepper

Prepare the vegetables, keeping the leeks separate from the rest: Trim the leeks (see page 125), then slice the leeks into chunks, about 5cm (2in) long. Scrub the carrots, halve lengthways and cut into 5cm (2in) lengths. Trim the celery and cut into 5cm (2in) lengths. Please don't be in any way too pernickety about these measurements. Finely chop the parsley stalks (keep the leaves). Trim the fennel bulbs and cut into eighths through the root.

Preheat the oven to 170°C fan/375°F/gas 5.

Season the pheasants. Heat the oil and butter in a large pot or casserole dish over a high heat and brown the pheasants all over. Remove and set the pheasants aside, then turn down the heat. Put the sliced leeks into the pot. Once they have softened, lightly crush the coriander seeds and add with the rest of the prepared vegetables (carrot, celery, parsley stalks and fennel). Season and cook for 5 minutes, stirring frequently, until they have softened too. Add the star anise, bay leaves, unpeeled whole garlic cloves and raisins. After another couple of minutes, stir in the sherry and 200ml (7fl oz) water, turn the heat up and bubble for just a minute. Sit the pheasants among the vegetables in the pot, cover and put in the oven for 1 hour.

WASTE TIPS: Leek, carrot, celery and fennel trimmings (see Stocks, page 340)

Remove the pheasants, cover and leave to rest. Strain the vegetables out of the broth. Squeeze the garlic flesh out of their skins, and mix with the veg; discard the star anise and bay leaves. Season and keep warm.

Measure out 300ml (10fl oz) of the reserved broth, topping up with water if necessary. Put the couscous in a heatproof dish. Bring the broth to the boil, pour it over the couscous and cover tightly. Leave for 10 minutes.

Fork through the couscous, season and spread over a large serving plate or platter. Spoon the vegetable mix over the couscous. Use a fork or your fingers to pull the pheasant meat off the bones and then scatter the meat pieces over the vegetables. Finish with the reserved parsley leaves, torn or roughly chopped.

Leek and Bean Broth with Grilled Hake

This hearty broth straddles the line between soup and stew. It would be lovely left as leek and bean without the fish, but the first time I made this we were in Newlyn in Cornwall in early November, and the fishmongers in town were abundant with local hake. See opposite for more on that.

This recipe lets the fish gently cook flesh-side down in the heat of the broth, while its skin crisps up under a grill. Serve with bread for soaking up the broth. You could serve leftovers as a soup, adding stock if it's too thick, blitzing to a smoother texture; and/or adding some greens.

Serves 2 hungrily as a main, with broth for leftovers

2 leeks

20g (¾oz) butter

2 tbsp rapeseed or olive oil

2 celery stalks

4 garlic cloves

1½ tsp coriander seeds

2 bay leaves

2 thyme sprigs

2 tarragon sprigs

2 tsp sherry vinegar

200ml (7fl oz) white wine

1 x 400g (14oz) tin cooked cannellini beans (250g/9oz drained weight)

100g (3½oz) samphire

2 skin-on hake fillets

salt and black pepper

Prepare the leeks (see page 125) and slice into coins. Heat the butter and 1 tablespoon of the oil in a large saucepan (or choose a dish that can go under the grill too, that will neatly fit the hake fillets). Add the leeks with a little salt, cover and let sweat. Meanwhile, chop the celery and garlic. Add to the pan just as the leeks are softening. Salt some more and let it cook, lid on, until the celery is softening too. Pestle the coriander seeds and add those with the bay leaves, thyme and tarragon. Give all that 2 minutes to get acquainted, then pour in the vinegar, wine and 200ml (7fl oz) water. Season, partially cover with the lid and gently simmer for 20 minutes.

Preheat the grill.

Lift out and discard all the herbs. Drain and rinse the beans, then add to the broth along with the samphire. Stir.

Transfer the broth to a baking dish if it isn't already in one. You need to choose one that will take the hake fillets in a single layer. Arrange the fish on top of the hot broth, skin-side up. Pour the remaining tablespoon of oil over their skins, scatter over some salt flakes, and put the dish under the grill for 10 minutes. The skin will crisp and the hake flesh will cook in the heat of the broth.

WASTE TIPS: Leek and celery trimmings (see Stocks, page 340)

Hake

A quick supper on a cold evening: Hake steaks seared skin-side down in a frying pan, into a hot oven for 10 minutes, and then joined in the pan by some halved late-season tomatoes, chopped garlic, anchovy fillets and fino sherry for another 10 minutes back in the oven. The hake then lifted onto plates, with the tomatoes spooned over, and the juices reduced to a sensationally intense sauce.

One forkful of that baked hake and I am transported to memories of eating merluza in Andalusia. Time was, each spring, my husband and I would go to the feria in a town called Rota in Cadiz. The merluza we used to have there contained all these flavours and we didn't even really know it. Although perhaps we should have done. The Spanish (and Portuguese) have long revered hake when the British really didn't.

We fished it – oh yes. And then we exported it. Until the 1990s hake was being hugely overfished for export and its stock levels suffering. Then a recovery plan for managing stocks of hake was brought in. It worked, and hake catches have grown to the point where fishermen can now call them both sustainable and abundant.

I can certainly vouch for their abundance at the fishmongers' in Cornwall when I'm there in the autumn. Every blackboard of wares proudly boasts Cornish hake. It's a local boast with meaning. The Marine Stewardship Council have now given its hard-won certification to Cornish hake that is fished by gill nets; and the Marine Stewardship Council gives all 'northern stock' (i.e. North Sea, Celtic Sea) hake the thumbs up too.

It is also absolutely and completely delicious. Hake is full of mild, sweet flavour and so succulent that to overcook it and dry it out should be a crime. It's also quite hard to do – hake is very cook friendly.

It likes a deep fry. If you find a fish-and-chip shop that offers hake, make friends with the owner. Or deep fry hake chunks in batter yourself, as on page 280. Add towards the end of curry or stew, as on page 120. Bake it in a parcel or pan fry. Steam into absolute sweetness, or roast a whole one for a feast. Some fishmongers will happily sell you a hake head for roasting (don't underestimate the amount of delicious meat on the head of fish like this), or using for stock.

Maincrop Potatoes

Autumn – Winter

Do I give a heavy sigh as summer's new potato season wanes? No, I do not. Because I know that the maincrop potatoes are coming right around the corner with their seemingly endless possibilities. They hold a special, ordinary-yet-extraordinary place in my culinary heart. The 'humble potato', as we so often say. Perhaps too humble by half. Potatoes are magical.

A potato would/could/should taste of the land from which it has come: the soil and the climate in which it has grown hugely affect its flavour. Some of the world's best potatoes come from coastal regions with salty air, rich soil, and often warming breezes. The variety will affect the flavour, too. There is a distinguished heritage of potato growers who carefully plot soil profiles and varieties to produce the best-tasting potatoes they can for whatever use cooks might have in mind.

All of which is why my heart breaks a little whenever I see bags of generic 'white potatoes'. They are symptomatic of just how far we have moved from wanting to know even the basics about what our food is and how it's produced. From acknowledging that wanting to know those things isn't just some romantic notion, but materially affects what you are going to cook. At least the bags of potatoes that declare what they are best for ('mashing', 'roasting', etc.) have a point. A helping hand in knowing just what to use for what is very welcome. There's more here on what varieties you might want to seek for different ways of using, but first some of the all-rounders:

Maris Piper – King Edward – Kerr's Pink – Desiree – Yukon Gold – Russet

Cyprus potatoes are not a variety, but (perhaps fairly obviously...) are potatoes grown in Cyprus. All I have said about coastal soil and climate being good for potatoes applies double to Cyprus potatoes.

Shop

- Only buy potatoes that are firm and smooth. Any green bits, sprouting or sponginess means they are past their best.
- A basic rule of thumb on what to buy for what: potatoes marked as floury will take on a fluffy texture when cooked, and collapse; waxy potatoes are firmer and hold their shape.

Store

- Potatoes are best stored somewhere cool and dark. But not the fridge – its cold will start to turn the potatoes' plentiful starches into sugar and give an odd bittersweet flavour on cooking.
- If your potatoes have any soil on them, leave that there until time to cook. The soil will help the potatoes stay fresh.
- As potatoes age they develop sprouting, which is a sign they are trying to go onto their next stage of life and grow more potatoes. Significant sprouting is bad, but the gentle nub of a small sprouting 'eye'? That's fine. Just rub/cut off and plough on.

Ways to Use

Sleeves up, shoulders back, stay focused – there's a lot to get through here.

Roast: Is there anything better than a well-roasted potato? Crisp on the outside, fluffy inside, salty as old heck. Turn to page 136 for guaranteeing all that, every time.

Mash: The only thing better than a well-roasted potato. See page 138.

Steam/Boil: Either way protects the potatoes' truest own flavour. Steaming is best of all. To boil, cook from cold water for potatoes that are equally tender all the way through. Adding potatoes to hot water might seem quicker, but all that happens is the outside cooks before the inside.

To serve a big bowl of steamed/boiled potatoes as a side: Cook all-rounders or floury varieties until very nearly tender, drain the water and return the potatoes to the pan with plenty of salt and butter or oil. Cut them, if needed, put the lid on and give them a big old shake to break them up a bit. Let them sit in the covered pan to finish cooking in their own steam and the fatty saltiness you've just added.

To cook with other flavours: Choose waxier potatoes, cube, cook until tender, drain, then cook off in a frying pan or wok with whatever spices or other flavours you fancy.

Leftovers: Crush into dumpling fillings; chop and use in a hash or soup; sauté.

Varieties: All-rounders; floury potatoes such as Arran Victory or Estima if you want them to collapse a little; waxy potatoes if that's not what you want.

Baked jackets: The goal is a salted crust and a fluffy inside. Preheat the oven to 200°C fan/425°F/gas 7. Wash the potato, prick in several places with a fork, then roll in salt while still damp. Bake, ideally sitting straight onto the oven's rack so the base gets crisp too. It will take about 1 hour to be fully tender, size depending. A skewer through the potato's middle can speed up the cooking time. As soon as baked, cut a cross to open the potato up and spoon/slice over your flavourings. Obviously you can't go wrong with butter and salt, but do also let your culinary mind roll free with flavour partners.

Leftovers: My childhood favourite of cheesy baked potato shells is what any extras are headed for in my kitchen. Halve them, scoop out the flesh and mix with grated cheese, salt and pepper, maybe some garlic that you've cooked off and crushed. Pile it all back into the shells and give a final dusting of grated cheese. Bake at 200°C fan/425°F/gas 7 for about 15 minutes (finish under the grill for extra browning).

Varieties: Only flouries will do.

Fry: We're talking chips. A deep-fat fryer is handy, but just as good really is a chip pan's mesh basket to put the potatoes into and then lower into hot oil in a saucepan.

Peel and slice the potatoes and immediately put into cold water. That's not just to stop them turning brown, but to wash away some of the starch and set you on your way to crisp chips. Choose your fat: dripping and lard are great choices for flavour and crunch, sunflower oil is fine. Dry the raw potato pieces and put into oil at 150°C/300°F. This moderately hot oil is fine for the first fry, as all you are trying to do is cook them through. Give them 6 minutes, lift out and drain, increase the oil to 185°C/365°F and return the chips to the pan for 3–4 minutes to crunch up. Lift out, drain, salt, eat.

For something altogether different: Try julienning peeled potatoes into thin matchsticks, wash and dry, then stir fry in a wok with perhaps sliced chillies, spring onions (scallions) and coriander seeds. Serve with dashes of sesame oil or Chinkiang vinegar.

Leftovers: Yeah, right.

Varieties: Golden Wonder are the ultimate pick for chips. They love fat, which means they crisp up brilliantly, deliver tender flesh and taste gorgeous. Mayan Gold are good, too.

Grate: For latkes, rosti, potato pancakes or potato breads, such as Irish boxty.

Slice and bake: If I write these down in one place, then hopefully I for one will keep this straight:

Pommes Anna: Very thinly sliced potatoes layered up in a pan (or a cake/loaf tin), each layer generously brushed with butter and salted. Bake, turn out, swoon.

Boulangère: Thinly sliced potatoes layered in a gratin dish whose sides have been rubbed with a garlic clove and some butter, with sliced onions or leeks to go between the layers. Tuck in herbs of your choosing. Cover with hot stock until the liquid is barely lapping at the top layer. Small knobs of butter over the top. A grating of nutmeg. Bake.

Dauphinoise: As per boulangère, but swap the stock for double (heavy) cream or a milk/cream mix. Add anchovies to head in the direction of Jansson's Temptation. I often do a hybrid version (dauphinère? boulangoise?) of 50/50 stock to cream.

Sarladaise: Sliced potatoes browned in duck fat, and then poached in more duck fat. Yes, indeed. With slivers of garlic and rosemary tucked in, too.

Flavour Partners

It is almost impossible to know where to start, or indeed stop. So many cultures offer their own takes on how to use potatoes to give and embrace flavour. But in the wise words of chef and food writer Samin Nosrat, it is broadly about: Salt. Fat. Acid. Heat.... And umami, too.

Salt: Potatoes love **salt**. So much so that they absorb it into their very being. You might need to season your potatoes twice to make sure your chips or roast potatoes give that lovely first salty hit as you bite in. More salty thoughts: **Anchovies**, **olives**, **capers**, **bacon** and **black pudding**, **caviar**.

Fat: **Butter**, **olive oil**, **duck fat**, **goose fat**, **beef dripping**, **lard**, **cream**, **crème fraîche**, **yoghurt**, every **cheese** imaginable....

Acid: **Malt** or **vermouth vinegar** over chips or crisps. A good squeeze of **lemon** into a skordalia.

Heat: Fry off cubed and cooked potatoes with **cumin**, **coriander**, **turmeric** and **paprika**. Paprika generally is excellent with potatoes. Add **horseradish** into the mash to top a cottage pie.

Umami: **Mushrooms** and **truffles**; **shellfish** and **smoked fish**; **pork** and **lamb**; **beef** (roast potatoes with beef rib; mash for a cottage pie; steak and frites); **tomatoes** (pass the ketchup with those frites).

Preserve

This isn't so much to do with preserving, but is more about what to do with your potato peelings: make crisps! Preheat the oven to 210°C fan/450°F/gas 8. Lay the peelings in a single layer on a roasting tray. Drizzle with oil, dust with salt, pepper and maybe some paprika or za'atar, and bake until crisp – 20 minutes or so. Or, give the peelings a stir fry in some hot oil (temperature and spice), with perhaps mustard seeds, chillies, turmeric and whatever other spicing you enjoy getting a toss round too.

The Crunchiest Roast Potatoes

And not just crunchy. Crisp on the outside, too, with the most gorgeous spectrum of golden browns showing how different parts have caramelised. Then, as you bite in, you reach the most delicious, tenderest, fluffy cooked potato. All, of course, perfectly seasoned. How hard can that be? Not hard at all is the comforting answer. Much is written about different ways of roasting potatoes, but there are some basic rules to follow that will always steer you true.

Choice of potatoes
Any of the all-rounders work well – King Edward and Maris Piper especially. Otherwise, go for a floury variety – Agria and Golden Wonder both make for excellent roasties.

Choice of fat
Beef dripping, lard, duck or goose fat are all great for flavour and achieving crispness. Vegetable, sunflower or rapeseed oils are fine. Light olive oils can work well, but are not ideal. Butter is, for once, an absolute no. It will just burn.

Prepare
Peel the potatoes and cut into whatever size you like your roast potatoes to be. I think that is ideally something that takes two bites. Go too small and they're going to become tough in the oven; too big and they're likely to collapse on you. Put them immediately into a large pan of cold water. If prepping the potatoes more than an hour before starting to cook them, change the water before carrying on.

Parboil
Salt the water and bring to the boil. Simmer the potatoes for just 7–10 minutes. They are ready when just about starting to feel tender to the point of a knife.

Drain and shake
Drain the water away completely. Return the potatoes to the pan, put the lid on and give them a really good strong shake to roughen up the edges. That is very important for achieving crispness later. If you are doing this ahead of time, take the lid off and check the potatoes aren't piled up on top of each other. If they are, transfer to a large plate or tray and set them out in a single layer. Otherwise they are going to carry on cooking in their own steam. Or simply carry straight on to roasting.

Roast

Preheat the oven to 200°C fan/425°F/gas 7. Use however many roasting tins you need to be able to fit the potatoes in a single layer with a little space between each one for air to circulate. Put a roughly 5mm (¼in) depth of your chosen fat (see opposite) into the tin(s) and put into the oven to get smoking hot. When hot, *carefully* transfer the potatoes to the hot oil, baste the potatoes with the oil and scatter with salt. Work fast, so the oil can't cool down. Put into the oven and roast for about 50 minutes, basting them two or three times while they cook.

Serve

Use a fork or slotted spoon to lift the potatoes out, taking as little fat with them as you can. Season well with salt and serve straight away. Or as quickly as you can hustle everyone to the table – in fact, start your hustling when you know the potatoes are getting close to being ready. It is very hard to keep roast potatoes warm without them losing the crispness you've worked so hard for. Your best bets are either keeping some uncovered in the oven you have just turned off and is cooling down; or sit a very loose dome of foil over them at the table.

Flavour boosts

Like this, they are the little black dress of the roast potato world: classic, simple, timeless, unbeatable. But sometimes we all want something a little racier than a little black dress and that's when you can add perhaps crushed coriander seeds, ground cumin, chaat masala, sesame seeds or olives as the potatoes roast.

Leftovers

Leftover roast potatoes are best eaten cold from the fridge. Perhaps secretly, perhaps with a lick of horseradish sauce, and just the right amount of guilt to give them an illicit thrill. Always worth it.

The Fluffiest Mash

And not just fluffy. Also creamy, comforting, and with a flavour that keeps you going back forkful after forkful.

Choice of potatoes
Fluffy mash requires floury potatoes. They are the ones that, in cooking, will want to give you the perfect creamy texture. Look especially for Arran Victory, King Edward, Maris Piper and Kerr's Pink.

Prepare
Peel the potatoes. Cut into even, largish chunks and put into a large pan of well-salted water. Don't be tempted into small potato pieces thinking they'll cook quicker. They might, but the resulting mash will be sloppy as they'll have taken on so much water. A bay leaf in with the water can be a nice addition, but remove before mashing. Or add a couple of peeled garlic cloves that will stay for the duration and get mashed in too.

Cook
Simmer the potatoes for about 15 minutes until fully tender.

Drain and dry
Drain the water away completely. Return the potatoes to the pan over a low heat for 30 seconds so that any moisture still on them can evaporate.

Mash
For 1kg (2lb 4oz) potatoes use the ratio of 100g (3½oz) cold unsalted butter and 50ml (1¾fl oz) warmed whole milk. Start by salting the potatoes and mashing in pieces of butter, then follow with the milk. Taste for salt as you go along, adding more as needed. A handled potato masher does the job well, as long as you finish with a final few beatings from a wooden spoon to get some lightness in there. A potato ricer achieves mashing and aerating simultaneously.

More on butter and milk
Successful mashing is about using the right balance of cold unsalted butter to warm whole milk. Too much butter can make for a heavy mash, too little is always a bit disappointing. The butter and milk both ideally need to be the most delicious versions of themselves you can find. It's not that basic versions won't make fine mash – they

absolutely will. But really good butter and milk make for really good mash. Unsalted butter gives you complete control over seasoning. As you warm the milk to use in your mashing, you might like to infuse it with some gentle flavour. Choose no more than two of: cloves, peppercorns, bay leaves, garlic, turmeric or paprika, and strain out before using in your mash.

Does it have to be butter and milk?

Not necessarily, no. You could swap the butter for olive oil or beef dripping. Try stock instead of milk. Or cream instead of milk, if you want something even richer.

Serve

Quickly. Mash goes cold fast. It is best revived in a microwave.

Flavour boosts

There are plenty of things you can do to amp-up your mash (although made this way it will already be quite glorious):

- Finish with a few gratings of nutmeg.
- Halve the amount of potatoes and, in a separate pan, boil peeled chunks of the same weight of celeriac or parsnips. Mash as above.
- For colcannon: steam 2 large handfuls of kale and mix into the mash along with spring onions (scallions), or sliced and fried leeks.
- Stir through a handful of chopped herbs (dill, tarragon or chervil work well).
- Stir through a tablespoon (or more, to taste) of mustard or grated horseradish.
- If using olive oil instead of butter, you might like to infuse the oil over a low heat with any of garlic, thyme, peppercorns, bay leaves or rosemary, and then strain out before mashing.
- Use barely a splash of milk and a beaten egg to stiffen the mash. Pipe or spoon small piles of the mash onto a lined baking sheet and bake at 200°C fan/425°F/gas 7 until crisped and golden. You've just made duchesse potatoes.

Leftovers

Mash makes for smooth soups; is versatile for potato cakes made with cooked fish, crisped black pudding or leftover veg; or use for potato breads, such as Norwegian lompe or the farls on page 323.

Pumpkins and Other Winter Squash

Autumn – Winter

One of the prettiest sights at this time of year must be the piles of pumpkins outside a grocer's. And our grocers are happily getting better and better at offering up an ever wider variety of squashes. Here's a quick run down on a few varieties – what's what and what's especially good for what:

Acorn: Looks like a large dark green or perhaps orange acorn. Deeply ridged, so takes on a scalloped-edged look when cut. Canary yellow flesh. Baking or roasting concentrates its flavour.

Buttercup: Small and sweet and a good choice to stuff per person. Similar to the delica, just smaller. Not to be confused with...

Butternut: Hello, old faithful. The proud precursor of fancier, trendier squashes. Butternuts are still a great kitchen asset, though: firm sweet flesh, easy to cut into, with a crater that is perfectly sized and placed for easy stuffing.

Crown Prince: In my kitchen, the prince and the prize of squashes. I've never yet managed to walk past a grocer's selling these and not given in to temptation. Large, with steely blueish-grey skin that encases flesh of the most vibrant orange. The skin is thick, so it can be tricky to cut into, but worth the effort. A great one for roasting and holds it shape well when cooked.

Delica/Japanese/Kabocha: Keeps its shape well when cooked so a good one to stuff and roast. Its dull, knobbly, ridged skin reveals beautifully bright yellow-orange flesh that is among the sweetest.

Onion: These are very cute teardrop shapes. Small, bright orange inside and out. Nutty flavour that is not so sweet as some. Good for roasting or mashing.

Spaghetti: Halve lengthways to roast cut-side down and you'll then be able to use a couple of forks to separate out the spaghetti-like flesh. That is often more exciting than the slightly bland flavour – this one needs some oomphing up.

Turk's Turban: Now these are fun. They look like a little squash that's squashed on top of a bigger squash. The flesh is a bit watery and the flavour a bit weak – best for soups, perhaps.

As a pumpkin is a type of squash, I'll be using the terms somewhat interchangeably from here on in.

Shop

- Give it a tap and it will sound hollow if ripe. It should feel heavy. If it has a stem, it should be firm and dry. If the skin has warts or is a little discoloured that is absolutely fine (even good), but any signs of mould are bad. The skin should be hard.

Store

- These beauties store brilliantly. Crown Princes especially can keep for months. The trick is to keep them at a cool room temperature, somewhere dark and dry. Check every so often to make sure they aren't going soft and give them a turn occasionally to distribute the pressure point of where the squash is sitting.
- Once you have cut into it, store unwrapped (clingfilm/plastic wrap will make it sweat) and just use a peeler to shave off the exposed edge when you next come to use it.

Ways to Use

- Take care when cutting in. Some, especially the large, dense ones like Crown Prince, can be tricky. It helps to cut a thin slice off at the base so it sits flat on your chopping board.
- Try not to peel unless your recipe really needs it. There is so much flavour in the skin. If roasting, the skin will be easier to remove after cooking. And if you do remove the raw peel, crisp it up in a hot 200°C fan/425°F/gas 7 oven with oil and salt for a delicious snack.
- The stringy insides are good for stocks. For the seeds, see page 143.

The best thing you can do with any squash is roast it, to caramelise its natural sugars. Roast wedges or slices at 200°C fan/425°F/gas 7 for 20–40 minutes, depending on the variety you are using and the size of the pieces. Toss first in your choice of oil, plus spices or other flavours. The roasted squash is then ready to use as it is – perhaps in a winter salad, or as a side. Roasted (peeled) cubes become a lovely pie filling.

Remove the skin after roasting if you want to blitz or mash the flesh into a purée that can then become a pasta filling, for gnocchi, to be used in pies and tarts, for soup, or as a bed for fish or mushrooms. Mash the flesh with a little flour, egg and some spices, shape into patties and you have pumpkin pancakes you can fry off in a little butter. None of those uses are going to welcome a watery purée. If you think yours is, spoon into a wide-based pan and let the moisture evaporate over a low heat.

Hasselback and roast a whole pumpkin. Or slice off a lid, scoop out the insides and bake. Then, stuff with a world of possibilities (see below) and bake some more with its lid back on. That is a fabulous centrepiece for a dinner.

Thin slices of squash can be roasted or griddled very quickly. Or tempura'd (see page 280) – that's a nice way to finish off a last unused wedge of a large squash you've been cutting into.

Steam or simmer squash pieces for 20 minutes or so until tender, then mash with lots of butter and black pepper.

Simmer squash in stock or broth for a soup (blitzing smooth entirely optional). Peeled cubes can be cooked directly in with a tagine, stew, dal or curry.

Grate squash to use for a bread or scone; for fritters; or to cook down with grated apple or pear and use as a topping for porridge or granola.

Flavour Partners

Bring any squash into your kitchen and in the balancing act of flavour you already have sweetness taken care of. Now it's all about the other elements.

Spices will work so well with that sweetness. Spoonfuls of **harissa** over roasted squash. Wedges tossed in **garam masala** or **dukkah** before they go into the oven. Cooking peeled and cubed squash in a dal or curry that is laden with any of the **curry spices**. **Cinnamon** and **nutmeg** tread a delicate path of bringing squash yet another edge of sweetness, but can absolutely work as long you add some bitter/acidic liveliness too.

That could come courtesy of **sherry vinegar** over squash before and/or after roasting. **Pomegranate molasses** over a winter squash salad. **Cavolo nero** or some **dried cherries** or **barberries** tucked into a filo pie filling, or as part of the stuffing of a whole squash.

Try a tart **apple**, too. And all the **citrus** family will help put some pep into pumpkin's step. **Orange** or **lime** best of all. Either make an excellent dressing or dipping sauce – and you are going to love some **soy sauce** in there, too, because that takes your balancing into the umami arena.

Umami flavours bring out the squash's innate earthy flavour. **Smoked tofu** into the stuffing for a whole pumpkin. Seasonal **mushrooms**, **scallops**, **prawns** or other **shellfish**, and **truffles**. They'll all love reclining somewhat louchely on a pumpkin purée bed.

An autumn/winter stand-by supper for me is roasting **sausages** and pumpkin wedges together with **red onion** chunks and whole **garlic** cloves for a one-tin wonder. I'll tuck some **sage** leaves or **rosemary** sprigs in there, too. They're flavours that aromatically lean into the sweet richness of pumpkin. You can do that for savoury pumpkin dishes as long as you have enough spice/acid/umami going on as well, to take the edge off. Perhaps toasted **walnuts** to finish a squash risotto that has plenty of **Parmesan** in there. Or into a pumpkin pilaf, which **pistachios** and **saffron** would also enjoy being part of.

For sweet pumpkin dishes you have no choice but to embrace the sweetness. Reach for the dense toffee notes of **brown sugars**, **dried fruits** and **Pedro Ximenez sherry**, noting that even then an orange kick or gentle spicing will be welcome.

More flavour thoughts: **Caraway**; **coconut**; **coriander** (seeds, stalks, leaves); **lavender**; **lemongrass**; **preserved lemon**; **salty cheeses**, such as the blues, Gruyère or feta; **Worcestershire sauce**.

Preserve

Seeds (pepitas): Scoop out and give a wash to remove the stringy fibres. Toss with olive oil and salt, transfer to a foil-lined baking tray and roast for 15 minutes or so at 150°C fan/325°F/gas 3. When they are ready, they will pop. So good for topping soups or salads, granola, flapjacks, or just to munch on. You could add flavour, such as soy sauce or orange, before roasting. Alternatively, toast the seeds in a dry frying pan with some honey or maple syrup and salt, and leave to cool before snacking on.

Jam: Follow a conventional jamming technique using peeled and grated flesh. Enhance the flavour with some orange blossom water or a little lemon into the syrup as it cooks.

Roasted Squash, Red Onion and Carnaroli Rice

This is summer's Pea and Tarragon Carnaroli Rice given an autumnal turn, with the freshly podded peas swapped for roasted pumpkin, and sage and nutmeg bringing their warmth. Making this is always one of my favourite, most relaxing times in the kitchen. Ideally, it's raining outside and I'm there at the stove. Music on, glass of wine in hand. Just stirring and chatting, stirring and chatting....

Choose a Crown Prince squash for this if you can, or another variety that is good for roasting and won't completely disintegrate. This recipe asks you to intentionally roast more than you need so that you can use it in any one or more of the myriad ways on page 141.

A nice addition that I often make is to tear in some cavolo nero, puntarelle or another bitter leaf at the end to temper the richness/sweetness of the squash.

Serves 2 as a main

1kg (2lb 4oz) Crown Prince squash

3 tbsp olive oil

500ml (17fl oz) stock (vegetable or chicken)

1 red onion

30g (1oz) butter

3 sage leaves

150g (5oz) carnaroli rice

150ml (5fl oz) white wine

¼ tsp chilli flakes

25g (1oz) Parmesan

whole nutmeg, for grating

salt and black pepper

WASTE TIPS: Onion skins (see Stocks, page 340), Parmesan rind (page 339), Pumpkin seeds (page 143)

Preheat the oven to 200°C fan/425°F/gas 7.

Carefully halve the squash, scoop out the seeds and fibres, and cut the flesh into slices about 2cm (¾in) thick with the skin left on. Toss in half of the oil. Season with salt, arrange in a single layer on a baking tray and roast for 20 minutes until tender and charred. Set aside. You could do this ahead of time.

Bring the stock to a low simmer in a small saucepan. Peel and chop the onion.

Heat the remaining olive oil and half of the butter in a deep frying pan and cook the onion over a low heat until just softening. Add the sage leaves, then the rice, and stir so that every grain is covered in the juices in the pan. Pour in the wine and let the rice take that on board for a minute or two, stir in the chilli flakes, season with salt and pepper, then add in a couple of ladlefuls of warmed stock. Allow the rice to absorb the liquid, then add more ladlefuls of stock. Keep going – stirring occasionally, rather than continuously as you would a risotto – until the rice is just about cooked and the dish has the consistency of a thick soup. It will take 15–20 minutes. You probably won't have used all the stock. While it is cooking, grate the Parmesan and set aside.

Cut the skin off about half of your roasted pumpkin slices and chop them. When the rice is very nearly ready, discard the sage leaves and stir the chopped pumpkin pieces into the rice so it all becomes properly integrated. Gently squash some of the squash, so it really sinks into the rest of the dish. Watch in wonder as the colour of the carnaroli is warmed by the pumpkin. You have extra roasted pumpkin to add if you want to. If it is all now a bit thick and you've lost the thick soup idea, then add more stock (or water if you've run out of stock).

Remove from the heat, stir in the remaining butter and half of the Parmesan. Grate over plenty of nutmeg. Serve without waiting, with black pepper and the rest of the Parmesan on the table for people to help themselves to.

Pumpkin Soda Bread with Rosemary and Caraway

This is a dense, savoury bread – earthy and sweet from the pumpkin, with rosemary and caraway enhancing those attributes. Such a good way to use up a leftover chunk of pumpkin or squash, or make this the reason you buy one.

Excellent with cheese (especially blue cheese), ham, butter, slices of apple... I'm thinking an autumn picnic.

Makes 1 loaf

150g (5oz) pumpkin or squash, peeled
 and de-seeded (prepared weight)
250g (9oz) wholemeal plain
 (all-purpose) flour
175g (6oz) plain (all-purpose) flour
1 tsp fine salt
1 tsp bicarbonate of soda
 (baking soda)
1 tsp baking powder
¼ tsp ground black pepper
1½ tbsp finely chopped rosemary
 leaves
1 tbsp caraway seeds
200–250ml (7–8½fl oz) buttermilk
1 tsp rapeseed oil

Preheat the oven to 175°C fan/375°F/gas 5.

Grate the pumpkin flesh into a bowl. Set aside, keeping the pumpkin seeds for later.

Combine all the dry ingredients in a large mixing bowl. Mix together, then add the grated pumpkin, using a fork to work it all in. Add the buttermilk in stages, working it into the mix to achieve a soft but not sticky dough. You may not need all the buttermilk. Don't knead, just bring it together into a round dome or more of an oval.

Brush a baking tray or large casserole with the oil. Sit the dough in. If it's a round shape, score a deep cross in the top; for more of an oval, just make 3 slashes across.

Clean a tablespoon of pumpkin seeds, removing the stringy fibres. Brush a little of the remaining buttermilk over the top of the loaf and scatter the seeds over.

Bake for 40–50 minutes until golden and risen. The base should sound hollow when you tap it and a skewer inserted come out clean. Cool the loaf on a wire rack for 30 minutes before cutting into it. Note that this bread is not really a keeper – best eaten the same day or the next.

WASTE TIPS: Pumpkin seeds and flesh (pages 143 and 341)

Apples, Pears and Quince

Summer - Autumn - Winter

There's a community orchard tucked away in our part of north London, where I've hosted Apple Day events over the years. I always start by asking people to name their favourite apples. The same six or so come up without fail: Delicious, Pink Lady, Bramley, Gala, Cox, Granny Smith. Maybe a Braeburn or Russet, too, but that is pretty much where it ends. Which is rather to ignore the literal thousands of varieties that make up Britain's apple heritage.

There are certainly 'good' commercial reasons why the big growers and stores focus on the same few varieties: the ones that are most dependable in how they crop, store, travel. They can be relied upon for year-round sameness. And that is what it is believed the buying public want. 'Yes but no' to that. Dependability is all well and good, but so are flavour and individuality. And the best way that apples with those qualities can be made more mainstream is if we can try to take the time to seek out the small growers and community orchards who are sticking with the more unusual varieties.

It's almost the same story with pears, and so partly why apples, pears and quince are grouped together here. As beloved as these pome family fruits have been century upon century, what has changed over that time is how they are produced and how we buy them.

Commercial pear production now centres around two varieties: the Conference and Williams. Both absolutely delicious. It's just, again, there was and could be so much more to our pear pleasures. Britain's pear orchards were decimated by 50% between 1970 and the end of the century. They have declined steadily since then, too, to the extent that 80% of pears consumed here have been imported. In recent years, there has been a burgeoning British pear revival. It is up to us to give it a helping hand when we can.

And then quince. A fruit that was madly popular right up until the mid-twentieth century when its (comparative) faff in the kitchen led to it falling out of favour. What a loss. Yes, a quince has to be cooked to be enjoyed. Surely that's not too much of it to ask.

These three fruits also share so much in terms of how we can cook and enjoy them. You'll see their common place in the kitchen across ways to use and flavour partners. Love one, love all. And I hope you will.

With so much to say about them individually, let alone together, the best I can hope for here is to pique your interest and send you on your way to find out more. For apples, head to Raymond Blanc and his Le Manoir orchards. The real thing if you fancy a treat, or his book *The Lost Orchards*. For pears, there is Joan Morgan's brilliant *Book of Pears*. Then, *Quinces: Growing & Cooking* by Jane McMorland Hunter and Sue Dunster. For more on quince, seek out recipes from Mark Diacono, who loves them more than anyone else I have ever met.

Shop

- Perfection can be boring. Look for apples with just the right amount of gnarl and character, which equal flavour.
- Pears are a little trickier, as ripe ones so easily bruise. Ideally, buy them just before they are fully ripe and ripen them up at home.
- As for quince, they are so rarely (albeit increasingly) available to buy that my best advice is if you see them, buy them.

Store

- Pears and quinces are best kept out of the fridge until fully ripe.
- A pear's ripeness will give itself away with a gently squeeze and by starting to give off its perfume. Once it is ripe, you won't have too long before it goes too far. The fridge will slow things down a bit.
- A ripe quince won't be especially squeezable, but it will smell amazing. All musky and rosy. And that's the reason for not keeping quinces in the fridge – their powerful, distinctive scent will transmit to everything else.

- Apples store well. Keep in the fridge to slow down their aging; out of the fridge to let the flavours develop. As apples age and their starches turn to sugar, they will sweeten up and the texture gets less crisp.
- The old rebuke about one bad apple spoiling the batch is absolutely true and why you should try to keep apples apart, without skins touching.

Ways to Use

The thing about an apple is that it can be hard to know by looking if it's one of the ones that upon cooking will keep its shape or collapse into apple froth. Find out by gently frying a sample slice in a little butter. Do more than a sample for pan-fried apple slices that can be taken in a sweet or savoury direction with a little sugar added to caramelise. Works a treat for pears, too.

The fluffy apple collapsers make the best apple sauces. Peel, core, chop. Put into a pan with a little water and cook until collapsing, then mash or blitz. Amp up in the flavour direction of your choosing. Pears and quinces work the same way, too.

Bake small apples or pears around a pork joint or game birds. Cutting just through the skin around the apple's equator will stop a fluffy variety exploding in the oven. Quinces will need chopping into chunks first. Or, for a dessert, bake halved pieces of any of these fruits with spices and sugar.

Stuff and then bake apples or quince for self-contained bundles of deliciousness: Cut off the top quarter for a lid; discard the core; scoop out the flesh, chop it and mix with whatever you fancy stuffing your fruit with (minced lamb, grains, spices...), pop the 'lid' back on and bake.

Grate apples or pears into autumnal soups or for a salad. Slice them raw for salads – remembering that they will want to go brown once cut into, so you need to dress them quickly with a citrus or vinegar dressing to help stave that off.

Poaching tends to be done mainly for pears and quinces, but there's really no reason not to poach apples, too. Whole or halved/quartered. Peeled or not. Play around with adding whatever of the fruit's flavour partners you fancy to the poaching liquor. Once the fruit is tender (and for quinces that really can take some time), lift the fruit out and then simmer the liquid in the pan over a high heat to reduce it down to a glorious sauce/cordial.

Raw apples and pears can be used interchangeably in recipes for cakes. Swap for quince, too – but poach them first to tenderise.

Also: pies, tarts, cobblers, crumbles – obviously.

Flavour Partners

Together, two or three of these pomes can work even better than any of them alone. Their flavours have enough in common, but enough difference, too. Quince especially seems to bring out the best in apples and pears. In fact, one of quince's main attributes is that just a little of it can lift other flavours and lend them sweet muskiness.

Those aspects of quince's character can be cheated into apple and pear dishes via other ingredients, too. Try a few drops of **rosewater** over baked pears; sprigs of **lavender** or **rosemary** into a pot for poaching; or a little **elderflower** cordial added to cooked-down apples (or pears) that might become a sorbet, ice cream, or be layered through zabaglione.

When these fruits are taken to their sweet musky max (either in the way they are used or what they are partnered with), you'll find that **spices** are your friend for balancing things out. **Cinnamon** and **nutmeg** are old faves. **Cardamom**, **cloves** and **star anise**, too. The zesty hit of **coriander seeds** plays very well with sharp apples. **Turmeric** is especially good with quince. The five-spice blend of **panch phoron** works for sweet or savoury dishes, as do its component seeds: **cumin**, **brown mustard**, **fenugreek**, **nigella** and **fennel**.

Lean into the innate sweetness of apples and pears with the richness of **dark sugars**. **Muscovados** and **demerara** are the ones to reach for, especially for a cake or tart. **Maple syrup** or **honey** are reliable partners for the same reason. A little of either over slices of raw apples and pears, or poached quince, can seem fairly ordinary until a smattering of **salt** takes it all in a different but brilliant direction.

That interplay of saltiness with the sweet sharpness of the fruits is why in Tuscany it is traditional to end an autumn meal with slices of pear and **pecorino cheese**. They are no fools there. A salty, creamy **blue cheese** will love a sharp apple or pear. As does a **soft cheese**, such as brie or the washed-rind **livarot**. Whenever serving slices of apple or pear with any cheese, I always like to grind some black pepper over the fruit for flavour contrast. Try apple pie with a **strong hard cheese** alongside or baked under the crust – best of all with some poached quince in there too.

More flavour thoughts: So many other flavours of the season, but especially **bay leaves**; **beetroot**; **blackberries**; **bourbon**; **butterscotch**; **celeriac**; **celery**; **chocolate**; **dill**; **fennel**; **figs**; **fortified red wines**; **game birds**; **goose**; **horseradish**; **juniper berries**; **mushrooms**; **nuts**; **pork**; **red wines**; **sesame seeds**; **shellfish**; **tahini**; **vermouth** (**sweet** and **dry**); **whisky**. Quince's origins in the Levant also lend it to all kinds of dishes and flavours of the region.

Preserve

Jam: Apples and quinces are high in pectin, so great for jamming.

In alcohol: Poached pears or quince can be bottled in the spirit of your choosing (plus flavour partners) and kept for several months. The result is a double-win of dessert + digestif. My preference is pears, calvados, cardamom and bay.

Cordial: There's so much flavour in the skin of apples, pears and quinces that I try hard not to peel them unless the recipe really needs it. But when I do have any pome peel around, I make it into a cordial: Put the skin into a pan and cover with water. However much water you used, add an equal weight of sugar and simmer to a syrup.

Jelly/paste: The traditional membrillo paste is made with quince, but apples make an excellent substitution, especially when partnered with musky plums that bring a fabulously rich and wintry purple colour. Cut 500g (1lb 2oz) apples into chunks and put into a large pan. No need to peel or core them first. Halve 1kg (2lb 4oz) plums and add those, along with their stones. Pour over 500ml (17fl oz) dry cider, cover the pan with a lid and cook gently for around 45 minutes until the fruit has collapsed. Cool slightly, then strain through a sieve using a spoon to really push at the fruit and get as much out of it as you can. Weigh the fruit purée, return it to the pan, and add the equivalent weight of caster (superfine) sugar to the purée. It will be around 800g (1lb 12oz). Put into a clean pan, stir in 2 tsp sherry vinegar and then bring to a rolling boil to reduce. Stir frequently. It will take about an hour – maybe more – and is done when a spoon run through the mix leaves a clear trail. As it gets close to being ready, keep a careful eye and stir more often to avoid it getting too thick or burning at the bottom. Use 1 tbsp sunflower oil to lightly grease some greaseproof paper and then use it to line a loaf tin. Pour the fruit mixture in. Once it has cooled and set, turn the paste out, wrap in more greaseproof paper, and store in the fridge. It should keep for up to 3 months and will be terrific to slice into and serve with cheese, or stir a small piece into the sauce of a stew for a sweet, fruity note.

Deep-fried Apple Rings with Cinnamon Sugar

I first made these for an autumnal Apple Day event at Borough Market. It was one of those days when the market (and London as a whole) is at its absolute best – cold but bright. I couldn't fry these fast enough to appease the market crowds. They've since gone on to be something I think of as a Bonfire Night treat. All warm and warming from the pan, as kids and grown-ups alike come in from oohing and ahhing at the sky.

No doubt, crisp batter wrapped around sweet, softened apple is a heavenly combination on its own. But a spoonful of ice cream alongside is very good too.

Serves 4

120g (4oz) plain (all-purpose) flour

1 tsp baking powder

1 egg

100ml (3½fl oz) semi-skimmed milk

100ml (3½fl oz) sparkling water

about 500ml (17fl oz) sunflower oil, for
  deep frying

3 eating apples

cinnamon sugar: 1 tbsp caster
  (superfine) sugar mixed with
  1 tsp ground cinnamon

Combine the flour and baking powder in a mixing bowl. In another bowl, whisk the egg with the milk, then whisk that into the flour. Add the water in stages until the consistency becomes like single (pure) cream.

Pour the oil into a deep-sided saucepan so that it is a few centimetres deep. Heat until 185°C/365°F (or when a small piece of bread dropped in sizzles and browns).

While the oil is getting hot, prepare the apples by using a corer to remove the core, then slice each apple into rings, 1cm (½in) thick. Expect to get 4 rings or so from each apple. Pat the apple rings dry with kitchen paper.

When the oil is hot enough, use a fork to dip an apple ring into the batter, let any excess batter drip off, and lower it gently into the hot oil. Repeat with the rest of the rings, deep frying the apples in 2 or 3 batches so that the pan doesn't get too crowded. Carefully turn the rings over after a minute or so, and remove each one from the oil with a slotted spoon when golden brown on both sides.

Rest each apple ring briefly on kitchen paper to remove excess grease, then transfer to a wire rack. Sprinkle cinnamon sugar over both sides and serve as quickly as you can, while the batter is still crisp.

WASTE TIP: Deep-frying oil (see page 338)

Pears in Red Wine with Bay and Thyme

One year, while on holiday in south-east France, we developed a deep and meaningful relationship with the local Pineau des Charentes fortified wine. We had it spritzed up with soda water, into champagne cocktails, and cooked with it too. The Pineau was the obvious choice of fortified wine when poaching some pears there. Back home, though, I use a Marsala or port. The point being that any and all of them will result in melt-in-the-mouth pears, with lightly decadent, deep flavour.

Serves 4–8

4 ripe Williams pears (or another
   in-season pear)
½ lemon
450ml (15fl oz) fortified red wine

4 tbsp mild honey, plus optional extra
2 bay leaves
3 thyme sprigs
crème fraîche, to serve

Peel the pears and rub with the lemon half to help stop them turning brown. Slice the pears in half through their length, cut out the cores and sit the fruit in a medium pan. Pour over the fortified red wine and 150ml (5fl oz) water. The pears should be just covered. Add the honey, a squeeze of the lemon, the bay leaves and two of the thyme sprigs. Bring to the boil, then reduce to a low simmer and leave to cook with a lid on for 15 minutes, or until the pears are very tender. Take them off the heat, remove the lid and let the pears cool in the pan.

Use a slotted spoon to transfer the pears to a bowl. Discard the herbs. Boil the poaching liquid in the pan over a high heat so that it reduces to about 150ml (5fl oz) sweet syrup. Taste it. You want it to be sweet but with some tart bite. Stir in a little more honey to taste, if necessary.

Let the syrup cool, then pour it over the pears and put it all into the fridge to chill for a couple of hours. Serve one or two pear halves per person in a bowl. Spoon over the syrup, sprinkle over some fresh thyme leaves from the remaining sprig, and finish with a spoonful of crème fraîche.

WASTE TIP: Lemon (see Citrus, page 338), Pear peelings (see page 152)

Blackberries and Elderberries

Summer - Autumn

Blackberries are one of the sure signs that autumn is on its way. Which is not necessarily all that welcome a feeling when they first appear ready to pick on the bush in mid-summer. Depending on the heat (and where you live – in London they always seem to disappear early), prime picking opportunities can be almost done and gone before summer is. Or months later you could still be finding good ones worth scrabbling for. It's always worth keeping an eye out.

I mean keep an eye out for wild ones on the roadside, or in the park as you're taking a walk. Shops will have cultivated blackberries a-plenty to see us through the season. Inevitably plumper and rather sweeter than the wild ones, their flavour doesn't quite bounce with the breadth of spice, rose, even tropical fruit notes that a wild blackberry can. On the bush they will get sweeter as the season progresses and that creates a conundrum for the blackberry picker. Do you get them early while still abundant or wait for them to ripen to their peak? Does waiting risk a) someone else getting there first, and/or b) them being so sweetly, ripely soft, they crush in your fingers while being pulled off the bush...? It's a balance of risk only you can answer.

Elderberries are a whole lot simpler. They appear squarely in autumn and are hardy enough to stay happily on the tree in their elegant clusters for quite a while. You are unlikely to have as much competition to pick these tartest of berries and you may be surprised at how abundant they are. Woods, roadsides, railway embankments – they are all likely spots for an elder tree. The prospect of elderberries makes it worth holding back a little on your springtime elderflower picking. Each elderflower head will only go on to produce berries if left on the tree. (And the bees and the butterflies will thank you too for not taking all their elderflowers away.)

Forage

- Go prepared. Tubs and bags to put your booty into – ideally broad tubs, so the fruits are not so heavily piled on top of each other they get crushed. For blackberries, you might be glad of gloves to protect hands and arms from the thorns, and your roughest jeans so it doesn't matter if they get snagged. For elderberries, you'll be glad of a pair of scissors to snip each head off the tree. An umbrella (and this applies to both) will help you get to the inevitable branch that looks like it has the best, sweetest juiciest berries going, but is always just that stretch too far out of reach.

- I have sometimes been confused on the bush between what's a black raspberry or a red (unripe) blackberry. Know the difference once you pick it: a raspberry will leave its core behind, but a blackberry's core will come away with it.

Shop

- You won't be able to buy elderberries. Not fresh ones anyway. Blackberries you can buy, of course. With the earlier caveats of their somewhat flatter flavour, but still fabulous. Look for blackberries that are mould-free and in shape.

Store

- Wild (i.e. foraged) blackberries don't keep well once picked. Neither do elderberries. So have a plan of what you are going to do with them.
- To keep them in the fridge: Gently wash in cold water and gently dry. You can prolong their life by washing in a mix of 1 part apple cider vinegar to 3 parts cold water and drying before putting into the fridge.

Ways to Use

Blackberries

Into an autumn fruit crumble, cobblers and pies – all the usual bakes you know well.

Think, too, of adding a few gently crushed blackberries to muffins, drop scones or American-style pancakes like the ones on page 81. Or fold them into a fool, like the one on page 163.

Make blackberry syrup to pour over vanilla ice cream for the speediest of desserts, or to dilute as a cordial drink: Combine 100g (3½oz) sugar (any type), 250g (9oz) blackberries and 25ml (scant 2 tbsp) water in a pan; cook until the fruit is collapsing; then strain, cool, bottle and chill.

Blackberries, with their tart sweetness and deep fruitiness, are perfect in so many savoury dishes, too. Some ideas to get you going:

- Add them into the stuffing mix for a joint of pork.
- Toss in at the end of roasting a tray of other autumn/winter veg.
- Quick-pickle with an apple balsamic vinegar to add to a salad or serve with meat.
- Blitz blackberries into a sauce for vegetable, meat or fish dishes – with oil, a little vinegar and whatever other flavour partners you are in the mood for.

Elderberries

When it comes to elderberries, use a fork to gently lift each berry free of its cluster. They are mildly poisonous when raw, so cook them and let their juicy tartness bring an edge to blackberries and other seasonal fruits in your sweet cooking.

Don't go all elderberry (you are unlikely to have collected enough, anyway), but add a few into a fruit crumble or autumn pudding.

For savoury cooking, elderberries are at their absolute best when added to a casserole or used in a gravy/sauce.

Flavour Partners

Blackberries and elderberries share an absolute love-in with other seasonal fruits. Late-summer **peaches**, **strawberries** and **raspberries** will cosily nestle up with a few of the first blackberries. Perhaps in a **goats' cheese** salad with some crisp **radicchio** leaves giving a peppery edge, too.

As the autumn fruits roll round, **apples** and **pears** make the most natural partners for both blackberries and elderberries. Try them together in a fruit crumble, cobbler or pie. You can elevate those from the expected to the 'wow' with the addition of one or more flavours that all these fruits will relish: **Vanilla** via extract, a few seeds from a pod or just some really vanilla-y ice cream or custard on the side; **orange** by way of its zest, juice or orange flower water; a teaspoon or so of **anise** or **fennel seeds** added to a crumble topping or pastry; or a sprinkle of **cinnamon**.

Lean even more into the warmth of spicing by mixing blackberry syrup (see previous page) with hot water, a dash of **rum**, a pinch of **nutmeg** and two **cloves** for a drink that should take the edge off any worries about the evenings drawing in.

I am drawn to **demerara** and all the **brown sugars** for these berries and blackberries especially. There's something about the toffee notes that works a treat. For similar reasons, a good deep **honey** or **maple syrup** works with a bowl of blackberries and the richest **cream** or **yoghurt**.

When it comes to savoury partners, the classics are going to be **beef** and **game**. The sweet tartness of blackberries and elderberries offsets the meat's sweetness. That logic means **white fish**, **scallops**, and sweet roots, such as **parsnips** and **beetroots**, are also excellent partners. Balance it all out with the salty kick of **capers** or some **smoked paprika**.

More flavour thoughts: **Almonds**; **bay leaves**; **chocolate** (especially **white chocolate**); **coffee**; **figs**; **green melon**; **hazelnuts**; **juniper**; **lime**; **liquorice**; **Marsala**; **red wine**; **saffron**; **sloe gin**; **thyme**; **za'atar**.

Preserve

Freeze: Wash and dry before freezing. To avoid them settling into one ginormous clump of blackberries or elderberries, lay them in a single layer on a tray in the freezer and only put into bags once frozen. Then you can just pull out a handful as you need them. The best blackberry smoothies use still-frozen fruit.

Jam: Neither of these berries is pectin-rich, so to set your jams you will need to use jam sugar that has added pectin, or include apple for its pectin as well as flavour.

Ferment: Blackberries and elderberries both make lovely fruity wines.

In alcohol: This one is for blackberries only. Use to infuse gin, vodka or whisky. After 4 weeks or so, you will have a fruitily infused spirit to use for cocktails, and can strain out the boozy berries for cooking with. They'll make for a lethal but lovely trifle.

Sauce: This one is for elderberries only. To make 350ml (12fl oz) pontack sauce, which is a sort-of elderberry ketchup: Put 500g (1lb 2oz) elderberries, 350ml (12fl oz) cider vinegar (or red wine vinegar) and 100g (3½oz) caster (superfine) sugar into an ovenproof dish that can go on the hob. Heat just until the sugar has dissolved. Off the heat, add 5 anchovy fillets rinsed of their oil, 4 finely chopped shallots, 5 allspice berries, 5 cloves, a blade of mace, a grated 3cm (1in) piece of fresh root ginger, 1 tablespoon black peppercorns and salt. Cover the dish and put into a 100°C fan/250°F/gas ½ oven for 8 hours, or overnight. Strain, pushing at the fruit to get all their juice out. Pour into a sterilised bottle and wait a week before using to accompany sausages, burgers or langoustines. It'll keep for ages in the fridge.

Autumn Salad: Beetroot, Fig, Blackberry, Radicchio and Hazelnut

This doesn't just taste of autumn, it looks like autumn on a plate. The burnished plum colours come together with depth from the beetroot, brightness from the quick-pickled blackberries, sweet musky figs and a bed of bitter radicchio leaves. With a tahini dressing and the crunch of a few seasonal nuts for the final flourish.

It's a good one to make ahead. Build it in readiness and just finish with the dressing when time to serve. Keep the pickling liquor from the blackberries to use in salad dressings.

Serves 4 as a small main
400g (14oz) raw beetroots
150g (5oz) blackberries
75ml (2½fl oz) red wine vinegar
1 tsp coriander seeds
1 tbsp caster (superfine) sugar

300g (10½oz) radicchio
3 ripe figs
100g (3½oz) white tahini
1 tbsp lemon juice
40g (1½oz) shelled hazelnuts
sea salt flakes

Steam or roast the beetroots until tender. Leave to cool, peel and set aside.

Quick-pickle the blackberries at least 1 hour before you want to eat: Put the blackberries into a bowl. In a small pan, heat the vinegar, coriander seeds, sugar and 75ml (2½fl oz) water just until the sugar dissolves. Pour all that over the blackberries and set aside for 45 minutes, mixing them round occasionally.

To build the salad: Choose either one large platter or individual plates. Separate the radicchio leaves and arrange as a base, roughly tearing any larger leaves. Cut the beetroots into wedges and arrange over. Cut the figs into wedges and add those, too. Lift the blackberries out of their pickling liquor and arrange over. Scatter over some salt flakes.

Make the dressing: Mix the tahini with 75ml (2½fl oz) water and the lemon juice. Give it some salt. Mix well.

Roughly chop the hazelnuts and scatter over. Serve with the tahini dressing on the side.

Blackberry and Cassis Custard Fool

Fools (the desserts, but I suppose this statement extends beyond that, too) come in various guises. Some are all cream; some cream + yoghurt; and others – like this one – custard + cream. Its more indulgent vibe suits, I think, the autumn mood and the blackberries that are being folded in.

Using pre-made custard is easier, obviously, than making your own from scratch. But that's not even the main reason for choosing pre-made here – it's that these bought ones tend to be vanilla-heavy in a way that suits this fool perfectly. Note that I do mean the posh, in-a-tub kind of custard, not the custard powder kind. Although....

Serves 4–6
300g (10½oz) blackberries
120ml (4fl oz) cassis
300ml (10fl oz) double (heavy) cream

1 x 500ml (17fl oz) pot ready-made
  custard
1 tbsp demerara sugar

Put the blackberries into a small saucepan and pour over the cassis. Gently simmer with a lid on for a few minutes until the blackberries are softened but still just about holding their shape. Turn the heat off and set aside to cool down thoroughly.

Whip the double cream in a large mixing bowl until firm. Ripple through the custard and the cooled blackberries with most (but not all) of the juices in the pan. Divide the fool between serving glasses or bowls. You can make these ahead and put into the fridge to firm up for a few hours, or serve immediately with a looser consistency. Before you hand them round, pour over more of the reserved blackberry cassis juices and scatter the demerara sugar over each serving.

Figs

Summer – Autumn

A ripe fig is a prize to be cherished. Not just for its deliciousness, but for the surprising rarity of having got hold of a fig in its absolute perfect moment of ripeness. When a little drop of its nectar is glistening where the fruit meets its stalk, the skin seeming barely able to contain the sweet fruit.

In that moment, figs are so unctuously soft they are nigh on impossible to transport. The challenge they pose to cook, shopper and greengrocer alike is well understood by any of us who have found the seemingly elusive perfectly ripe figs on a market stall, and transported them oh-so-gingerly home, only to find they've got slightly sadly mushed in their brown paper bag. That is why figs are picked and transported while not quite ripe. It's the level of not-quite-ripe that causes the problem. Too much so and they will never go on to ripen. You will be stuck with under-ripe figs. But buy them the right amount of almost ripe and in the sunshine of your kitchen they become the figs of your dreams.

Our chances of finding figs in their ideal state of ripeness are heightened when buying in season. For UK figs, the season is late summer/early autumn, so basically August and September. I know – short. Mediterranean figs stretch through July to October. The figs you see being sold year-round will have been harvested while under-ripe so they can be stored a long time/transported a long way. Leave them alone.

Shop

- I think I've already made the case for buying figs in their perfect state of not-quite-ripeness. How will you know? Have a look at the skin. If it already has that nectar 'eye' and bulging skin, it is absolutely ripe. Buy and eat it there and then, its juice running down your chin and onto the white top you are now regretting wearing for this shopping trip. Otherwise, give it a squeeze if you are allowed/can do it without being seen. You are hoping for a little give, but not a squish. And/or buy from a grocer you trust to sell you and tell you what's what.

Store

- If your figs need a little final ripening, keep them out of the fridge on the work surface, ideally in the sunlight. Keep fully ripe figs in the fridge and use quickly.
- Crucially, avoid the figs' skins touching other. That's a sure fire way to them going mouldy quickly.

Ways to Use

Any slightly not-quite-ripe figs will benefit from ways of using that draw out their natural sugars. Grilling fig halves or slices is good for that, as long as you keep a close eye that they don't go too far and burn. You just want the heat to lift the sugars to the surface and caramelise them.

Roasting achieves the same goal. Do them whole and embrace how they will burst open with juicy, sticky flavour. Or halve/slice and roast. You just always need to make sure there's enough liquid with them in the dish as they roast, to make sure that 'sticky' doesn't become 'stuck'. There are so many different ways you could roast figs, ingredients to roast them with, and flavour partners to finish them with once out of the oven. Head to Flavour Partners, below, for more on all that.

Baking – which implies a lower oven temperature and the figs somehow covered – doesn't give you the caramelisation, but the heat still does its lovely job of tenderising the figs and maximising their potential. The covering might be a dish lid, some kitchen foil – or sponge. A fig cake or clafoutis is heavenly.

Ripe figs make for great compôte. Just roughly chopped and simmered with a little water and your choice of flavour partners.

Only properly ripe figs should be enjoyed raw. That could mean layered into a simple salad, blitzed into a fig tapenade, or just as they are.

Flavour Partners

A ripe fig will be sweet with berry notes and a deeply musky flavour that comes through in its taste as well as smell. It wants to mature into a fig that is headily intoxifying, and almost boozy. Take that idea and run with it by pouring **Marsala** or **Madeira** over figs that have been opened with a crossways cut, given a little sprinkle of sugar and then baked. Serve warm from the oven with **cream** or **ice cream**, and perhaps some grated **lime** zest over the top for lift. Figs when dried are often described as taking on notes akin to **Pedro Ximenez sherry**, so try using some of that when baking fresh figs too.

You want your figs musky? Then give them some extra musky. With **bay leaves**, **lavender**, **rosemary**, **rose**, **violet** or **raspberry**. Go steady, though – it's a high wire act of layering musky flavours that could land too heavily in the territory of a 1980s perfume if you aren't careful.

Figs also bring their own honey notes, so using that with figs is again a way to embrace and amplify their natural flavours. Use **honey** (or **maple syrup**) as the flavour base for what you might grill/roast/bake your figs with, and then take it in different directions according to your mood. On the savoury front, that could be mixing honey with a **balsamic** or **sherry vinegar** and **olive oil**; or with **soy sauce** and **Chinkiang vinegar**. You're trying to get the right balance of sweet and sour, and it's why I love to pile slices of ripe figs atop quick-pickled thinly sliced **red onions**, which get finished with a little olive oil and salt, and maybe some feta, too, because...

Salty cheeses are one of the umami big-guns that figs love. Try raw figs opened up with a cross-cut, stuffed with **mascarpone**, given a drizzle of honey, a drop or two of **rosewater** and some salt to finish. Could that be dessert or even breakfast on a warm autumn day? Very often, yes. And just as lovely are baked figs with a soft cheese, such as **gorgonzola** or **mozzarella**.

Punchy flavours that can not only stand up to figs but be improved by them, include **capers**, **black olives** and **anchovies**. Together, they can become a fig tapenade, or be used in any combination for dressing cooked figs. Raw figs, too, come to think of it (as long as – but I think you've got this message now – they are fully ripe).

Chop figs into a stuffing for a **pork** loin or leg, with other flavours that love both pork and figs along for the ride. I'm thinking some crushed **walnuts** to thicken the stuffing, **orange** for its acidity that can temper the sweetness, **thyme**, and just a little **cinnamon**.

That last is one of many **warming spices** for sweet and savoury fig incarnations. Perhaps **star anise**; or whole **cloves** added to a dish of figs and baked, or ground and dusted over. **Vanilla**, too – it's why fig sponges and clafoutis win over pies and tarts. With the absolute exception of my Fig, Chocolate and Pecan Frangipane Tart on page 168 that nestles figs in among the warm nuttiness they love – meaning look to **walnuts**, **hazelnuts**, **almonds**, **pistachios** and **pecans**, too.

More flavour thoughts: **Basil**; **blackberries**; **chocolate** (especially **dark**); **coffee**; **elderberries**; **fennel**; **game birds**; **liquorice**; **mint**; **radicchio**; **rocket** (**arugula**); **tahini**; **tarragon**; **venison**.

Preserve

Pickle: For fig chutneys.

Jam: Yes, but it's another of the low-pectin fruits, so you'll either need to amp up the pectin (with jam sugar or apple) or embrace it as being just a looser set of preserve to spoon on top of your toast or scone.

Dry: This is the best thing to do with an excess of ripe figs, because a dried fig is very nearly as lovely as a fresh one (and a whole lot lovelier than an under-ripe fresh one). Wash, dry, give them the cross cut previously mentioned, and sit on a tray in a 60°C fan/150°F/gas ¼ oven for 8 hours or so. If it is hot, hot, hot where you are, then have a go at drying them in the sun: Slice in half lengthways, onto baking paper on a baking sheet with cheesecloth or more baking paper over the top to protect from flies. Leave out in the heat of the day, bring inside overnight, repeat for perhaps 5 days until dried. Then feel exceptionally happy and smug with having made your own sun-dried figs.

Fig, Chocolate and Pecan Frangipane Tart

Frangipane is more usually made with almonds, but switching for pecans gives a gorgeously warming, toffee-esque flavour and texture that is perfect with the chocolate and figs. This tart is dense and rich. Fabulously so. All you'll need with it is a spoonful of lush cream, yoghurt or vanilla ice cream.

Serves 8–10

For the pastry

270g (9½oz) plain (all-purpose) flour, plus extra for dusting

pinch of salt

1 orange

150g (5oz) cold butter

For the frangipane

200g (7oz) pecans

85g (3oz) dark chocolate, minimum 70% cocoa solids

3 star anise

200g (7oz) butter, at room temperature

100g (3½oz) golden caster (superfine) sugar

100g (3½oz) soft light brown sugar

2 eggs

25g (1oz) plain (all-purpose) flour

½ tsp baking powder

pinch of salt

about 200g (7oz) ripe figs

icing (confectioners') sugar, for dusting

22–23cm (9in) loose-bottomed tart tin

First, make the pastry: Sift the flour with the salt into a mixing bowl. Grate in the zest of the orange. Dice the butter, add to the bowl and mix into the flour with your fingertips until it looks like breadcrumbs. Add cold water to help it come together, but as little as you can get away with to form a smooth dough – start with just a couple of teaspoons. Shape into a disc, wrap and chill for 1 hour.

Use that time to make the frangipane: Finely grind the pecans using a pestle and mortar or grinder, and set aside. Break the chocolate into a heatproof bowl suspended over a pan of simmering water (make sure the bowl isn't touching the water). Add the star anise. Once the chocolate has melted, take the bowl off the pan so it can cool and the star anise can subtly infuse its flavour into the chocolate.

Meanwhile, use a wooden spoon to cream together the butter and sugars in a large mixing bowl until light in colour and texture. Add the eggs, one at a time, incorporating well after each addition. Mix in the flour, baking powder and salt. Add the melted chocolate (discard the star anise) and lastly the ground pecans. Mix together and set aside.

recipe continues overleaf...

WASTE TIP: Orange juice (see Citrus, page 338)

Lightly dust the work surface with flour and roll the pastry until generously large enough to fit the tart tin. Ease the pastry over your rolling pin and carefully lift over the tin, gently pressing it in. Let it overhang the tin as the pastry will shrink as it cooks. Prick the base a few times with a fork and chill for 30 minutes.

Preheat the oven to 170°C fan/375°F/gas 5, with a large baking sheet inside.

Sit the tart case on the hot baking sheet, line with a large piece of baking paper and fill with baking beans or rice. Bake for 15 minutes, then remove the paper and beans and return to the oven for another 5 minutes. Take out of the oven and sit on a wire rack to cool, then trim the pastry before filling with the chocolate frangipane. Spread it over evenly. Cut each fig into slices or wedges, as you prefer, and arrange on top of the frangipane, gently pressing the figs in a little.

Turn the oven down to 160°C fan/350°F/gas 4 and bake the tart for about 40 minutes until the surface is just about firm to the touch. Start checking at 30 minutes. If the pastry or topping is getting too dark, loosely cover with foil. Remove from the oven and cool for at least 15 minutes on a wire rack before releasing the tart from its tin.

Dust with icing sugar and serve at room temperature, or while the warmth of the oven's breath is still upon it.

Fig and Bourbon Ratafia

Infusing bourbon with figs, star anise and orange zest creates a deliciously sweet and musky ratafia. Serve as it is over ice; or use in cocktails, such as an Old-Fashioned, or a champagne cocktail like the one on page 173.

Makes 500ml (17fl oz)
500ml (17fl oz) bourbon
300g (10½oz) fresh figs

1 star anise
1 orange

Pour the bourbon into a sterilised jar or wide-necked bottle. Cut the figs into eighths and add those to the bourbon along with the star anise. Make sure the figs are just immersed in the alcohol. Set aside somewhere cool and dark (but not the fridge) for 2 weeks, giving it a shake every couple of days to move the figs around.

After 2 weeks, add broad strips of zest from the orange. You should get a gentle scent of figs as you open up the jar or bottle to do that. Leave for another 3 days, then taste. Leave a little longer if you want a more heavily infused fruit flavour.

When it is ready, strain out the figs, star anise and zest through a fine sieve and store the ratafia in a sterilised bottle where it will keep for up to 3 months.

A few feasting menu ideas

Puy Lentil, Beetroot and Baked Feta (*small plates/sharing plates*)

Zarzuela

Pears in Red Wine with Bay and Thyme

Pumpkin Soda Bread with Rosemary and Caraway
with charcuterie and pickles

Baked Za'atar Meatballs with Tomato Sauce and Beetroot Tops

Fig, Chocolate and Pecan Frangipane Tart

Pulled Pot-roasted Pheasant with Leek and Celery Couscous

Deep-fried Apple Rings with Cinnamon Sugar

Autumn Salad: Beetroot, Fig, Blackberry, Radicchio and Hazelnut

Leek and Bean Broth with Grilled Hake

Fennel and Lime Bundt with Mascarpone

Braised Beef Short Ribs with Honeyed Figs
and The Fluffiest Mash

Blackberry and Cassis Custard Fool

Fig and Bourbon Ratafia Champagne Cocktail

For 1, to scale up

1 sugar cube

4 dashes Angostura bitters

25ml (1fl oz) Fig and Bourbon Ratafia
   (page 170)

100ml (3½fl oz) champagne

Sit the sugar cube in a champagne saucer or flute. Douse with the dashes of bitters, pour over the ratafia and then top with the champagne, tilting the glass slightly so it doesn't over-fizz. Serve immediately while the bubbles are still rising up in an excited stream from the sugar at the bottom of the glass.

- Small vases of cyclamen, dahlias, chrysanthemums or Michaelmas daisies. Those last three are also beautiful as a single flower on a place setting or napkin, perhaps with a sprig or two of woody herbs like rosemary or bay leaves. Try floating flower heads in shallow bowls.

- In early autumn you might get lucky with the last of the hydrangeas. Luckier still, these heads manage to still look magnificent even when the first flush of their beauty is waning.

- Lay autumn grasses, eucalyptus or dried autumn leaves along the table, woven among your candles and other bits and pieces (being cautious of flames near foliage, of course). Nestle rosehips or crab apples among them. Personally, I'd hold off on holly and ivy for the more festive tables ahead, but both are fabulous for autumn too.

- Small ornamental squashes arranged in a bowl for a centrepiece, or just dotted along your table among the greenery.

Winter

Bring on the carrots and the parsnips. The celeriac and the kales. Sprouts! And the glory of winter oranges. Immersing myself in these and yet more of winter's produce has been for me – and maybe it can be the same for you – a needed reminder of how much potential there is in this season's cooking and eating, and in the joy these foods bring to a winter malaise the increasing cold and dark can make hard to shake.

Use winter's wealth of deeply green (or purple, or red) leaves to wrap up bundles of deeply savoury fillings. Shred them for dumplings and serve with an aromatic broth. There'll never be a better excuse to make or eat pies. Embrace the carby comfort of roots and mash with butter and spices, then let them soak up the sauces of stews and braises; or layer them into creamy bakes. Let the oven take care of one-pots where the flavours of the season that nature chose to grow together can reunite and bring the best out of each other. Relish the relief of a winter salad. And if things ever threaten to get a little too heavy, citrus abounds to pep it all up. It's all enough to kick any culinary ruts right out of the kitchen window and into the cold.

In Season

Autumn		Spring
Beetroot	**Brussels sprouts, kales and more dark winter greens**	Asparagus
Celery		Broccoli – purple and white sprouting, and Calabrese
Fennel	**Cabbages**	
Leeks	**Carrots, parsnips and salsify**	Elderflower and other spring blossoms
Hake		Lettuces
Maincrop potatoes	**Scallops**	New potatoes
Pumpkins and other winter squash	**Cauliflower**	Radishes
Apples, pears and quince	**Celeriac and swede**	Goats' and sheep's cheeses
Blackberries and elderberries	**Chard – Swiss, rainbow and ruby**	Soft herbs
Figs	**Kohlrabi**	Watercress and baby spinach
	Waterfowl – duck and goose	Trout
	Oranges – Seville, blood, bergamot and mandarins	Wild garlic
	Venison	Gooseberries
	Rhubarb	

Featured Recipes

Brussels Sprouts, Kales and More Dark Winter Greens

Cavolo Nero and Pearl Barley Broth

The Basics of Winter Broths

Sautéed Brussels Sprouts and Kale

Cabbages

Cabbage Leaves Stuffed with Mixed Mushrooms and Potato

Braised Red Cabbage with Chestnuts and Sloe Gin

Carrots, Parsnips and Salsify / Scallops

Carrot and Orange Salad with Saffron Aioli and Scallops

One-pot Fragrant Spiced Lamb with Parsnip and Spinach Rice

Cauliflower

Cauliflower, Leek and Coconut Soup

Roasted Cauliflower with Pork, Ginger and Shallots

Shaved Cauliflower, Sultanas, Preserved Lemon and Chilli

Celeriac and Swede

Celeriac and Horseradish Rosti with a Fried Egg and Walnut Oil Dressin

Mixed Roasted Roots with Black Pudding (or Butter Beans)

Chard - Swiss, Rainbow and Ruby

Filo Tart of Mixed Greens and Feta

Swiss Chard Dumplings, Broth and Crisped Sage Leaves

Kohlrabi / Duck

Kohlrabi 'Fries'

Kohlrabi and Sprout Winter Slaw with Spatchcock Roast Duck

Oranges - Seville, Blood, Bergamot and Mandarins / Venison

Bergamot Crème Brûlée

Venison Osso Buco with Mixed Herb and Citrus Gremolata

Rhubarb

Quick-pickled Rhubarb and Labneh Toasts

Rhubarb Sponge with Orange Blossom Crème Fraîche

Winter Feasting

Rhubarb Gimlet

Brussels Sprouts, Kales and More Dark Winter Greens

Winter

Kalemonath. That's what the Anglo-Saxons called February. 'Kale month'. No surer indication is needed of the importance kale has long held in winter cooking. With autumn's produce all eaten, and winter's crops running sparse, there was kale. Not just surviving the cold but relishing the way it concentrates its sugars and forces it to grow slowly, drawing up into its leaves as many flavoursome nutrients as possible from the soil.

Nutritious, delicious, fashionable kales fall broadly into two types: There's the curly kale, with its green or purple frills. And then the more elegant, plume-like flat-leaf kales, such as black cavolo nero, or Red Russian with flashes of silver among its pinks and purples.

Is it harder for me to claim Brussels sprouts as being fashionable? I'd like to think not. Certainly the sprout top rosettes that crown each sprout stalk bring enough panache to the kitchen that they're being sold more and more as a green leaf in their own right, not 'just' a bonus from buying sprouts on the stalk.

Look closely at a Brussels sprout and see a cabbage in miniature form. They're orbs of tasty joy and deserving of far higher status in the kitchen than the Christmas Day apologies they're too often served with. People claim not to like them... that they're there for tradition not flavour.... Forget all that. Do them right and your family and friends will be clamouring (okay, keen) for you to cook sprouts all winter long. Like kale, sprouts taste all the sweeter for growing in the cold.

Here are some quick thoughts on a few other wintry greens to keep an eye out for (and to which the notes to come will also very much apply):

Collard greens: Large, blousy green leaves shot through with white veins. You might buy them still attached to the central stem from which they grow, or as loose leaves.

Turnip tops/broccoli rabe/rapini/cime di rapa: All just different names for the same thing. Think of these as being something between a very leafy broccoli or a kale with small flowers and florets.

Mature spinach: The delicate crops of young spinach grow into leaves that are distinctly larger, with considerable stems and a much more bitter taste. They are packed with potential and much of it coincides with these thoughts on winter greens. Remember, though, that spinach will release lots of moisture when cooked.

Shop

- When buying loose Brussels sprouts, check their bases for any signs of drying out. Sprouts on the stalk will stay fresher longer as the stalk 'feeds' the sprouts.
- Any signs of yellowing leaf edges are signs of, again, drying out and of older sprouts. You want your sprouts to look perky and firm.
- Those bags of pre-cut kale might seem a good idea, but the leaves in there will already be on their way to drying out. Buy whole leaves if you possibly can.
- Look for vibrancy and life in the leaves of kale or sprout tops, etc. Nothing sad or wilting.

Store

- For Brussels sprouts: The key thing is to keep them clear of any moisture that might cause them to go mouldy. That includes not washing them. Loose sprouts will do well in the fridge's crisper drawer. For sprout stalks find a nice cool, dark, dry place. Keep the sprouts on the stalk until you come to use them.
- For kale, sprout tops, etc.: Again, it's the fridge crisper or somewhere cool, dark and dry. If they are in bags, get those open to let the leaves breathe. Preferably even take the leaves out of the bag and sit them on kitchen paper in the fridge crisper.

Ways to Use

- Sprouts on a stalk should be twisted off. Try if you can to use the larger ones lower down the stalk before the smaller ones towards the top, as they will have been the first to grow and so the first to age. Remove any discoloured leaves. Trim the bases if particularly large or woody. Wash only just before using.
- Kale leaves need to be stripped off their ribs. Don't throw those away, though. When the ribs are very finely chopped they are a lovely addition to cooking down with onion, celery, etc. in the base of a dish.

And then you are all set for:

Cooked sprouts

When boiling sprouts to serve straight away: Resist any temptation to cut a cross into the base of the sprout. All that is going to do is make your sprouts soggy and that is categorically not the plan. Cook them quickly, in rapidly boiling salted water for sprouts that are bright as buttons, just about tender, lushly green and – definitely – not smelling old and eggy. That only happens when they are overcooked. The sprouts need to be of roughly equal size to cook at the same rate. Halve/quarter larger ones as needed. They'll carry on cooking when drained, so dress and serve quickly. Boiled sprouts are also very good crushed or puréed, with your choice of flavour partners.

To blanch sprouts and get their cooking started: Follow the notes above but with two differences: Take them out of the water before they're tender and refresh them in cold water straight away to stop them cooking in their own steam. Blanched sprouts could then be:

- Baked into a gratin: Roughly chop the sprouts, mix with double (heavy) cream, put into a dish and cover with Parmesan and breadcrumbs before baking.
- Sautéed or stir fried.
- Added to a winter salad.
- Fried or roasted at high heat so their sugars caramelise as the sprouts char.

Small sprouts: These are best just simply steamed to protect their sweetness. Again, serve them quickly once done.

Raw shredded sprouts, sprout tops, kale leaves and other winter dark greens

Larger raw sprouts will be that bit more bitter than the tiddlers. This is really where you need to think of sprouts as mini cabbages. It's also where their tops, the kales and other winter dark greens come in. All great to:

- Use in a winter slaw.
- Ferment into kimchi.

- Blitz into pesto.
- Dress into a winter salad, giving them enough time in the dressing for its citrus or vinegar acidity to relax the leaves. They're especially useful at the tail end of winter, when spring's produce hasn't yet made an appearance but the culinary mood has definitely shifted into wanting fresher flavours and lighter dishes.

Another way to relax de-ribbed kale leaves, and other greens, for using raw in a salad is to give them a nice massage. As a bonus it's such a calming, therapeutic kitchen job. Put the leaves into a bowl, add salt, and massage away, breaking down the cell structure.

Cooked shredded sprouts, sprout tops, kale leaves and other winter dark greens

This is about fast and hot.

Simplest of all is boiling. Shredded sprouts and torn leaves will need barely a minute in fast boiling water. Drain, dress and serve straight away. I'll often add some torn kale into a pasta pan for its last minute of cooking, so when the pasta is drained the kale is already cooked and mingled in with the pasta. It just needs oil and salt.

All these leaves are mainstays of winter broths. Add the leaves to wilt only when the soup is nearly ready. Same for folding leaves into an almost-ready dal, risotto or stew. When adding kale to any of these, cook down its finely chopped ribs into the dish's base at the same time as adding chopped celery or garlic.

Stir frying is a great way of delivering fast high heat to leaves. Make sure the leaves are thoroughly dry before adding to the wok, and don't overload the pan or all they'll do is cool the wok's temperature and slowly braise rather than quickly stir fry. Similarly, salt draws moisture out of the leaves and means they cook in that rather than the heat – add salt at the end.

Sauté torn leaves in a little butter and oil, the roasting juices of a joint of meat, or in the pan after doing some chops and while they rest.

Deep frying may take away some of the virtuosity that the leaves were bringing, but chopped kale pakoras are far too good to let that put you off.

Roast leaves in a hot 200°C fan/425°F/gas 7 oven. Perhaps added towards the end of roasting other vegetables. Or solo on a roasting tray, tossed in oil and salt, spread in a single layer and roasted until crisped. I love to tear kale leaves onto a pizza, then let the oven's intense heat crisp them up.

Steaming works especially well for sprout tops, keeping the rosettes whole. Dress and serve as soon as they come out of the steamer. Or, once steamed give them a quick sauté in butter and other flavour partners to take on colour.

Flavour Partners

Next time you roast a **chicken** grab any of these greens and cook them in the umami-laden juices of the roasting tin. They'll be the best greens of your life. Try that and then tell me sprouts aren't a great combo with **turkey**. They absolutely are. The sprouts give the bird (and the rest of the feast) a much-needed bitter note; and the turkey gives the sprouts that same sweet umami hit the roasted chicken juices give.

It's also why these greens love anything in the **pork** line. Perhaps an Italian **sausage** pasta salsicia with torn greens swapped for the broccoli that is more usually there. Top stir-fried or steamed greens with **'nduja**. Roast **black pudding** on a bed of Brussels tops.

Add leaves at the end of sautéing **mushrooms** (add too soon and they release moisture that will make the mushrooms soggy). Stir fry blanched sprouts or raw leaves with **tofu**. Toss boiled or stir-fried sprouts or leaves with **soy sauce** or chopped **black olives**.

It might seem counter-intuitive to temper the bitterness these greens bring with acidic flavour partners but it absolutely works. Dress any of these, cooked any way, with **sherry** or **Chinese black vinegar**. Give them a spritz of **lemon**, **orange** (especially winter's **blood oranges** and **clementines**) or **grapefruit** juice – all of those are very good for dressing the raw leaves, too. **Preserved lemons** are similarly great for these veggies when raw or cooked.

Give your greens some heat with **chilli**. Spice them up with **caraway**, **cinnamon**, **cumin**, **nutmeg**, **juniper** or **liquorice**.

For a simple supper that brings a few of these ideas together: Marinate chicken thighs in soy sauce, **honey**, orange juice and a little ground cinnamon. Roast the thighs, take them out to rest, and then roast your greens in the marinade left behind in the tin.

Tahini is a sprout and green leaf go-to. Stick with the sesame vibe and toss **sesame seeds** into stir-fried or roasted greens. Use **sesame oil** to dress.

Chestnuts are the classic with those Christmas Day sprouts. It's a good call for how the smooth nuttiness takes the edge off the bitterness. **Almonds**, **hazelnuts** and **walnuts**, too. Perhaps cooked or raw leaves tossed with toasted flaked almonds, plus some **raisins** soaked for a few minutes in sherry vinegar for a sweet-sour flourish and with a dusting of ground cinnamon.

More flavour thoughts: **Anchovies**; **apple**; **bacon**; **bay leaves**; **bottarga**; **capers**; **coconut**; **cream**; **egg**; **feta**; **halloumi**; **labneh**; **leeks**; **mackerel**; **maple syrup**; **mustard**; **nori**; **pancetta**; **Parmesan**; **plum**; **root ginger**; **sage**; **smoked garlic**; **thyme**.

Preserve

Freeze: Raw sprouts freeze pretty well. Lay them on a tray to freeze in a single layer, before transferring to a freezer bag. Kales and other leaves should be chopped before freezing – again, raw rather than cooked.

Cavolo Nero and Pearl Barley Broth

I make versions of this broth on a regular basis throughout the winter. What goes in it equally determined by what food I want to use up and what I am in the mood for.

I hope you'll think of the recipe here as being the basis for all kinds of wintry broths and use the guide overleaf to keep on making the ones that suit you. They'll all be reliable, nutritious bowlfuls of warmth and comfort and flavour.

Serves 6

40g (1½oz) dried porcini (or other) mushrooms

1 large (or 2 smaller) carrots

2 medium leeks

3 tbsp olive oil

200g (7oz) cavolo nero

2 fresh bay leaves

1 rosemary sprig

1.5 litres (50fl oz) vegetable stock

100g (3½oz) pearl barley

whole nutmeg, for grating

1 tbsp sherry vinegar or balsamic vinegar

salt

Put the dried porcini into a bowl and pour over 500ml (17fl oz) very hot water. Set aside to rehydrate while you start the rest of the soup.

Scrub the carrots and finely dice. You only need to peel them if the skin looks very tough. Trim the leeks, halve lengthways and chop.

Heat the oil in a large pan over a medium heat. When it is good and hot, add the carrots and leeks. Stir round, turn the heat down a little and let them cook while you prepare the cavolo nero. Strip its leaves from the stalks and set the leaves aside. Trim off and discard any very woody ends on the stalks, then very finely chop what is left. Add the chopped stalks to the pan with the bay leaves and rosemary sprig. Add salt and sauté for 10 minutes or so to let the vegetables soften but not colour.

Lift the rehydrated porcini out of the water, squeeze them over the pan, then put onto a chopping board and chop. Add to the pan along with the water they steeped in. Pour in the stock and the pearl barley, turn the heat up to bring to the boil, then cover and reduce the heat so the broth gently simmers for 25 minutes until the barley is tender. Remove the bay leaves and rosemary sprig.

Chop the cavolo nero leaves – not so fine that they disappear, but small enough to be easy to eat in a broth. Add to the pan and gently simmer for 5 minutes over a low heat for the flavours to mix, then add a few good gratings of nutmeg and the vinegar. Taste for seasoning and serve straight away or store in the fridge/freezer.

(You will need 3 litres' worth of containers for this recipe. I go for 500ml/17fl oz pots and don't fill them to the rim – leave space for the liquid to expand as it freezes. This can be reheated straight from frozen.)

WASTE TIPS: Carrot and leek trimmings (see Stock, page 340)

The Basics of Winter Broths

As reassuring as it is to follow a 'proper' recipe, I often think the best broths are the ones that are made up on the go, using whatever bits and pieces are leftover from other cooking, That is certainly how the Cavolo Nero and Pearl Barley Broth recipe on page 185 started. Its basic principles could be amped up in any number of ways – here are a few that I think about in broth making.

Alliums

Take your pick of leeks, onions or shallots. Chopped small enough to almost disappear as they cook, or into more chunky pieces. I don't think garlic goes brilliantly here – you might disagree.

More roots

Dice a peeled or unpeeled medium potato and add at the same time as the diced carrot. Similarly, any last kitchen stragglers of parsnips, celeriac or swede are great to add then.

Flavour boosts

Dice a celery stalk and, again, add along with the carrots. Towards the end of the sauté time add your flavour bedrocks of herbs or spices. The bay and rosemary here could have thyme as well. Or, instead of the herbs, go for more of a fennel seed/grated root ginger/chopped chilli vibe.

Umami

A broth has to have at least one element that is bringing umami-ness. Skip that and it will feel weak. In the broth on page 185, that is the job of the dried mushrooms. Other options:
- Add a Parmesan end into the simmering soup, then remove before serving, or a grating of Parmesan to serve.
- Drain 4 anchovy fillets of their oil, chop, and add with the herbs.
- Add 100g (3½oz) diced pancetta/streaky bacon to the sauté.
- Shred in the last bits of meat from a roasting joint.
- Add dashes of Worcestershire sauce at the end.

Acidity

To lift the flavours and bring them together. The acidity in the recipe on page 185 comes at the end by way of vinegar but that could instead be added as the soup cooks. Try a small pour of dry sherry added with the stock and/or finish the soup with gratings of lemon or orange zest.

Stock

Swap the vegetable stock for chicken (best of all the dark chicken stock of page 228) or beef. Try adding a tablespoon of tomato purée with the stock. Note that those options each add umami, too.

Greens

Swap the cavolo nero for kale, Swiss chard (silverbeet) or rainbow chard. Or swap the cavolo nero for spinach but forget about sautéing the stalks, and tear the leaves rather than chop. The spinach will give its moisture to the pot; the other greens will absorb it. Kale seems to especially thicken a broth.

To fill you up

Swap the pearl barley for lentils. Or for cooked beans or chickpeas, or broken-up dried pasta, those added at the same time as the cavolo nero leaves.

Seasoning

Keep tasting, keep seasoning.

Garnish

Maybe a drizzle of balsamic or Chinese black Chinkiang vinegar; some grated citrus zest or Parmesan; soy sauce or Worcestershire sauce. Any of these don't just look pretty: they deliver acidity/umami with the very first spoonfuls.

Leftovers

Broths freeze well. Just don't fill containers to the rim – leave space for the liquid to expand as it freezes. They can be reheated straight from frozen.

Sautéed Brussels Sprouts and Kale

This recipe can take itself in a few different directions: With the cream finish as a side for, perhaps, a joint of roasted pork loin. Without the cream finish if serving with lots of other fairly rich dishes – so perhaps if doing this as part of your Christmas Day feast (for which it would work very well). Or, I sometimes do it with a poached egg atop each portion to turn it from a side into a light main. The egg a little soft so its yolk sinks into the sprouts and kale.

Serves 4 as a side

400g (14oz) Brussels sprouts	6 bushy thyme sprigs
150g (5oz) kale	1 tbsp sherry vinegar
25g (1oz) butter	1 unwaxed lemon
2 tbsp olive oil or rapeseed oil	125ml (4fl oz) double (heavy) cream
8 anchovy fillets, drained of their oil	(optional)
(equivalent of 1 x 50g/2oz tin)	1 tbsp walnut or hazelnut oil
	salt and black pepper

Trim off the woody end of each sprout, halve them (unless small) and put into a medium pan of salted water. Bring to the boil over a high heat and let them cook for 2–3 minutes until only barely becoming tender. Drain in a colander, rinse in plenty of cold water, then set aside to drain. They should be the brightest, freshest green you could hope for. To this point can be done up to a day ahead of time – keep the blanched sprouts in the fridge if made more than a couple of hours ahead. Only finish the dish right before you want to eat it.

Strip the kale leaves from their core/ribs. Tear the leaves and set aside.

Melt the butter with the oil in a large deep frying pan over a medium heat. When bubbling, add the drained anchovy fillets. Stir them with a wooden spoon so they disappear, taking care not to burn the butter/oil. Turn the heat up to high and add the sprouts. Stir well. Strip the leaves from the thyme sprigs and add those too. Just as the sprouts start to colour and become fully tender, stir in the sherry vinegar, then add the kale and toss to quickly wilt. Turn the heat down to low and grate in the zest of the lemon. If using the cream, stir it in now.

Serve straight away, finishing with a drizzle of the nut oil and lots (I do mean lots) of freshly ground black pepper.

WASTE TIPS: Anchovies (page 338), Kale ribs (page 341), Herb stems (see Stocks, page 340; Soft Herbs, page 341), Lemon juice (see Citrus, page 338)

Cabbages

Winter – Year Round

Is there a vegetable more beautiful than a January King cabbage? I'd struggle to name it. There's certainly not a cabbage more beautiful. And while the opportunity to talk about the January Kings is not entirely why the year-round delight of cabbages features here in winter, it's not not why.

The cabbages you can get at different times of the year cleverly, and perfectly, suit their seasons. The summer varieties tend to be smaller, with softer leaves and sweet flavour. By the winter these varieties have traded up in shape, colour and flavour; bringing endless options that suit the mood of the season. These are just a few:

January King: As delicious as this cabbage is there's no doubt its real appeal lies in its huge, dramatic leaves. They're deeply veined, in some places the richest purple and in others a forest green. These cabbages are works of art as much as ingredients. The leaves get paler as you work your way inside the cabbage and are blistered, like its close relation the better-known Savoy...

Savoy: Different varieties of the Savoy are available all year. In the winter it's often the hardy Tundra that you will find. The Savoys are great everyday cabbages but more tasty than that might make them sound. A good, deep green, blousy winter Savoy can be nearly as much as a head-turner as a January King.

White cabbage: These have tightly packed, hard heads and a crunch that means they're often the choice for raw cabbage dishes or stir frying.

Red cabbage: Their gorgeous garnet colour just screams winter, as does the kind of braising and slow cooking these tight leaves are most suited to.

Shop

- Smell your cabbage. A light essence of itself is fine, but a strong smell might mean it is starting to go off inside.
- Loose-leaved cabbages (like January King or Savoy) should look perky and full of life.
- Hard white and red cabbages should feel heavy.

Store

- Your cabbage will store best if you keep it together. As soon as you start to take leaves off, or cut into it, it will start to age more quickly.
- Store somewhere dark and cooler than typical room temperature, or in the fridge crisper.
- Hard, tight-headed cabbages will store for longer than the loose-leaved varieties. I've had some that have kept for weeks, even months.

Ways to Use

When it comes to chopping/shredding, the loose-leaved January King or Savoy requires a different strategy than a white or red hard-headed type.
- *For the loose-leaved varieties:* Pull the leaves away from the stalk, roll them up together, and cut. When you get right down to the heart of the cabbage and can no longer peel off leaves, just slice through.
- *For hard white and red varieties:* Cut the whole cabbage in half and then into quarters. Cut out the core and then slice through the leaves.

The core itself is packed with juicy, crunchy flavour. Finely chop it to steam, sauté or stir fry as you could/would/should the leaves. Those are three of the fastest and best ways for preparing cabbage as a side, and for each of them the cooking time is barely minutes. Just long enough and no more for the heat to tenderise and leave the leaves shining with flavour.

This is a good time to clear up that boiled cabbage is the stuff of food nightmares. Cooking it that way somehow inevitably means over-cooking, and that is when cabbage turns sulphurous, smells eggy, and gives off a distinct hospital-food aura. It smells and tastes like the butt of jokes it otherwise does not deserve to be. The only time you should be boiling cabbage leaves is to blanch them so they are pliable enough to work with.

Back to happier cabbage ways: braising. Chopped leaves will be superb when added to some sautéed onion and garlic, then given enough wine, vermouth or cider that they can enjoy lapping up its flavours but are categorically not boiling in it. Season well and finish with cream or butter to serve.

The harder cabbages can be braised as wedges, core and all. The goal is for the core to tenderise and the leaves be a mix of just about cooked-through to crisped and wilting.

Quarter loose-leaved cabbages and tease the leaves open, then lay them on a roasting tray to make a superb bed for roasting other things on. Small game birds, perhaps, that will take about as long to cook as the cabbage, their juices sinking into the cabbage folds.

Cabbage leaves are great to stuff. Varieties like January King or Savoy with their large soft leaves are easiest to work with but will still need the leaves blanching for just two minutes first. See the recipe on page 194 for more tips on cabbage leaf-stuffing.

Try a chou farci, stuffing a whole cabbage. Savoys work best. You'll need to parboil the whole cabbage first for 10 minutes (making this another of the few times it is okay to let your cabbage near boiling water), then – once cool enough to handle – gently ease the leaves apart enough to be able to fill their gaps with your choice of stuffing. Scoop out the heart and stuff the space it leaves, then bake in a snug-fitting pan that will help the cabbage hold its shape, on top of some sliced onions and carrots.

Use cabbage leaves as the walls, floor and ceiling of a pie. Again, it's about first separating leaves, blanching and drying. Grease a springform cake tin, then lay the leaves in at angles to cover the base and sides (a very similar idea to working with the filo pastry for the tart on page 226). Fold over more cabbage leaves for a lid after piling in your filling, then brush with butter and bake.

Shredded cabbage leaves turn up in dumplings all over the world. Or try shredded cabbage in a Japanese okonomiyaki. I do that no justice by describing it as a sort of shredded-cabbage-led omelette/pancake/frittata.

Shredded cabbage is often how cabbage turns up raw. The hard whites and reds are better suited here than the loose-leaved types. Look to slaws, sauerkrauts and kimchis.

Flavour Partners

My biggest cabbage triumph came when serving up a vegetable medley of cabbage and **celeriac** to my nephews when they were pretty young and it was so enjoyed (to frankly everyone's surprise) that years later it is still the one they both, now in their mid-twenties, expect/want me to roll out. I will admit the lashings of **cream** and **bacon** probably helped things along, but also maintain it was the marriage of the celeriac's **anise** flavours with cabbage that worked its magic. Look similarly to **dill**, **fennel** and **tarragon**.

The bacon in that dish was crucial. Its saltiness balancing some of cabbages more bitter edges. It's why **anchovies**, **blue cheeses**, **smoked fish**, **dried shrimps** and **soy sauce** are all cabbage go-tos.

Sometimes that bitterness of cabbage is a good thing. It can give **potatoes** more flavour life; or balance the sweetness of **pumpkin** or **scallops**. Even better if there is some grated **ginger** in the pan with the cabbage and/or the finished leaves are given a squeeze of fresh **lemon** or (blood?) **orange** when they are done.

Red cabbages in particular love fruity flavours like **apple**, **pear**, **blackberry** or **fig**. Any of those as **vinegars** will bring helpful acidity.

Cabbage can take **spices** well. When roasting wedges, toss them in oil and salt along with your pick of a spice blend before they go into the oven. Perhaps **chaat masala**;

berbere spice; **ras-el-hanout** or **za'atar**. A drizzle of **honey** or **maple syrup** part way though the roasting will sweetly round things out.

Nuts and **nut oils** are very useful for cooking with or finishing cabbage dishes. Look to **chestnut**, **walnut** or **hazelnut**. Spoon a little **coconut cream** into braised cabbages or green leaves before serving.

And then for the raw slaws and salads, you just really have to think about hitting all the angles:

- *Texture:* Raw cabbage will give you crunch but would you like more? Think about raw **apple**, or mandolined **fennel/celeriac**, or ribboned **carrot**. Remembering the longer all these sit in their dressing, the more relaxed (i.e. less crunchy) they become. You could add extra crunch at the end with **toasted almonds**.
- *Dressing:* Oil + citrus or vinegar for acidity? Lovely. Or go for something creamier by adding any of **yoghurt/sour cream/buttermilk**. Coleslaw traditionally calls for a heavier, **mayonnaise**-based dressing.
- *Round out the flavours:* With maybe **capers**, lots of fresh **herbs**, some finely chopped raw **red onion**, **poppy seeds** or **sesame seeds**. Sweeten things up with a little **sugar**, **honey** or **raisins**.

More flavour thoughts: **Barberry**; **beetroot**; **black lime**; **burrata**; **cardamom**; **cinnamon**; **cumin**; **egg**; **horseradish**; **juniper**; **Marsala**; **mushrooms**; **mustard**; **paprika**; **quince** and **quince paste**; **raisins**; **rosemary**; **sage**; **sesame oil**; **sumac**; **tamarind**; **thyme**; **vermouth** (**sweet** or **dry**).

Preserve

Ferment: Sauerkraut and kimchi are what you will want to know about. Two different yet similar, and similarly ancient, ways of lacto-fermenting cabbages into feisty condiments. The technicalities of getting these right need more attention than I can give here, but that is absolutely not to say these are at all complicated. Recipes abound in books and online. I find the food writers Olia Hercules, Mark Diacono and Tom Hunt especially clever on these.

Cabbage Leaves Stuffed with Mixed Mushrooms and Potato

Two cabbages might feel extravagant for this but it's so you have roughly equal-sized large outer leaves to use. I find the smaller leaves near the cabbage heart too much of a faff to stuff, but head to pages 191–2 and I promise you won't be short of things to do with them....

Serve with some simply dressed radicchio and/or double carb it with bulgur wheat or couscous alongside.

Serves 3–4 as a main

250g (9oz) potatoes

2 large Savoy or January King cabbages

2 small/medium onions

3 tbsp rapeseed or olive oil

2 garlic cloves

1 large eating apple, ideally one that's quite tart

2 tsp juniper berries

1 tsp black peppercorns

1 tsp yellow mustard seeds

75ml (2½fl oz) cider, wine, stock or water

300g (10½oz) mixed seasonal mushrooms

1 tbsp malt vinegar

300ml (10fl oz) stock (vegetable, chicken or beef)

salt and black pepper

Peel the potatoes and cube into pieces about 1cm (½in) square. Put into a pan of well salted cold water, simmer until just about tender, drain in a colander, rinse with cold water, drain again and set aside uncovered.

Pull the largest leaves away from the cabbages – you need 8 in total. Bring a large pan of salted water to the boil, immerse the cabbage leaves for 2 minutes, then drain and refresh in cold water. Dry the leaves flat between pieces of kitchen paper.

Peel and chop one of the onions. Set a medium saucepan over a medium heat and get 2 tablespoons of the oil hot. Add the onion and cook until softened and just taking on colour. Meanwhile, peel and crush the garlic cloves, and peel, core and chop the apple into similar size pieces to the potatoes. Perhaps a little smaller. Add to the pan. Pestle the juniper berries and peppercorns and add to the pan with the mustard seeds. Cook for a minute, then pour in the 75ml (2½fl oz) liquid. Roughly chop the mushrooms and stir into the pan. Season with salt, partially cover with a lid and gently cook for 5 minutes. Stir in the potato cubes, season, taste and season again, if needed. To this point can be done ahead of time, or carry straight on.

WASTE TIPS: Onion skins (see Stocks, page 340), Potato peelings (page 341)

For the broth the cabbage leaves will bake in: Peel the remaining onion and slice into thin half-moons. Heat the remaining tablespoon of oil in a small saucepan and cook the onion until softening. Pour in the malt vinegar and the stock and simmer for 10 minutes to thicken and reduce. To this point can be done ahead of time, or carry straight on.

Preheat the oven to 200°C fan/425°F/gas 7.

Lay the cabbage leaves out flat. At each stalk end, cut out a 'V' pointing up the leaf (this makes them easier to roll). Sit spoonfuls of the stuffing mix in the middle of each and tightly roll or bundle up, tucking the sides in as you go. (If there's excess filling, either wilt more leaves to stuff or serve the filling hot alongside.) Pour the broth into a baking dish that will nearly fit the stuffed leaves. Sit the leaves in the stock and bake for 20 minutes.

To serve, scatter over salt flakes and grind over some black pepper.

Braised Red Cabbage with Chestnuts and Sloe Gin

Sloe gin is genius with red cabbage. A single pour delivers fruity flavour, juniper and gentle spicing that the cabbage absolutely adores. This is a terrific side for any meat, or with a big bowl of Puy lentils.

Fresh chestnuts are in season at the same time as red cabbage and I find them fun to cook with, even if a little on the labour-intensive side of things. Of course feel free to use the handy vacuum-packed pre-prepared ones instead, especially if this part of a larger feast (Christmas Day? Boxing Day?) and there is a lot else being juggled. Just maybe try to give the fresh chestnuts a go at some point.

Serves 6–8 as a side

1 red cabbage
50g (2oz) butter
1 tbsp olive or rapeseed oil
1 tbsp soft brown sugar
100ml (3½fl oz) sloe gin
1 cinnamon stick
3 thyme sprigs
400g (14oz) chestnuts in their shells
  (or 180g/6½oz prepared chestnuts)
1 tbsp sherry vinegar
salt

Prepare the cabbage first: Remove only any very damaged outer leaves. Cut the cabbage into quarters and cut out the core. Slice the leaves about 2.5cm (1in) wide, then cut the core into thin lengths. Wash well and drain.

Melt the butter in a large casserole dish. Add the oil, then the cabbage leaves and core, and stir round until the leaves become glossy and start to wilt. Add the sugar and the gin, sprinkle over some salt, tuck in the cinnamon stick and thyme, and cover the dish with a lid. Let it gently cook for about 30 minutes, giving it a stir every so often and adding a little water if it looks at all dry.

Meanwhile, prepare the chestnuts if using fresh ones. Use a small sharp knife to carefully score a cross into the flat side of each nut and simmer them for around 12 minutes in salted boiling water. Test one to check you can easily peel the shell away. Once they are ready, drain the chestnuts, run under cold water so they are cool enough to handle, and peel.

Discard the cinnamon stick and thyme sprigs from the cabbage. Roughly chop the peeled chestnuts (or the pre-prepared ones) and add to the cabbage with the vinegar and give it all another 15 minutes. Taste for seasoning before serving.

Carrots, Parsnips and Salsify

Autumn - Winter

Carrots crop up twice in this book: For summer over on page 49, and then here in winter. Twice because, I think more so than most other vegetables or fruits that are around across seasons, they are so very different from each other.

By winter, the slim, tender-as-they-are summer carrots mature into much larger, thicker ones. Their flavour develops more character and is now more earthy, even nutty. Those attributes are especially amplified with (my favourite) 'sand carrots'. Sadly not quite literally carrots that have grown in the sand, but in very sandy soil that is so packed with nutrients it protects the carrots' own flavour while giving an extra flavour boost.

Alongside the orange carrots we all know are the heritage varieties that are getting more popular, too. Keep an open mind and shopping basket with carrots that are yellow, all shades of purply-plum, or white.

Those white carrots might easily be mistaken for a parsnip. That would be a shame as parsnips deserve love in their own right, and don't get nearly as much of it as they used to before potatoes nudged them out of the way as a mainstay of the diet. They're terrific when chipped, crisped, mashed, roasted, baked, braised, or stuck in around a roasting joint to soak up the delicious meat juices. So basically all the things you might do with a potato – or indeed a carrot. Parsnips have a more complicated flavour than either. The old line that they're best after the first frosts of winter holds true, as soil temperatures drop the starches in the roots turn to sugar and the whole vegetable gets sweeter.

Potential confusion in the long root identity parade continues with parsnips and salsify. The latter are longer and thinner, but similar at first glance. Especially if that glance isn't so acquainted with salsify. It – and the black salsify you might also see called scorzonera – are deserving of wider recognition and use than currently. They share the same sweet, earthy, nutty profiles that have made carrots and parsnips so beloved. Worth seeking out. (And from here on when I say 'salsify' that includes black salsify.)

Shop

- Fresh-tasting comes from fresh-picking. Ideally, you'll be buying carrots, parsnips or salsify that have had the least time out of the ground. They should be firm across their length. Nothing soft, limp, bendy or withering – they are all signs of drying out.
- Roots with hairs on them are a sign of age. They will be absolutely fine to cook with, just that bit woodier of taste and texture. Any hairy veg definitely needs peeling.
- If you can, buy them with soil still on as that helps protect the moisture.
- You should be able to smell the promise of their flavour. Lacking in smell likely means lacking in flavour.

Store

- Storing somewhere cool and dry is best, wrapped in a paper bag. The fridge is good, but a cool cupboard or larder is good, too.
- Keep any soil on until it comes time to use your roots. If they are very soil-y (even muddy, lucky you) that might count out storing in the fridge.
- Winter carrots are less likely than summer carrots to come with their tops attached. If they do have them, remove the tops or they will just try to feed themselves from the carrots' nutrients. (Winter carrot tops will be gritty and bitter. They're still fine to wash and whizz into a pesto, but not so good as summer's carrot tops for enjoying raw as a herb.)

Ways to Use

- First thing is to wash any soil off.
- Only peel carrots if they really look like they need it, as so much goodness and flavour lies just under the skin. Parsnips and salsify are more likely to have a woody skin that needs peeling. Black salsify definitely needs peeling. All three of those will go brown as soon as their pale flesh meets the air, so put the peeled veg straight into a bowl of cold water with lemon juice added to stop the oxidising.

Roasting caramelises and intensifies the roots' natural sugars. Roasted together or singly they can be a side, amped up into a main, used for a winter salad, or blitzed into a dip or soup. Whatever their destiny they'll need a hot oven, at least 190°C fan/400°C/ gas 6. Slice into lengths of roughly the same size but non-uniform shapes, toss in plenty of oil and salt before roasting, and then look to the flavour partners overleaf as to what herbs, spices or vinegars you might add. If you want an extra edge of sweetness by way of honey or maple syrup, only add that halfway through the roasting time to avoid any burning. You want them caramelised, not cindered. Parsnips, which as they age develop a woody core, can benefit from a quick steam or blanch first to get them on their way to cooking through. That's not necessary if you're cutting them into thin pieces, but worth it for larger chunks.

The joy of hasselbacking these roots left whole is that by cutting very thin slices right the way along their length the oven's heat penetrates into their centre. Who am I kidding – that is only one of the joys of a hasselback. There's plenty more joy in how the oil, salt and other flavours sink into every slice.

There's much you can do with a simmered long root. Salsify especially is good just lightly boiled and then finished under the grill with some lemon juice, butter and breadcrumbs over the top. Or add a little sugar and butter to the pan when simmering chopped carrots or parsnips – if the roots are only barely covered by liquid you can reduce the simmering liquor to a glaze for pouring over the roots to serve.

To use parsnips in gnocchi, push chunks that have been simmered to tenderness through a ricer and use them 50/50 with similarly riced potatoes.

Crush simmered roots so they retain a little texture, or go the full way and mash them smooth. Simmering in milk, rather than water or even stock, gives an extra-creamy edge to mashed parsnips or salsify. In the mashing they'll benefit, too, from plenty of butter. Older, tougher parsnips, with that woody core I mentioned, are more successfully processed into a purée rather than hand-mashed.

Boulangères/dauphinoises bring out their silky succulence. Thinly slice and layer, then sink under stock and/or cream, and bake. Again, go for a single choice of these roots, or mix them up. Slices of garlic, onion or potato tucked in will help things along.

Carrots and parsnips bring sweetness to mirepoix/sofrito. Salsify less typically so for that, but it can certainly join in for adding chopped chunks of roots to braises or casseroles.

Older, woodier, wintry roots don't work quite so well raw for a salad as their younger selves do. A ribboned carrot can still bring sweetness, crunch and colour but it will need punchy dressing and some time in it to relax (as with the salad on page 202).

Look to grated carrot, parsnip or salsify for fritters, latkes or rosti; stir through a pilaf; or bake into a bread. Any of these roots could be very happily swapped for the pumpkin in the soda bread recipe on page 147.

And... cakes. I'd say parsnips are right up there with carrots on the sweet bake front.

Flavour Partners

Whether you are looking to wrap up with some comfort food, or give your taste buds a kick, these roots can handle almost anything with aplomb.

Spices work especially well. Try dusting a little ground **cumin** into a root dauphinoise or finishing that up with a hearty grating of fresh **nutmeg**. Toss the roots with any mix of **mustard**, **caraway** or **nigella seeds** before roasting and/or some **garam masala**, **chaat masala** or ground **cinnamon**. Ground **cardamom**, too, or whole pods added to the water or stock you are simmering the roots in.

Add **thyme**, **sage** or **bay leave**s into the pot when cooking carrots, parsnips or salsify. Dress the roots with chopped **tarragon**, **chervil** or **dill** – they'll all play happily with the **anise**-like notes already present in the roots, and in parsnips especially.

These long roots are all carb-tastic. They are inherently comforting to eat. But it's cold out. Maybe it's been cold out for week after week, even month after month. Layer up the comfort like a couple of your favourite jumpers and add some lush **dairy** to your roots. Serve hasselbacks with a **butter** rippled with **miso** paste; don't stint on the **cream** or butter in your root mash. Lean into creamily rich root dauphinoise with grated **Parmesan** over the top. Dairy-free yet delivering the same comfort: Envelop roasted roots in a **tahini** sauce or serve that alongside some root fritters.

Extra sugar brings out the roots' sweetness and flavour. **Demerara sugar**, **date syrup**, **honey** or **maple syrup** added to roasting roots. A pinch of **caster (superfine) sugar** into the water when simmering. **Raisins** added to a winter root salad. **Scallops**, **langoustines**, **cod** or **hake** to swap sweetness and nuttiness with the roots.

Parsnips and **pork** are a classic combo. Puréed parsnips the unbeatable partner to a **pig's cheek** that has been cooked ever-so slowly with **onions**, **garlic**, **juniper** and a rich **fortified wine** like **Marsala** until it is almost falling apart. These roots are otherwise interchangeably as good as each other for most meats.

If this is all sounding just a touch too soporific, here are the flavours to know for kick: **Vinegars**, especially **sherry** or **Chinkiang**; **chillies** in any form and including **harissa**; **root ginger**; **horseradish**; **wasabi**; **orange**, **lemon** and **lime**.

More flavour thoughts: **Aioli**; **apple**; **blackberry**; **celeriac**; **coconut**; **coriander seeds**; **garlic** (especially **smoked** or **black**); **mushrooms**; **nuts**; **paprika**; **pear**; **rosemary**; **rosewater**; **saffron**; **sage**; **sesame seeds**; **watercress**.

Preserve

Freeze: Any of these roots can be chopped and frozen raw. Or cook them off in a little oil/butter and then freeze in portions.

Pickle: Carrots will work better than either of the other two to pickle – they can lose their colour and become rather unappealingly grey.

Scallops

The best scallops of my life were the ones had after a 10-mile walk on Camber Sands – cooked in the fat of some chorizo sausages; the scallops and chorizo then tucked together between plain white bread. I can't see them ever being beaten.

They were nowhere near as fancy as how scallops often appear in restaurants and cookbooks – cooked as treats, not least because they're so expensive. When hand-dived there is good reason behind the price. We are literally talking about divers picking scallops off the seabed. But that only accounts for a very, very small minority of the scallops for sale. Any hand-dived scallops at the fishmonger's will wear those credentials with pride. If they don't say it, you can be sure those scallops have been dredged.

That's one of those words that raises all kinds of environmentally sustainable alarm bells. Scallop dredging, at its worst, means large trawlers with metal rakes are essentially scraping scallops off the sea bed. In the process they wreak havoc with it, and with the sea life that lives and depends upon it. Some fisheries do dredge using smaller boats, with the fishermen using chains or ropes to steer the scallops into a net that is towed along the seabed. The beds are regularly checked and, when necessary, closed to allow regeneration. That way is distinctly less damaging but such 'sustainable' dredging is again applying to a minority of scallops. The point is to try to take the time to think about – and find out about – what you are sourcing. If you can, make a choice that helps the way we feed ourselves cause as little damage as possible to our ecology.

Spawning time is to be avoided, which is why winter is so good. King scallops, at least 10cm (4in) across in their shell, are typically twice the size of Queens. If you are somewhere with scallops coming in fresh from the water you might be able to get them alive, in their shell. Eat those raw, just thinly sliced, given a pinch of salt and maybe a drop of vinegar. Sublime.

Mostly our scallops come opened, or out of the shell completely, and therefore dead. They'll need cooking. I know some people are squeamish about the coral roe. I don't know if that is down to the colour (probably not); the creamy texture (maybe); or that it's where the scallop keeps its sperm and eggs. Yes, sperm and eggs. Clever scallops can do it all.

Cook your scallops hot and fast enough that they take on some colour but don't overcook into rubber. They'll love olive oil, butter, bacon fat, chorizo oil (like those ones I did in Camber) or really any fat to cook in. Give them a kick of lemon, lime, Seville orange or vinegar. And lots of salt to bring out the flavours of the sea.

Carrot and Orange Salad with Saffron Aioli and Scallops

This carrot and orange salad turns up in my kitchen in all kinds of ways – and often – throughout the winter. It's one for those times when I need something sparkier and fresher of flavour, a little crunchier of texture, and with a burst of colour too. I have it on its own, with some steamed fish, with just a few nuts crumbled in, as a side to a pork chop....

Here that favourite winter salad gets a bit fancy. Not too fancy, just a bit.

Serves 4 as a main

For the salad

2 medium carrots

50ml (3 tbsp plus 1 tsp) muscatel or other white wine vinegar

25ml (1 tbsp plus 2 tsp) extra-virgin olive oil

1 tsp caster (superfine) sugar

¼ tsp ground cinnamon

large pinch of salt

2 sweet or blood oranges

leaves of 2 tarragon sprigs

black pepper

For the saffron aioli

pinch of saffron threads

1 small garlic clove

1 large egg yolk

1 tsp Dijon mustard

2 tsp sherry vinegar

pinch of salt

100ml (3½fl oz) rapeseed oil

100ml (3½fl oz) extra-virgin olive oil

For the scallops

12 scallops

2 tbsp olive oil

Use a vegetable peeler to first peel the carrots and then slice them into ribbons and into a bowl. Mix together the vinegar, extra virgin olive oil, sugar, cinnamon and a large pinch of salt. Toss the carrot ribbons in the dressing and set aside for 2 hours (or in the fridge for up to 24 hours).

To make the saffron aioli: Soak the saffron in 1½ tsp warm water in a small cup and set aside. Peel the garlic and grate into a mixing bowl. Add the egg yolk, mustard, vinegar and a pinch of salt. Whisk in the oils, going slowly at first. Once all the oil has been incorporated, season and whisk in the saffron and its water.

Prepare the oranges by cutting off their tops and bottoms so they stand flat, then use a small sharp knife to cut around the circumference of each orange, removing the peel and white pith. Now use the knife to carefully cut close to the membranes

WASTE TIPS: Carrot peelings (see Stocks, page 340), Egg white (page 338), Herb stems (see Stocks, page 340; Soft Herbs, page 341), Orange rind (see Citrus, page 338)

between the segments to release them. Add the orange segments to the carrots, along with any juice that comes from the oranges as you are cutting them. Divide the salad between plates. Chop the tarragon leaves and scatter over.

Dry the scallops on kitchen paper. Heat the olive oil in a large frying pan over a medium heat. Sit the scallops in the hot oil, let them cook for a couple of minutes then turn them over and cook for a few minutes more. They are ready when browned on the outside with the flesh turning opaque. Give them a pat and feel a nice bounce.

Lift the scallops on top of the salad, spooning over any oil left behind in the pan. Finish with freshly ground black pepper and serve with the saffron aioli alongside.

One-pot Fragrant Spiced Lamb with Parsnip and Spinach Rice

What a winner of a wintry dinner. Diced lamb that cooks with parsnips, spices, onions, garlic and greens in a big pot of rice. All the flavours meld together and the result is a feast and treat. Comfort food at its most fabulous. Just don't expect it to hold its shape when you turn it out – this isn't one of those. What you get instead is an elegant collapse.

Serves 4–6 as a main

400g (14oz) basmati rice

1 lemon

2 parsnips

2 tbsp olive oil

800g (1lb 12oz) diced lamb shoulder

2 red onions

40g (1½oz) butter

2 tsp coriander seeds

2 tsp fennel seeds

2 tsp ground cumin

½ tsp saffron threads

1 tsp smoked paprika

1 cinnamon stick

1 garlic bulb

150g (5oz) spinach leaves (or chard leaves, or beetroot tops)

2 tbsp any or all of: chopped flat-leaf parsley, pomegranate seeds, chopped pistachios

salt and black pepper

Rinse the rice, then put into a large bowl, cover with cold water and set aside. Squeeze the juice of the lemon into a large bowl of cold water. Wash the parsnips, trim, peel them only if really needed, and cut into batons. Put the batons into the lemon water and set aside.

Heat the olive oil in a large, heavy-based casserole dish over a medium heat. Brown the lamb in two batches, removing it from the dish with a slotted spoon when the meat is golden all over. While that is happening, peel and slice the onions into thin half-moons. Put half of the butter into the casserole, then cook the onions until softening. Rub at the base of the dish with a wooden spoon to release any sticky bits from searing the lamb. Add all the spices and cook for a minute, stirring, to release their flavours. Drain the parsnip batons and sit them on top of the onions, then return the lamb (and any juices that have come from it) to the dish. Don't stir to combine – this is about creating layers. Break the garlic bulb into cloves and nestle those into the dish, unpeeled. Season, sit the spinach leaves on top and put a lid on. The spinach will release moisture as it cooks and keep the lamb tender. Cook over a very low heat on the hob for 40 minutes.

Drain the rice and spoon it over the spinach layer, level with a spoon, then pour in enough boiling water to come 1cm (½in) above the rice. Bring to the boil, cover with a lid and cook for 15 minutes over a low heat.

Take the lid off the dish and, working quickly, make 4 holes in the rice. Drop a piece of the reserved butter into each hole. Cover the dish with a clean tea towel and leave off the heat for 10 minutes.

To serve, either turn the dish out onto a large serving platter for it to prettily fall and finish with whatever mix of parsley, pomegranate, pistachios you fancy; or garnish the casserole with those and spoon it out of the dish.

Cauliflower

Year Round

What a renaissance the cauliflower has had. Thanks in large part to the passion and creativity of Yotam Ottolenghi it has gone from being a bit of an also-ran vegetable to centre-stage.

It's a source of year-round fabulousness, which begs the question why are cauliflowers appearing here in winter? Mainly because summer and winter varieties are not the same. Those growing in the warmer climate of the summer months tend to be that little bit sweeter than their wintry brethren. Cooks don't need to try quite so hard to get the best out of them. A winter cauliflower, on the other hand, is a little flatter of flavour. There are plentiful rewards to be had with it right though the season – cauliflowers are very well suited to winter cooking – they are just going to need that bit more effort to be enjoyed to their max again and again.

Beyond the standard white cauliflower look out for ones that are green or purple. They'll all cook the same. And while we're talking varieties, I'd long thought that Romanesco, with its slightly futuristic-looking florets, was a modern cross-breed between cauliflower and its close relation broccoli. Not so. Romanesco is a member of that family in its own right, and has been enjoyed in kitchens in the Lazio region of Italy since at least the sixteenth century. Lazio's capital, Rome, giving it its name. For cooking Romanesco see the notes here and on Calabrese broccoli (pages 276–9).

Shop

- Look for cauliflower heads without discolouration across the florets. Dark spots mean the cauliflower is getting old and tired. The florets should look firm and tight.
- Perky and vibrant leaves are a good sign of a fresh cauliflower.
- If the base of the stalk looks dry, it is likely to be older, and could well be drier throughout. Whereas brightness is a sign that it has been relatively recently cut.

Store

- Remove the leaves and keep them separate in a damp towel in the fridge.
- Cauliflowers are best kept in the fridge crisper drawer.

Ways to Use

When preparing cauliflowers it can sometimes feel like they generate a lot of waste. Yet that is absolutely not the case – it is all usable.

- As you cut the florets away from the central stalk, what you reveal is its sweet core. You might need to peel away some of its tough outer layer but somewhere there is a heart you can grate into a slaw, stir fry, cook and blitz into soups, or roast.
- The larger, tough leaves can be kept for stock or kimchi.
- Medium leaves are good to stir fry, tempura, or roast. Think of them like kale.
- The very smallest, most delicate leaves can be enjoyed raw.

Cooked

The main thing to know is that cauliflower loves a high heat to caramelise its sugars. In the summer that might mean over fire; it could be under a grill; but best of all it means roasting. At its very simplest: Get the oven good and hot at about 200°C fan/ 425°F/gas 7, toss cauliflower florets in oil, sprinkle with salt and roast for 30 minutes or so until tender and taking on as much colour as you want. (I like it best when the small florets, or the curds that fall away, get really properly crispy.) The flavour partners to follow will give you lots of options for months of amping-up that basic idea.

Roasting a whole head of cauliflower gives an impressive centrepiece for a meal. You will want to make sure it is tender all the way through, so give it a head (pun intended) start by scoring the base and boiling the cauliflower for a couple of minutes before draining, giving it its flavour partners, and then roasting.

Cauliflower loves a deep fry for how it delivers high heat quickly. A cauliflower pakora should convert any and all cauliflower sceptics. Try deep frying florets in a chickpea flour (besan) batter or perhaps buttermilk. Large florets might need a quick blanch in boiling water first to make sure they cook through.

Cauliflowers are brassicas like cabbages, which means any over-cooking runs the same risk of making the cauliflower smell eggy and deeply unappealing. Keep a close eye and nose on what's happening when blanching, boiling or steaming the florets. Florets of white cauliflower benefit from a little squeeze of lemon juice beforehand to help keep them beautifully creamy coloured. They can go a little grey otherwise.

Florets boiled or steamed all the way to being tender are ready to be dressed and served. Perhaps simply covered in nut oil or butter and black pepper; or tossed in olive oil, toasted breadcrumbs and other flavour partners for a side or to run through pasta; or blitzed to a purée with butter and milk.

Options for the further cooking of nearly tender blanched florets:
- Crush them with the back of a fork and fry off as fritters.
- Shallow fry the florets in a little oil to give them colour and finish off cooking.
- Turn into soup, using the water the cauliflower cooked in as stock.
- Layer up the florets in a parmigiana-style bake.

Raw

Enjoying cauliflower raw isn't just to be reserved for the sweeter summer varieties, so long as you have a nicely fresh cauliflower to use. Shave it (with a mandoline or just a knife) and use in all kinds of winter salads. You will, though, need to give the sweetness that winter cauli lacks; and also give it time to relax a little in its dressing. Head to page 212 for Shaved Cauliflower, Sultanas, Preserved Lemon and Chilli.

Flavour Partners

A cauliflower in and of itself doesn't really taste of very much. But I always think it has enough aspirations of deliciousness to make it great at taking on flavour.

Reach for the **spices** and you are well on your way. They'll marry with the musky notes that cauliflower takes on once cooked, and emphasise its sweetness. Add a mix of spices to your florets before roasting – perhaps **allspice**, **ground cumin**, **ground cinnamon** and **ground coriander**. Try **garam masala** or **berbere spice**.

Those spices and others will serve you well for a rub over a whole cauliflower head before roasting it. Mix them with salt and oil into **yoghurt** or **kefir**, rub over your blanched cauliflower head, and bake.

For when you really want to turn up the heat, think **harissa**, **paprika**, **cayenne**, chopped **chillies** and **root ginger**. All, again, excellent when roasting cauliflower (whole or florets) or for dressing after cooking.

Soy sauce/tamari and **miso** are also great ways to deliver the necessary oomph, whether before cooking or after. **Anchovies**, **capers**, **garlic** and **black olives**, too. I'll often shallow fry blanched florets with any (all?) of those and some **breadcrumbs** added for crunch.

A squeeze of **orange**, **lime** or **lemon** over all that would round things out. And in a similar vein, **preserved lemons** are an absolute cauliflower winner.

When you're adding bold flavours like really all of the ones I've mentioned so far, you are going to want to temper and mellow things out a little. That could be with **buttermilk** into a dressing or for a curried sauce; **potatoes** cooked alongside, as in aloo gobi; or **shellfish**, such as **scallops** or **crab**. Cook with **coconut milk** or finish dishes with toasted **coconut chips**.

Nuts suit cooked cauli's earthiness. **Hazelnut** or **walnut oils** to dress cooked cauliflower; blitz toasted **walnuts** into a **tahini** sauce – or just go for the tahini sauce as it is.

I can't quite believe I've made it this far with cauliflower without mentioning **cheese**. Take the British classic of almost submerging florets in a heavy cheese sauce in a more modern direction by shaving **Parmesan** over roasted florets before serving. Or grate **Gruyère** over blanched or steamed florets and then put under the grill so the cheese can just gently melt around the cauliflower with the whole thing taking on a gorgeous golden hue.

To give winter cauliflower the hit of sweetness that it lacks compared to summer cauliflower: **Rosewater**; **raisins** or **sultanas (golden raisins)**; **honey** or **maple syrup** into dressings or to finish roasted florets; **apple** or **pear**.

More flavour thoughts: **Bottarga**; **capers**; **dill**; **fennel seeds**; **figs**; **fish sauce**; **mustard**; **nigella seeds**; **nutmeg**; **oregano**; **pesto**; **quince** and **quince paste**; **saffron**; **sesame oil**; **sherry vinegar**; **sloe**; **sriracha**; **star anise**; **tarragon**; **tofu**; **truffle**; **turmeric**; **watercress**; **za'atar**.

Preserve

Pickle: Perhaps an achaar pickle of cauliflower with white wine vinegar, mustard oil and spices. Or add in other mixed veg and swap in malt vinegar to make piccalilli.

Ferment: Cauliflower stalks and the tough outer leaves work well in kimchi. And there's a wonderful Cypriot dish called moungra, which ferments cauliflower florets in bread dough, that is well worth seeking out.

Cauliflower, Leek and Coconut Soup

This is a bowlful of true winter-warming comfort. It is equally great straight from the pan when freshly made, as to make ahead and freeze in portion sizes. It is then the work of moments to reheat on one of those days when something like this is very much needed but there isn't quite the time/will to get out from under the blanket long enough to make it from scratch.

Serves 4

1 cauliflower, around 800g (1lb 12oz)

2 leeks

1 celery stalk

2 tablespoons olive oil

20g (¾oz) butter

3 garlic cloves

2 bay leaves

1½ tsp ground cumin

1 mild red chilli (optional)

8 anchovy fillets, drained of their oil
  (equivalent of 1 x 50g/2oz tin)

500ml (17fl oz) chicken or
  vegetable stock

400ml (13fl oz) coconut milk

1 orange

salt and black pepper

oil (extra-virgin olive, nut, or a herb/
  spice-infused oil), to serve

Trim away the leaves and woody base of the cauliflower. Chop the florets and stem and set aside. Trim and finely slice the leeks and celery.

Heat the olive oil and butter in a large saucepan over a medium heat. Add the chopped leeks and celery, season with salt, put the lid on and gently cook, stirring occasionally, until the vegetables are soft but not colouring. Peel and crush the garlic cloves and add to the pan with the bay leaves. Gently cook for a further 5 minutes. Add the cumin, chilli (if using) and anchovies, and stir so they can release flavour. Once the anchovies have softened in the heat, put the cauliflower florets into the pan and pour over the stock. Stir and gently simmer with the lid on for about 20 minutes until the cauliflower is thoroughly tender.

Remove the bay leaves and chilli, and pour in the coconut milk. Blend the soup to be as smooth or not as preferred. Season, being careful with salt as there are all those anchovies and generous with the pepper. Reheat if needed.

While the soup is cooking, grate the zest of the orange and set aside for garnish.

To serve: Ladle the soup among bowls, scatter over orange zest, give each serving a small pour of oil, and then some freshly ground black pepper.

WASTE TIPS: Anchovies (page 338), Cauliflower (page 341),
Celery and leek trimmings (see Stocks, page 340), Orange juice (see Citrus, page 338)

Roasted Cauliflower with Pork, Ginger and Shallots

A one-tin triumph. My very favourite way to cook cauliflower is always to roast it so that it chars and gets even better at taking on other flavours. In this dish there are some hefty flavours available to it. Some kind of rice is good with this – perhaps Jasmine or sticky.

Note that the weight given is of prepared florets cut away from their stalk and leaves. You can find out what to do with those on pages 207 and 341.

Serves 4 as a main

600g (1lb 5oz) cauliflower florets

3 banana shallots

4 tbsp toasted sesame oil

400g (14oz) pork mince

1 red chilli

15g (½oz) root ginger

1 tbsp fish sauce, plus extra to serve

1½ tsp tamari/soy sauce, plus extra to serve

3 spring onions (scallions)

small handful of fresh coriander (cilantro)

1 lime

1 tbsp roasted black sesame seeds

salt

Preheat the oven to 200°C fan/425°F/gas 7.

Slice the cauliflower florets along their lengths, thinking about what size of piece you'd like in your finished dish. Peel the shallots and slice into thin lengths. Put the cauliflower and shallots into a large roasting dish, then toss with the sesame oil and a little salt. Roast for 15–20 minutes. You want them beginning to become tender and also starting to take on some lovely colour.

Meanwhile, put the pork into a large mixing bowl. Finely chop the chilli and add most of that to the pork, keeping some back for garnish. Grate in the ginger – there's no need to peel it. Add the fish sauce and tamari or soy sauce, then mix together well. The idea is to break the mince up, not bring it all together. Dot the pork mixture over the part-roasted cauliflower and shallots, and return to the oven for 15 minutes.

For the garnish: Trim the spring onions and slice into very thin lengths. Chop the coriander. Cut the lime into wedges.

When the pork has cooked (both it and the cauliflower should have browned really nicely), scatter over the spring onions, coriander, sesame seeds and the reserved chopped chilli. Serve with the lime wedges to squeeze over; with more fish sauce and tamari on the table to be added to taste.

WASTE TIPS: Cauliflower (page 341), Ginger (see Horseradish, page 338), Shallot skins and spring onion trimmings (see Stocks, page 340)

Shaved Cauliflower, Sultanas, Preserved Lemon and Chilli

I love this most as a winter salad but in truth it's just as good when made with any cauliflower you find across the year. It has it all: crunch from the cauliflower; sweetness from the sultanas; salty zestiness from the preserved lemons; and heat from the chilli. The key is to be sure to make it ahead of time so the flavours can get acquainted, and the yoghurt/oil mix can slightly relax the raw cauliflower.

Serves 6 as a side or 4 as a main

100g (3½oz) sultanas (golden raisins)

1½ tbsp sherry vinegar

¼ tsp ground cinnamon

1 cauliflower, about 800g (1lb 12oz), with its leaves

225g (8oz) plain full-fat Greek yoghurt

4 tbsp extra-virgin olive oil

½ mild red chilli

3 preserved lemons

40g (1½oz) flaked almonds

small bunch of fresh mint

salt

Put the sultanas into a shallow bowl with the vinegar and cinnamon, and mix. As you prepare the cauliflower, remember to give these another occasional mix round.

Pull off the large outer leaves of the cauliflower. Trim away and discard the cauliflower's base. Pull away and keep the small delicate inner leaves. Cut off the florets and then slice down their lengths just 3mm (⅛in) or so thick. Put into a large mixing bowl or serving dish, along with any of the cauliflower 'curds' that have come away as you cut. Add to them the small cauliflower leaves. Spoon the yoghurt and 2 tablespoons of the olive oil over the cauliflower. Lightly season with salt and mix together well.

Add the sultanas and any of the cinnamon or sherry left behind in the bowl. Finely chop the chilli and add that, then finely chop the preserved lemons and add too. Mix well again. Set all this aside for at least 2 hours or up to 24 hours. Put it in the fridge if more than a couple of hours.

To serve: Bring the cauliflower back to room temperature if it has been in the fridge. Toss everything round and transfer to the dish/plates you'll be serving it in. Toast the flaked almonds in a dry frying pan over a medium heat until just becoming golden. Scatter them over the cauliflower. Discard any tough stalks on the mint, roughly chop and scatter over too. Pour over the remaining 2 tablespoons of olive oil and serve.

WASTE TIPS: Cauliflower (page 341), Herb stems (see Stocks, page 340; Soft Herbs, page 341)

Celeriac and Swede

Winter

Give me a cold winter's day and a big bowl of hot, buttery, saffron-hued swede mash that has a grating of nutmeg stirred through it, and I could almost (*almost*) not care if spring never comes.

Cooked like that a swede takes on more glamour than its raw state gives the promise of. Same with celeriac. And what's even worse for poor old celeriac is not only that it looks distinctly 'rustic' but it looks difficult. With its tangle of roots that are often holding so tightly onto their soil. So off-putting are those roots that some celeriacs are being bred that can be sold without the roots, or less of them. If that helps more cooks feel more comfortable about cooking this beautiful vegetable then all to the good – although I can't help also feeling the roots are a distinctive part of a celeriac's character.

Celeriac is sometimes called 'celery root' and that unsurprisingly leads to the assumption that it is, literally, the root of celery. Almost, but not quite. Celeriac is the bulb of *a* celery plant. Just not *the* celery plant that gives us the celery stalks we cook and eat. Celeriac's flavour is more subtle, more rounded than celery itself. Even people who may not love celery can be persuaded into celeriac.

While we're playing the name game, a swede is sometimes called a turnip. It's sometimes called a swede-turnip. The classifications are confused and confusing. It's a tangle that seems more intricate than the roots of a celeriac, so let's just settle on what I mean here: The large, round vegetable with a purply-green skin that reveals yellowy-orange flesh. In contrast to a true turnip, swedes get sweeter as they get bigger through the season. Actually, somehow not just sweeter but more peppery at the same time. If you encounter large winter turnips you can follow the swede notes here. But for the small, summer/autumn turnips you'll be better helped over at kohlrabi on page 230.

I tend to think of celeriac and swede as being like potatoes, but (even) more interesting. Whatever a potato can do, a celeriac or swede can do too – and then some.

Shop

- If leaves are attached make sure that they are nicely perky. Lack of leaves is no particular sign of anything negative – it is pretty unusual (but lovely) to find celeriacs or swedes with their stalks and leaves still attached.
- They should feel heavy for their size. Check that the skin feels firm.

Store

- Don't wash soil off celeriac until it's time to use it.
- Both celeriacs and swedes are fine in the fridge, or anywhere cool and dark. If they come wrapped in plastic get that off straight away and let them breathe.

Ways to Use

- Sit celeriac in a bowl of cold water for 10 minutes to encourage its soil to float away, then give it a rinse under cold water. It should hopefully now look like you don't have to cut away quite so much of its roots to get at its flesh.
- The skin of both celeriacs and swedes is edible. If you don't want to peel it just be sure to give them a good wash. Swedes often come waxed to stop them drying out – remove that with warm water and a gentle scrub with a brush.
- Celeriac's flesh wants to turn brown quickly upon being revealed. Either head it straight into however you are using it, or have to hand a bowl of water with lemon juice in it that you can put the naked celeriac into.
- Celeriac skins are good for stocks; swede skins not so much – they're in the cabbage family so will become sulphurous.

The very clever trick that swede pulls off is to intensify its colour as it cooks. That's how the swede mash this all started with is the colour of saffron. Make your swede mash just like you would any potato mash, although you might find you don't have to try quite so hard to make it lustrously fabulous. Swede mash is inherently fabulous, so long as accessorised with lots of butter.

Celeriac tends to make a sloppy mash. A 50/50 combo of celeriac to potato gives it firmer texture. Cook them separately, as the celeriac pieces will almost certainly become tender before the potato does; if they were together in the bubbling water you'd have over-cooked celeriac and be back to sloppy mash problems.

A mixed root mash is a great way to use up leftovers or random amounts.

Thin slices of (peeled or unpeeled) celeriac and swede make for glorious gratins and dauphinoises. They are interchangeable with each other whenever you see them in these recipes, and interchangeable, too, with potatoes for the same.

Very thin slices of either/both of these veg can be used in a tian. Or put on top of some cheese on top of some puff pastry for a quick tart.

Steam peeled cubes for a light side that will be thirsty for dressing as soon as they come out of the steamer. Sauté peeled cubes in butter and oil, then pour over stock or wine and let them gently simmer until cooked. The cooking liquor can then be reduced over a high heat into a sauce to serve with the tender veg as a side.

Cubes of these veg are terrific to cook into pies, curries, stews.... Cut the size of the pieces according to whether they are playing a leading role or rather supporting cast.

Celeriacs and swedes are very much the stars of any meal when roasted whole. The simplest way is to wash but don't peel, pierce all over with a fork going in about 1cm (½in) deep and then sit on a roasting tray before smothering in oil, salt and your choices of other flavours. Roast in a 200°C fan/425°F/gas 7 oven, basting every 30 minutes or so. It could take up to two and half hours until tender right the way through. Well worth the wait once you slice through to reveal tender, delicious flesh.

An only slightly more complicated version is to wrap the vegetable in a salt dough for its baking. That protects it from the direct heat of the oven, giving more of a steaming than a roasting. Yes, loosely wrapping it in kitchen foil would achieve the same result but you wouldn't then have the wow of taking a salt-crusted vegetable to table. For one celeriac or swede: Mix 500g (1lb 2oz) plain (all-purpose) flour with 150g (5oz) salt and some chopped herbs of your choosing, then use a little water to enable it to come into a dough. Wrap that around the celeriac/swede and carry on as just above.

Note that the cooking times of both these ways of roasting whole celeriac/swede can be reduced if you parboil the veg first. Personally, I think there is greater depth of flavour the slower way.

And all that's all before we even get to thinking about using these two raw. There's celeriac remoulade, of course, which is the gateway to using celeriac in all kinds of salads and slaws. It would be perfect instead of either the sprouts or kohlrabi in the slaw recipe on page 234. Try swede mandolined into thin slices, or peeled into ribbons, and tossed in a citrus or vinegar dressing.

Flavour Partners

Butter.

More? Well okay, but butter is certainly the one I keep going back to. As celeriac and swede cook they have a sponge-like ability to absorb other flavours. Melted, possibly browned, butter doesn't just dress them, it becomes part of them.

Take advantage of that characteristic by immersing pieces of celeriac and swede in the slow cooking of a stew perhaps with lots of **herbs**, such as **thyme**, **bay**, **rosemary** or **sage**; chunks of **leeks**; and rich **chicken** or **beef stock**. Or simmering them in herb-infused **white wine** or **dry vermouth**.

Celeriac and swede like being cooked with each other, and with other root veg. Roast wedges with **parsnips**, **carrots** or **potatoes**. Arrange a medley of them all as the bed for roasting a joint of **chicken**, **pork**, **lamb** or **venison**. Tuck some pieces of **celery** in there, too. It might seem that would be too much celery-ness alongside celeriac but in fact their partnership is a happy one, rounding each other out.

Celeriac and swede make excellent partners for all kinds of **fish** and **shellfish: white fish**, **scallops**, **prawns**, **crab**.... One of the best fish pies I ever made was topped by a mix of leftover celeriac and swede mash.

Apple gives celeriac a real lift. Both these veg like apple, actually. Put them together in a soup or winter salad. I'd love a couple of **blackberries** in there as well – especially if quick-pickled like the ones over on page 160. That recipe's **red wine vinegar**, or **sherry vinegar** or **balsamic**, are the best choices for pouring over celeriac and swede as they roast.

Freshly grated **nutmeg** makes celeriac and swede sing. Look to other **spices**, such as **black pepper** (and lots of it), **anise seeds**, **turmeric**, **fenugreek**, **ground ginger**, **coriander seeds**, **dukkah**, **sumac**.... Grate **root ginger** over cubes as they steam, add chopped fresh **chilli** into the steamer, then douse with **soy sauce** once they're done.

Use **Parmesan** to top a celeriac/swede gratin. It brings the umami that is behind why **mushrooms** and **truffle** also work. Try just a little grated truffle over a celeriac or swede mash and feel your taste buds swoon.

I know, mash again. I'm sorry. And I'm going to end there, too, with this idea from Fergus Henderson and Justin Piers Gellatly's transformative book *The Complete Nose to Tail:* Make a buttery celeriac mash, spoon it into a baking dish and make indents to break **eggs** into. Season, add more butter, and bake. Heaven.

I did say it always comes back to butter in the end.

More flavour thoughts: **Beef**; **blackcurrant**; **black sesame seeds**; **bottarga**; **capers**; **game birds**; **horseradish**; **lamb**; **lime**; **mustard**; **nuts**; **orange**; **pomegranate molasses**; **rosewater**; **sumac**; **tahini**; **wasabi**; **watercress**.

Preserve

Freeze: Peel and chop cubes of celeriac or swede, then spread on a tray and freeze before transferring to bags. Good for swede, invaluable for celeriac when you might find you don't use the whole thing at once, but know that once it's been cut into it will start going brown.

Celeriac and Horseradish Rosti with a Fried Egg and Walnut Oil Dressing

Most of the time taken in making these rosti is just letting the celeriac and potato drain away their juices. The rest is the work of a few minutes – great for a quick and light, yet satisfying, dinner. Once prepped but not yet fried they freeze well, too. I'll often defrost a couple and cook for a weekday lunch on one of those days when I want to feel like I've made a bit of effort, but time is still a little short.

A few salad leaves are good alongside to soak up some of the walnut oil dressing and egg yolk.

Makes 8 rosti (serves 4 as light main or lunch)

For the rosti

800g (1lb 12oz) celeriac

300g (10½oz) potatoes

2 tsp salt

2 large eggs

20g (¾oz) horseradish root

45g (1¾oz) plain (all-purpose) flour

small handful of mixed fresh soft
  herbs of your choosing: dill,
  tarragon, mint, chervil, parsley...

salt and black pepper

2 tbsp oil, for frying

For the dressing

75ml (2½fl oz) walnut oil

1½ tbsp muscatel or other white wine
  vinegar

½ tsp English mustard

salt and black pepper

For the fried eggs

2 tsp oil, for frying (optional)

4 eggs

WASTE TIPS: Celeriac peelings (see Stocks, page 340), Herb stems (see Stocks, page 340; Soft Herbs, page 341), Horseradish (page 339), Potato peelings (page 341)

Peel the celeriac and potatoes, then coarsely grate into a large mixing bowl. Add the salt, mix, and tip it all into a colander or sieve lined with a cloth. Bring the cloth's ends up to tighten the bundle and sit the colander/sieve over a bowl for 30 minutes, then give it a good squeeze, or even wring, to get out as much liquid as you can.

Meanwhile, make the dressing: Whisk together the walnut oil, muscatel vinegar and mustard in a small bowl. Season and set aside.

Beat the eggs for the rosti into a mixing bowl. Peel and grate the horseradish – you are aiming for about 2 tablespoons – then add to the egg along with the flour. Finely chop the fresh herbs and add those, too. Season and mix well. Add the drained celeriac and potato, and bring it all together. Shape into 8 rosti, about 10cm (4in) in diameter. You can then carry straight on to cook the rosti, put them into the fridge for a few hours, or freeze individually.

To cook the rosti: Preheat the oven to 100°C fan/250°F/gas ½. Heat the oil in a large frying pan over a medium heat. Once hot, sit 4 rosti in the oil and cook for 3 4 minutes, then carefully turn over and cook for another 3–4 minutes. You want them gently browned on each side. Lift out of the pan, put them onto a plate and into the warm oven, uncovered. Repeat for the rest of the rosti.

Only add more oil to the pan to fry the eggs if needed. Break the eggs into the pan and cook however you prefer. Perhaps runny, 'sunny-side up', turned over.... You know how you like your fried eggs.

Plate up 2 rosti per person, with a fried egg balanced on top and the dressing spooned over.

Mixed Roasted Roots with Black Pudding (or Butter Beans)

Many is the cold winter's night I've served this at home just for the two of us (often the whole dish for four disappearing...), with just a bottle of red and some good bread on the side. And I've done it for friends and family too, plus a large bowl of lightly dressed radicchio leaves for a burst of freshness. This dish seems to be able to carry things off whatever the crowd. So long as they're hungry, and definitely if it is cold.

The proportions of the root vegetables can change depending on what you have around. You could swap in carrot or salsify or potatoes. It's a good recipe for using things up that might otherwise be in danger of being wasted. Switching the black pudding for butter beans isn't in any way a vegetarian 'concession'. It's an alternative that I enjoy every bit as much as the original.

Serves 4 as a main
Total 1.8kg (3lb 15oz) root veg:
  600g (1lb 5oz) celeriac
  600g (1lb 5oz) swede
  600g (1lb 5oz) parsnips
1 large leek
2 rosemary sprigs
5 garlic cloves
100ml (3½fl oz) olive oil

100ml (3½fl oz) dry white wine
1 tbsp sherry vinegar
¼ tsp chilli flakes
300g (10½oz) black pudding OR
  1 x 400g (14oz) tin butter beans
100g (3½oz) crème fraîche
2 mint sprigs
salt

Preheat the oven to 200°C fan/425°F/gas 7.

Trim the three root vegetables. Peel the celeriac and swede but only peel the parsnips if they are looking hairy and woody. Cut the vegetables into uneven chunks. Trim the leek and cut into chunks. Tumble all the vegetables together into a large baking dish.

Tuck in the rosemary sprigs and the (unpeeled) garlic cloves. Pour over the oil, wine and vinegar. Add the chilli flakes and season with salt. Mix together well and put into the oven for 40 minutes, tossing everything round once or twice in that time.

Remove the skin from the black pudding. Crumble it among the roasted roots, pushing some underneath and leaving some on top. Roast for another 15 minutes.

(*For the butter bean option:* Drain and rinse the beans. Give the roots 50 minutes in the oven rather than 40, before adding the beans to the dish and gently mixing them through the roots. Return to the oven for just 5 minutes.)

Remove from the oven, spoon over the crème fraîche and let it sink around the roots. Pull the mint leaves from their stems, chop and scatter over. Serve straight away.

WASTE TIPS: Celeriac and parsnip peelings, leek trimmings (see Stocks, page 340), Herb stems (see Stocks, page 340; Soft Herbs, page 341)

Chard – Swiss, Rainbow and Ruby

Winter – *Spring – Summer – Autumn*

It's their beautiful plumes that do it. That make chard – in all its forms – look so enticing. Even when I know deep in my soul it is not a vegetable I find myself naturally enjoying in the kitchen, or on the plate. I'm sorry to admit it. But there we are. We can't all love everything.

Which isn't to say I can't see the point of chard. Nor that it is a stranger to my kitchen. It's just I have to work that little bit harder to enjoy it. Not so much with the young chard of summer whose stalks and leaves are so small and delicate you need only think of them like a lovely lettuce. But by the time winter comes, chard has matured into a stronger character that can not only handle cooking and flavour but needs both.

Its ribbed stalks are now thicker and coarser. Colour builds in intensity along the length of the stalk until it finally releases into a burst of brightness across the huge leaves. On a dark winter's day they are impossible to turn away from, in all their varieties:

Swiss chard (silverbeet): With broad stalks that might be snow white or more creamy, right up until they get near the leaf and then the green starts. And what a green. The greenest wintry green of joy.

Rainbow chard: Even within the same bundle you might find them with stalks that are yellow or orange or red or pink. So very bright with those colours, too. As the stalk meets the leaf the colour turns into shooting veins that run across the leaves.

Ruby chard: No less exciting than rainbow, just more consistent of colour. With lushly red stems and deeply green leaves.

Don't I just sound like I love chard?! I hope very much that you might be the beneficiary of my hours spent learning to.

Shop

- Brightness is the key here. Bright stalks with bright leaves. Discolouration is a sign they're drying out with age. Same if they are too sadly limp. Your chard should look alive.

Store

- The fridge is the best place for storing chard, wrapped in a bundle in kitchen paper. Keep the leaves and stalks together until you want to use both/either, but don't wash them for storing as that can just speed up the chard going off.

Ways to Use

Chard with a stalk broader than a finger's width (so that is most winter chard) needs to have its leaves and stalks cooked separately from each other. Otherwise the leaves will be overcooked while the stalks are still on their journey to tenderness. Neither takes especially long to cook at all, but minutes matter. Whether the stalks and leaves end up together in the same dish is entirely up to you. They can do, but they don't have to.

Leaves

Chard leaves are so often given a shorthand of 'cook like spinach'. I am not sure I totally agree with that. For summer's chard, yes. Winter's chard, only sort of. It's so much larger, tougher, bitter-er than spinach. And so needs not just more cooking, but smarter cooking.

Swiss chard (silverbeet) leaves are as good as spinach in any recipe for a very green, and very tasty, soup. That's largely due to both having high water content. That also means, depending on what you're cooking, you might need to squeeze away the excess water that comes out of the leaves once cooked. Definitely needed for the dumplings over on page 228, or for baking chard into a loaf of bread. That's one of my favourite things to do with chard: Chop the leaves, sauté in oil with garlic, squeeze away the excess moisture, then mix with cheese, herbs and pepper for the loaf's stuffing.

Same for a chard leaf omelette – you need to cook off and drain the chard leaves before they go anywhere near any eggs. When I first gave this a go it was a recipe from an old book by the brilliant food writer, Elisabeth Luard. She calls for a whopping 500g (1lb 2oz) chard leaves for a 6-egg omelette. I was initially wary and then sold. The leaves reduce just as spinach does.

The size of winter's chard leaves makes them very useful for stuffing as you might cabbage leaves (see page 194). Choose leaves without holes or the filling will fall out. I'll often cook the stalks into the filling somehow, but if that proves just too chard-y I know I can keep the stalks to cook in their own right, too.

Stalks

Chard stalks are terrific when gently sweated in butter and/or olive oil. Let them take their time and their bitter edge will mellow itself out. Cut to be still quite large (perhaps 10cm/4in long) and sweated into almost tenderness, they can become the base for a lovely gratin. The celery version on page 112 could easily and deliciously have chard swapped in.

Try poaching the stalks in a little water, wine or stock, cooking them nice and slowly until absolutely tender, then drain and serve with the flavour partners of your choosing.

Chard stalks take well to stir frying, but thicker Swiss chard ones will need to be quickly blanched first for a couple of minutes. Make sure they are fully drained and dried before adding to your wok, where they'll need only a few minutes more. Blanching is good too if you just want to roast or griddle Swiss chard stalks, or cook them over fire. They'll benefit from having had that head start on the cooking. A squeeze of lemon juice into the blanching water for Swiss chard will help the stems keep their gorgeous colour.

Where the stalks aren't so broad you are detaching them from the leaves: Steam the chard for a couple of minutes, with only the stalks actually in the steamer and the leaves hanging over the sides. Or toss them in oil, salt and spices, spread on a roasting tray and roast in a hot oven for 12–15 minutes until the stalks are fully tender and the leaves crisped.

Just quickly, if you are here with summertime chard in your hand: Its small, bitter-sweet leaves are lovely raw for a salad, so head to Lettuce on pages 288-95 for more there. As the leaves get that bit bigger, let them have some time in an acidic (vinegar or citrus) dressing so they can relax a little. Small stalks no wider than a finger just need trimming but can stay on.

Flavour Partners

Winter chard – even once cooked – is bitter, in its stalks and its leaves. Know it, use it, and embrace it in how you layer up flavour.

A little smoothing out is often a good thing. That's why chard stalks, especially, will enjoy hanging out with their seasonal buddies **potato** and **celeriac**. In a soup, or a stew of some kind, or all of them thinly sliced into a gratin.

That gratin would be heavenly with **coconut milk** and/or **cream** in there. Both bring calm. Look to more smooth **dairy** by way of **butter** for cooking, smooth sauces like **hollandaise** or **mayonnaise** to serve with chard stalks; a side of cooked stalks with **yoghurt** or a lush spoonful of **labneh** or **mascarpone**, that's been given some heat (see opposite...) for further balancing.

For other **cheeses** with chard steer towards the creamier end of things. A rich salty **blue cheese** works a treat crumbled over poached stalks before popping under the grill; or try chard with **feta** or any similar **goats'/sheep's cheese**. The really strong, hard cheeses, like a **Cheddar** or **Parmesan**, are best kept for a fairly minimal grating.

Eggs are exceptionally versatile in how they can make all things chard work. There's the chard/egg omelette mentioned over on page 223; or try wilting chard leaves instead of spinach for Florentine eggs.

Fatty meats continue the calming theme. Chard is not the place for strong game – not unless you do some serious smoothing out. Rich **pork** is more the vibe: chard stalks roasted with **sausages**, **pork mince** with chopped-down chard stalks as stuffing for the leaves or into dumplings; or a rich bake of **pork chops** with chard stalks and cream.

None of which is to say that chard can't take – or enjoy – strong flavours. You are going to need them for balance. Just make sure you head towards flavours that bring heat, zest, and/or brightness:

Stir fry blanched chard stalks with **celery**, the greens of some **spring onions (scallions)**, lots of fresh or dried **chilli**, **root ginger**, and **coriander** (**seeds**, **stalks** and **leaves**). Give extra pep via **mustard seeds** or **wasabi**. Reach for the **soy sauce** or **mirin**. And whatever you do, don't forget the **garlic**. Chard – its stalks and leaves, and however you are doing it – loves loves loves garlic.

Give sauces, or cooked chard itself, a burst of **paprika**, **cayenne** or chilli for heat. For more of a comforting warmth look to **cumin** and **cinnamon**. Ground versions of either/both are great over blanched stalks before roasting; with leaves as they wilt; or partnering with chard in a green shakshuka. (You see – eggs, again.)

Finely chopped **preserved lemon** makes for an uplifting way to finish any chard dish. As would a grating of fresh **lemon** or **orange** zest. The juice of either is useful, too, for adding in when cooking the stalks.

More flavour thoughts: **Allspice**; **almond**; **anchovies**; **blackcurrant**; **black olives**; **buttermilk**; **capers**; **clementine**; **date syrup**; **dill**; **harissa**; **lime**; **nutmeg**; **parsley**; **raisins**; **saffron**; **tarragon**.

Preserve

Freeze: You'll need to separate the leaves and the stalks. The stalks are best blanched and dried before freezing. The leaves you can freeze raw.

Ferment: Chard kimchi? Oh yes.

Filo Tart of Mixed Greens and Feta

Winter's fabulously bitter leafy greens (of which chard is here the star, ably supported by cavolo nero) have their edge smoothed out by baking them with cheese. The ratio of nutritious to comforting is just right. You could happily switch round the proportions of the greens here. Or swap in whatever leaves you have hanging around – spinach, kale, beetroot tops, turnip tops, collard greens – they'd all be just as lovely, just as green.

Serves 6 as a main

400g (14oz) chard

200g (7oz) cavolo nero

1 medium onion

4 tbsp olive oil

½ orange

1 tsp ground cinnamon

3 eggs

200g (7oz) feta

40g (1½oz) leafy herbs
 (any mix of dill, mint, coriander
 [cilantro], parsley)

1 tbsp honey

nutmeg, for grating

1 tbsp plain (all-purpose) flour

4 sheets of filo pastry

salt and black pepper

23cm (9in) springform cake tin

Separate the stalks and the leaves of the chard and cavolo nero. Trim and finely chop all the stalks. Wash all the leaves, drain and shred.

Peel and chop the onion. Heat 2 tablespoons of the oil in a deep frying pan. Gently cook the onion until just about softening, then add the chopped stalks. Season, squeeze in the juice of the orange half, stir round and cook for 10 minutes until soft. Add the cinnamon, then the shredded leaves. Cook for 5 minutes to wilt, then take off the heat. Let it cool a little before spooning into a fine sieve set over a sink or bowl to drain away any excess liquid.

Beat the eggs in a large mixing bowl. Crumble in the cheese. Chop the herbs and add too, keeping just a few back for garnish. Mix well, adding the honey and a good grating of nutmeg. Add the drained chard mix and combine thoroughly. Taste before seasoning. Up to here can be done ahead of time.

Preheat the oven to 190°C fan/400°F/gas 6. Brush the cake tin with some of the remaining oil and dust with the flour. Lay one sheet of filo in the base, overhanging the sides. Brush it with oil, then lay another sheet of filo on top, going crossways to cover the other sides of the tin. Oil and repeat with 2 more sheets. Fill with the cheesy greens filling. Bring up the overhanging pastry and scrunch to form an edge to the pie (not a lid). Bake for 25 minutes until the pastry edges are golden.

Cool in the tin for 5 minutes, then remove and serve warm or at room temperature with the reserved chopped herbs scattered over.

WASTE TIPS: Feta brine (page 339), Filo pastry (page 339), Herb stems (see Stocks, page 340;
Soft Herbs, page 341), Onion skins (see Stocks, page 340), Orange (see Citrus, page 338)

Swiss Chard Dumplings, Broth and Crisped Sage Leaves

These are the strangolapreti of where northern Italy borders Austria and Switzerland. The Swiss connection isn't my only reason for switching the more usual spinach for chard – I think the chard just simply tastes better here. The Austrian influence certainly comes through in the style of these dumplings. They are made of breadcrumbs and flour yet light as anything. *Strangolapreti* translates as 'priest stranglers', referring to the effects of how quickly (many?) the priests ate. I share their pain/joy.

The broth here is a basic dark chicken stock. Switch it for 750ml (25fl oz) vegetable stock if you prefer. Pages 223–4 have ideas for using the chard's stalks that don't make it into this recipe.

Serves 4–6 as a main

For the broth

500g (1lb 2oz) chicken wings

1 onion

2 carrots

1 celery stalk

½ tsp coriander seeds

½ tsp black peppercorns

5 green cardamom pods

1 rosemary sprig

salt

For the dumplings

200g (7oz) breadcrumbs

200ml (7fl oz) milk

500g (1lb 2oz) Swiss chard (silverbeet) leaves (weight of leaves only)

2 large eggs

75g (2½oz) Parmesan

80g (3oz) plain (all-purpose) flour, plus 2 tbsp extra for dusting

nutmeg, for grating

salt and black pepper

For the crisped sage leaves

60g (2oz) butter

about 12 sage leaves

WASTE TIPS: Bread (page 338), Carrot peelings, celery trimmings and onion skins (see Stocks, page 340), Parmesan rind (page 339)

Make the broth first: Preheat the oven to 200°C fan/425°F/gas 7. Lay the chicken wings in a single layer in a roasting dish, without any oil added, and roast for 1 hour, turning halfway.

Transfer the wings to a stockpot or very large pan. Pour a splash of water into the roasting dish so you can rub at the base to deglaze it and add any browned bits and juices to the stockpot. Peel the onion, chop into chunks and add to the pot. Wash and trim the carrots and celery (only peel the carrots if really necessary), cut into chunks and add those too, followed by the coriander seeds, peppercorns, cardamom, rosemary and a large pinch of salt. Pour over enough cold water to just about cover everything, put on a partial lid, bring to the boil and then gently simmer for 1½ hours. Occasionally strain off any scum at the surface. Strain the broth, taste for seasoning, and set aside.

For the dumplings: Put the breadcrumbs into a large mixing bowl, pour over the milk, stir and set aside.

Bring a very large pan of salted water to the boil, add the chard leaves and quickly simmer for 3 minutes. Use tongs to lift the wilted leaves into a colander (you want to keep the water in the pan). Refresh the leaves in cold water. Then squeeze, squeeze and squeeze some more to get all the moisture out of the leaves.

Beat the eggs and add to the breadcrumbs. Grate in the Parmesan and stir in the flour. Chop the chard as finely as you can and add that too, along with seasoning and a few gratings of nutmeg. Bring into a sticky dough. Tear off pieces the size of large walnuts or golf balls, roll in your hands, and put on a tray dusted with extra flour.

Preheat the oven to 100°C fan/250°F/gas ½ with a large baking tray inside it. Bring the pan of water the chard cooked in back to the boil. Lower the dumplings into the water, taking care not to crowd the pan. They are ready when they bubble to the water's surface in 2–3 minutes. Lift out with a slotted spoon and onto the tray in the oven. Repeat for the rest of the dumplings.

Reheat 750ml (25fl oz) of the broth in a small saucepan.

Meanwhile, crisp the sage leaves: Melt the butter in a frying pan and once it is frothing sit the sage leaves in to crisp up.

To serve: Divide the broth and dumplings between shallow bowls. Top with the crisped sage leaves, pour the melted butter over, and serve straight away.

Kohlrabi

Summer - Autumn - Winter

Kohlrabis tend to come with excuses. When they are being written about, anyway. Excuses for their alien-esque form, how little loved they tend to be, and a general vibe of setting the bar quite low on how fabulous kohlrabis are. Them being part of the cabbage family doesn't exactly help. I'd like to take all those expectations of kohlrabi having limited appeal or uses, and of it looking a bit odd (who cares?), roll them up into a prejudiced ball and throw them out of the kitchen window. The prejudices, not the kohlrabi. And let's start again.

Summer's kohlrabis tend to be not much larger than a golf ball. It's easy to love a tender and sweet summertime kohlrabi – slice them thinly, dress with oil plus lemon/vinegar, and let the kohlrabi relax. Or finely chop/grate them into a slaw. Easy peasy.

As summer turns to autumn and then winter the kohlrabi get bigger; and so grows the potential for what you might do with them to make the most of their size and stronger, gorgeously sweet, flavour.

Most kohlrabis are greeny-white to look at, with white flesh. Some have a gorgeous purple skin instead, and the flesh inside will still be pure white. Their colour contrast is striking, and especially joyous in the dark days of winter. Grab these whenever you can.

Shop

- Bulbs with stalks and nicely perky leaves still attached will be freshest.
- Look for bulbs that feel weighty for their size, and full of life. Winter kohlrabis tend to have acquired more gnarls than in their summertime youth. I like that about them. Gnarls can mean flavour and character. Any yellowing or bruising is not so good.

Store

- Removing the leaves will help the bulbs stay fresh longer.
- Keep the kohlrabi bulbs in the fridge crisper drawer, and the stalks/leaves there too but wrapped in some damp kitchen paper. The stalks/leaves won't keep nearly as long as the bulbs so use those quickly if you can.

Ways to Use

Summer's kohlrabis are so delicious as they are that using them raw is best. Come winter you'll still find that useful. Quick-pickle kohlrabi matchsticks. Shaved as thinly as you or a mandoline can manage they'll be sublime in salads alongside other seasonal goodies. Similarly for winter slaws – like the one on page 234.

Cooking winter kohlrabis really brings out their sweetness. First thing to do is see if it needs peeling (in summer they don't, their skin is so thin). If unsure have a little nibble of one of their antennae. If it's tender, you are fine to put the peeler back in the drawer unused. If it is a little woody, then get peeling. The skin isn't any good for stocks, I'm afraid – it would just make the stock taste and smell sulphurous.

When kohlrabi has some leaves attached, think of those like spinach or kale. Roast in a hot oven, add towards the end of cooking soups or dals, or stir fry with the stalk.

Batons, or slices, of the bulb are lovely to sauté in plenty of butter, with some stock or wine. Semi-cover with a lid and let them cook through until tender, being sure to serve the cooking juices too.

Kohlrabi slices bring a sweet edge to indulgent gratins or dauphinoise. In any recipe for those just switch all or some of the potatoes for the same weight of kohlrabi.

Roasting – as ever – serves to caramelise and enhance the vegetable's inherent sweetness. Anything from small 2.5cm (1in) cubes to large wedges can be very happily tossed in oil, your choice of flavour partners, and roasted in a hot 200°C fan/425°F/gas 7 oven. Give chunks 20–30 minutes; cubes barely 10 minutes. And turn them a couple of times so they colour all over.

Or how about a deep fry? Perhaps thin slices dipped in a batter, or the kohlrabi cut into batons and just rolled in seasoned flour before hitting the hot oil. The trick is to have the oil temperature a bit lower than is usual for deep frying, so they can cook through without the outside scorching. Look for oil at 160°C/320°F on a thermometer. Easier/quicker/tastier still is to head to page 233 and make kohlrabi 'fries' in a wok.

Steaming cubes of kohlrabi makes for a light side when simply dressed. Their flesh can also be grated for rosti.

Flavour Partners

Kohlrabis like their seasonal friends, which means by the time we get to winter the produce they are most going to love hanging out with will include winter's bitter **oranges** over on page 237. Perhaps some **Seville orange** juice in a dressing for a kohlrabi salad; with **blood orange** segments in there instead or as well as.

Brussels sprouts, too. Together raw in a slaw, or kohlrabi cubes roasting with some blanched sprouts. When they come out of the oven, some **capers**, **sherry vinegar** or **soy sauce** are the only things that will need adding to the roasting juices.

A winter veg gratin is a good way to use up bits and bobs of various things you might have hanging around. That could mean slices of kohlrabi nudging up with **celeriac** or **parsnip** and all their creamy colours melding into creamy flavours; or wedges of kohlrabi roasting with **carrots** or **cauliflower**.

Kohlrabi's sweetness loves some spicing and can take it well. I can't think of many **spices** or **spice blends** that wouldn't work, but I find myself especially drawn to **cumin seeds**, **coriander seeds**, **ground cinnamon**, **dukkah**....

Mustard seeds too, and perhaps especially. If sautéing some thin slices of kohlrabi in butter and a little **white wine**, you'll fine some yellow or black mustard seeds in there will give a lovely pop of flavour as the kohlrabi soaks up the butteriness. And for similar reasons my dressing of kohlrabi salads tend to be heavy on the **Dijon**.

More flavour thoughts: **Apple**; **bottarga**; **caraway seeds**; strong **cheeses** (like **gorgonzola**); **Chinese black Chinkiang vinegar**; **dill**; **hazelnut oil**; **garlic**; **root ginger**; **juniper**; **lemongrass**; **mint**; **oregano**; **peppercorns**; **pesto**; **raisins**; **sesame** (seeds and oil); **spinach**; **truffle**.

Preserve

Pickle: Slices or batons of kohlrabi pickle well, as do the stalks. I'd go for a sweet vinegar like muscatel.

Ferment: Kohlrabi kimchi.

Freeze: The bulb can be frozen as cubes, batons or wedges but blanch them first, then freeze in a single layer on a tray before bundling into freezer bags.

Kohlrabi 'Fries'

Don't imagine these as being like potato fries (they don't have the firmness), but do imagine them as being almost preposterously good.

I rather love that a vegetable that can seem so very virtuous will – admittedly once deep fried and dusted in salt and smoked paprika – so readily take on a whole different personality.

Serves 4 as a side
1 kohlrabi, about 500g (1lb 2oz)

150ml (5fl oz) rapeseed oil
½ tsp smoked paprika powder
salt

Trim and peel the kohlrabi. Cut into matchsticks and sit those in a single layer between kitchen paper to dry out for 10 minutes.

Put 50ml (3 tablespoons) of the oil into a wok and get it very hot. Take a handful of the kohlrabi sticks and put them into the hot oil. Be careful as it will be very hot – do not turn away or get distracted. They'll need barely a minute to turn deep brown. Use a slotted spoon to lift out the kohlrabi sticks onto kitchen paper.

Repeat with the rest of the kohlrabi, working in batches and quickly. Add more oil to the wok when you need to and always get it hot again before it meets kohlrabi.

Dust the fries with salt and smoked paprika while they're still hot, and serve quickly.

Kohlrabi and Sprout Winter Slaw with Spatchcock Roast Duck

If raw sprouts in a slaw seems at all surprising, just remember that sprouts are really mini cabbages. Then it will all make sense. Their partnership here with kohlrabi gives this a lovely lightness. The slaw will be good with all kinds of things, but I do very much like it with duck – its bright zesty flavour marries with the richness of the meat.

Spatchcocking is always such a great way to roast duck. By flattening it out, the breasts and legs cook at the same rate. It's quicker too. You just need strong kitchen scissors and confidence.

Serves 4–6 as a main

For the slaw

1 unwaxed orange (sweet or blood)
100ml (3½fl oz) extra-virgin olive oil
½ tsp English or Dijon mustard
250g (9oz) Brussels sprouts
250g (9oz) kohlrabi
½ tsp sumac

2 tarragon sprigs
salt and black pepper

For the duck

1 x 2–2.5kg (4lb 8oz–5lb 8oz) duck
1 tsp dukkah
1 tsp flaky salt

Make the slaw at least 2 hours before you want to eat, or up to 24 hours ahead. Use a vegetable peeler to pare 4 broad strips of skin from the orange, taking as little of the white pith as possible. Set the peeled skin aside. Juice the orange into a large mixing bowl and whisk in the olive oil and mustard. Season well.

Cut away the base of the sprouts and pull off the outer leaves. Slice the trimmed sprouts as thinly as you possibly can. Toss with the dressing.

Pull off and keep any kohlrabi leaves. Trim away the top and bottom of the kohlrabi, then peel it. Now cut the kohlrabi into matchsticks ('julienne' it). Add to the sprouts and toss.

Very thinly slice the strips of orange zest and the kohlrabi leaves. Add those, too, along with the sumac, and mix well. Tear in the tarragon leaves and toss again. Make sure it is very well mixed. Set aside until needed – in the fridge if for more than 2 hours.

*WASTE TIPS: Duck carcass and fat (page 338), Herb stems (see Stocks, page 340;
Soft Herbs, page 341), Orange rind (see Citrus, page 338)*

For the duck: Preheat the oven to 180°C fan/400°F/gas 6.

Sit the duck breast-side down on a large chopping board. Use strong kitchen scissors to cut along either side of the backbone and remove it. Turn the duck over and press down hard on the breast bone to flatten the duck. Sit it on a rack in a roasting tray. Pierce the skin all over. Pestle the dukkah to make it slightly finer, mix with the salt, and scatter over the skin. Roast for 30 minutes. (The internal temperature you are looking for on a meat thermometer is 60°C/140°F.) If the skin isn't quite crisped to your liking, just put it under the grill for a few minutes. Rest the duck for 30 minutes before serving.

To serve: Bring the slaw back to room temperature if it has been in the fridge. Toss it well to revive. Slice the duck and serve with the slaw for people to help themselves to.

Waterfowl – Duck and Goose

When duck can be had all year round, is there really much point any more in thinking of it as being seasonal? The answer, for me, is very much 'yes'. Stepping away from simply accepting that duck can be had whatever the month reminds me to take a moment and think about how the duck I might be about to buy, cook and eat has been reared. Because not all ducks are equal, by any means.

The technical winter seasonality of duck in the UK really relates only to wild duck that can only be shot through autumn and up to the end of winter. Those ducks might have been wild all their lives, or sometimes they will have started out farmed and then been released into the wild later. But whichever way round, these birds are definitely seasonal and have had the benefit both of grazing on land and enjoying what the water can offer.

Theirs will have been a very different experience to the intensively farmed ducks that make up the majority of ducks on sale across the year. The occasional exposé is done of conditions in these farms and it is pretty harrowing. Think what you know about intensive chicken farming and it is the same idea. It might seem overly romantic – even naive – of me to think that ducks should be near water for at least some of their life, but shouldn't they?

As so often, there is a middle way. An increasing number of farmers produce ducks that are free-range and organic. I know, those are terms that can be bandied around rather too loosely sometimes. I urge us all – you, me, all – to look behind those words when buying to find producers who are working responsibly and sustainably, proud to have let their ducks enjoy land and water alike. Many of these producers will follow the seasonality of having the ducks available in the winter.

Geese don't take so well to being kept indoors, so intensive farming is far less of an issue for them. The goose was once the most favoured of feasting birds until turkeys shunted them out of the way. Geese keep trying to make a Christmas comeback but I am afraid I am not their advocate here. The one time I did go for doing a Christmas Day goose, dealing with the sheer amount of fat that comes off it was a level of faff that day did not need.

Not that I wasted a drop of it. Obviously. Duck fat and goose fat are gold when they come from your own cooking and from a bird you have carefully sourced. The rest of your winter cooking – I think especially root vegetables of all kinds, but the greens, too – will love you for having cooked a goose. Or a duck.

Oranges – Seville, Blood, Bergamot and Mandarins

Winter

Winter oranges are to this season what asparagus is to spring, or strawberries to summer: Their arrival is properly exciting, properly seasonal, and gifting cooks bounteous brightness of colour and flavour.

I'll admit that perhaps part of their allure is that they only appear relatively briefly. Squarely in the winter months, when a bit of lift is welcome. Much more a factor, though, is that the oranges we can get all year round are the sweet ones. They're lovely and useful, of course – my kitchen is rarely without them – but flatter of flavour and just somehow more obvious compared to the complexity of the bitter-sweet spectrum their winter cousins offer. A hit of citrus can so often be the needed flavour accent in a dish, and all the better if one of these:

Seville oranges: Marmalade oranges! Yet so much more than that, too. These are bitter, tart and deeply aromatic of both zest and juice. Beyond marmalading, I find it helpful to categorise them in my culinary brain as being in temperament rather closer to lemons or limes than sweet oranges. They are still very definitely oranges, though. Just more complicated ones – as a good fruit should be.

Blood oranges: Stand poised with your knife and wait to see what your slice will reveal. The flesh could be the dramatic deep purple-black of a good goth's eye make-up; or the delicate blush of a medieval maiden's cheek (they're sometimes called blush oranges). Or anywhere in between. It's the balancing act of low night temperatures and warmer days that develops the blood oranges' colour as they grow. The juice is exceptional whatever the shade, falling on the sweet-sour spectrum in a place that makes it both very delicious and very useful.

Bergamot: These look a little more like a typical lemon than a typical orange, but the orange family is claiming them. They are most prized for their zest, with its scent and flavour that lovers of Earl Grey tea will be familiar with. It is musky, floral, intensely heady in its citrussy hit – and so to be used judiciously. The sourness of the juice makes it not so great on its own but fabulous to (literally) tart up other flavours.

Mandarins: The sweeter, dinkier side of winter oranges and also where things get a little complicated. The lines are distinctly blurred between the clementines, satsumas and tangerines of the mandarin family. This is how I try to remember it...

Mandarin: Both a fruit in its own right and the umbrella term for the others. A mandarin is in itself gorgeously complex of flavour. It starts off as 'just' sweet, then gets a bit more floral. Its zest is great, too.

Tangerines: These ones are a little tarter than their pals.

Clementines: The skins are quite tight, the flesh definitely sweet. Seedless. The skin has a lovely red tinge to it and is more bitter than you might expect (in a good way).

Satsumas: These are the ones with a baggier skin, making them easier to peel. Sweet and seedless.

Some of those names may be there on the labels of 'easy-peelers'. But if no variety is named an easy-peeler is more likely to be a carefully honed hybrid of these small fruits, as producers try to get just the right combination of sweet flesh, easy to peel skin, not much pith, seedless, and with extended seasonality that will make them a go-to for lunchboxes everywhere.

Shop

- For Sevilles/blood/bergamot oranges (and this applies to year-round sweet oranges too): Look for firm oranges that feel heavy for their size – that is likely to mean they are nicely juicy. They should be unbruised and unwrinkled, with skin that is tight to the fruit.
- The shade of red/purple of a blood orange's skin is no indication at all of the depth of colour its flesh will be. Which is either a shame or exciting, depending on your take.
- For the mandarins you are, again, looking for unblemished, unwrinkled skin. Satsumas are the most delicate of the family and prone to bruised flesh that can be hard to spot from the outside due to the general bagginess of the skin. So take an extra-long look at satsumas before buying, to try to spot any bruising.

Store

- Producers wax oranges to help protect them on their journey from harvesting to your kitchen. That waxing will also prolong their life once you have them and so the oranges can be happily stored in or out of the fridge. Unwaxed oranges should be kept in the fridge.

Ways to Use

You'll find the usefulness of year-round sweet oranges peppered right through this book. They pop up to bring lift to other produce, and brighten/sweeten recipes. So what I am going to focus on here is specifically how to get the best out of the winter oranges that are with us for a short time. BUT, remember that the broad scope of uses here will apply to sweet oranges, too. Bearing in mind they are, well, sweeter and so balancing them accordingly.

Skins

Any and all oranges carry so much flavour within their skins. Having a little taste is the best way of understanding their varying profiles. The skin of Sevilles is very bitter. To use it in strips or pieces, blanch the pieces for a minute first in boiling hot water to take off the tendency towards over-bitterness. Blood orange skin is closer in flavour to a sweet orange, just more aromatic and often with that colour 'wow'. Bergamot skin is the best bit of the fruit – deeply musky and floral in its uplifting bitterness. Of the mandarins, clementines or mandarins themselves are optimum for zesting or otherwise using the skins, as they bring the most enjoyably complex flavour.

Most oranges are bought waxed and if you intend to use the skin you should remove the wax first: Wash in hot water and gently rub the skin with a vegetable brush, then rinse and dry.

Salad dressings, sauces and marinades

Seville oranges work exceptionally well in salad dressings in place of lemon or lime. The acidity will not only balance the other elements of the dressing but relax the leaves (or whatever else you are dressing). A Seville-orange-based salad dressing will need a little sweetening up, while a blood-orange one will already be bringing its own sweetness. Taste to get the balance just right. A touch of bergamot juice can be great in a salad dressing, so long as you marry it with another orange or other citrus. Don't go all bergamot.

Look to Sevilles, blood oranges or clementines – their zest or juice – to add varying degrees of aromatic citrussy flavour to sauces and marinades.

Tuck strips of peel into a casserole where they can release fragrance and flavour into the sauce and help bring it all together.

Ceviche

The high acidity of Seville oranges makes them excellent for ceviching fish. A sweet orange, or a blood, or any mandarin would need lemon or lime juice added to have enough acidity to 'cook' the fish, but the Seville orange can do the job on its own. You can ceviche with bergamot, too, adding another citrus partner just to temper quite how sour the juice is.

Roasted with meats, fish, vegetables

Chunks/slices of unpeeled blood orange or clementine are great for adding to the roasting tin for any of these. If I don't have a lemon to hand, a halved orange will often find its way inside my roasting chicken. (My Christmas Day turkey is stuffed inside with orange halves, leek ends, garlic, an abundance of herbs, and I swear it is the orange that makes the meat extra-delicious.)

Curd

Make yourself a pot or two of Seville or blood orange curd to have in the fridge and you will have weeks to enjoy finding ways to use it: for toast, on crumpets, to layer a sponge with, or for a Seville or blood orange meringue pie.... A Seville orange curd will (sorry for the repetition) be more bitter.

Cakes

A winter orange drizzle cake is going to make the trad lemon suddenly seem deadly dull. This is perhaps best of all with Seville orange juice, poured over the cake while the sponge is still hot from the oven and keen to soak it up. You can switch clementines into any cake recipe that calls for sweet oranges. And sticking with the sponge theme, try the zest of any winter oranges into the batter of a clafoutis. Use a little bergamot juice for making icing.

Sorbets/ice cream/granitas

The blood orange finds most favour here. For their colour but also the complexity of their bitter-sweetness.

Cocktails

Again, this is blood orange territory. And again, it's the combination of their colour pop and flavour that does it. Their juice is a superb ingredient, a slice or a paring of skin a gorgeous garnish. Cocktails are also a place for bergamots to come to the fore and for once it's the sour punch of its juice that you might find the most interesting, rather than the aromatic skin that would too easily overwhelm a drink. Cheers to a bergamot margarita.

Flavour Partners

Often the best partners for winter oranges are each other. In a salad you can build layers of their flavour and bitter-sweetness by using them in different ways. Perhaps blood oranges segments in the body of the salad, with a dressing that might include a balance of bergamot and clementine juice (which, if you follow page 242, will be easy to gather just a little of from your freezer) whisked with **olive oil**, **mustard**, and a careful gauging of just enough **honey**, but no more than that. Finish with a smattering of **salt flakes**.

Or how about this lovely idea for a sweet winter orange salad from Frances Bissell's *The Scented Kitchen*: Segments of blood oranges and a few different types of mandarins macerated in any juices they release on cutting and tossed in **icing (confectioners') sugar** to bring out more juiciness, plus **rosewater** and **orange flower water**. Chilled and then topped with toasted flaked **almonds**.

These kinds of combos work because you are playing with, and balancing, different levels of bitterness. It's why winter oranges love anything in the aniseed line of flavour. **Fennel** could be mandolined into a winter orange salad; or chunks roasted with blood oranges, mandarins or clementines. **Dill** or **tarragon** as garnishing herbs.

Lean towards orange with bitter leaves. The sautéed **sprouts** and **kale** on page 189 could easily have their lemon zesting switched for orange. **Radicchio**'s pink-purple leaves are a colour as well as flavour match for blood oranges. Raw **chicory** (witlof) or **endive** could have winter orange slices/segments tucked in among them, or their roasted leaves be finished with an orange-laced dressing. Even just a squeeze of orange would on its own bring so much flavour lift there. A few **pomegranate seeds** or **pomegranate molasses** work well added to any of these, too.

The carb-fest root veggies of **celeriac**, **parsnips** and **beetroots** also enjoy winter oranges. Zestings of blood orange or mandarin/clementine to garnish their soups; into dressings; or squeezes of the fruit over them when they come out from roasting.

That's a very good trick for roasted/baked **fish**: As soon as it comes out of the oven, spritz over some fresh winter orange straight from the fruit. It's going to delicately play on the surface of the fish and give your taste buds a buzz as you start to eat. Think also of winter oranges for marinating **shellfish** and **squid**. A little bergamot juice is especially good with shellfish.

Campari is very fun with blood orange. Try a negroni, with blood orange taking the place of the red vermouth – so equal measures **gin**, Campari and blood orange juice stirred over ice. As a bitter-fiend, I'd pop a **rosemary** sprig into the glass to stir it all together.

Nuts are handy to balance out orange's flavours. **Walnuts** become a lovely sauce when pestled with orange juice and zest, a few **anchovies**, and enough olive oil to bring it all together. For a sweet dish, I'd be more inclined to partner orange with **pecans**, **almonds** or **pistachios**.

Any desserts that threaten to be a bit too sweet, or a bit too creamy, or in any way just a bit too rich will thank you for reaching for a winter orange. Take a pavlova: So often a bit of all those things, what with the sweet meringue and whipped cream; but give it a swirl of blood orange or, even better, Seville orange curd (perhaps infused with **cardamom** or **saffron**) and you not only have extra beauty but added complexity and depth of flavour, too.

It's why the crème brûlée opposite is better than it even usually is thanks to bergamot zest. Same with whipping orange zest through **labneh** or **mascarpone**. Or, in the same vein of cutting through richness, adding blood orange juice when making a **hollandaise** and you've got Maltaise sauce. That is going to be sensational with those first spears of **purple sprouting broccoli** that edge into season just as the last of the winter oranges ebb out.

More flavour thoughts: **Bay leaves**; **black pepper**; **chicken**; **chilli**; **chocolate** (dark or white); **cinnamon**; **duck**; **figs**; **lamb**; **pumpkin**; **quince**; **rhubarb**; **rum**; **sage**; **thyme**; **vinegars**, especially **sherry**, **vermouth** and **red wine**.

Preserve

Winter oranges are for cherishing and, therefore, preserving. I am going to touch on a couple of ideas here, but beyond these – and to find out about more ways of preserving them in much more depth – you can do no better than head to Catherine Phipps' book, *Citrus*. There, you'll find oil, salts, rubs, dried whole fruits....

Freeze: These oranges all freeze well and you can do them in varying forms to suit different purposes when it comes to using.
- Freeze juice in ice-cube trays/bags or tubs, depending how much you have and how you are likely to want to use it. The ice-cube sizes are so handy for when you just need a bit of winter orange juice for a dressing.
- Freeze slices or wedges in a single layer on a tray before bundling into a freezer bag. You can use those straight from the freezer to put into drinks.
- Parings of zest can be frozen in the same way.

Sugar: Blitz or pestle any winter orange zest with granulated sugar for the most fragrant, delicious aromatic sugar to bake with.

Bergamot Crème Brûlée

The very first time I made crème brûlées was before I was working in food, before being that much of a confident cook, really – and, oh yes, for about 20 people at a birthday dinner for my husband. I'm not too sure what I was thinking but the point is: thank goodness crème brulées are the easiest of make-ahead, luxe desserts.

Those were the classic vanilla-infused crèmes. Now I look forward each winter to making them with bergamot instead of vanilla. The bergamot's delicate yet distinctive zest giving extra depth of flavour. (With love and thanks for the inspiration to the brilliant London chefs Honey & Co., whose heavenly bergamot posset first made me think of doing this.)

Serves 4
500ml (17fl oz) double (heavy) cream
1 bergamot
4 egg yolks
50g (2oz) golden caster (superfine)
   sugar, plus 2 tbsp
pinch of salt

4 x shallow crème brûlée dishes or
   150–175ml (5–6fl oz) ramekins

Preheat the oven to 130°C fan/300°F/gas 2.

Pour the cream into a medium saucepan and grate in the zest of the bergamot. Put the pan over a low-medium heat and warm just until you start to see a few bubbles (about 70°C/158°F on a thermometer). Take the pan off the heat and set aside.

In a medium mixing bowl, lightly whisk together the egg yolks, 50g (2oz) of sugar and salt. Now begin to pour in the cream. Go very slowly at first so as not to curdle/scramble the eggs. This is the only painstaking part of the recipe (and hardly all that painstaking), so it is worth taking time over. Stir the cream into the eggs after each pour. Carry on until all mixed together – you can speed up a little as more goes in.

Sit the crème brûlée dishes in a large roasting tin. Pour into the tin enough hot (not boiling) water to come about two-thirds of the way up the dishes' sides. Now pour the crème brûlée mixture among the dishes. Carefully lift the tray into the oven.

Bake for 25–30 minutes if using shallow dishes; 35–40 minutes for deeper ramekins. They are ready when set but with a gentle wobble in the middle. Lift the dishes onto a wire rack to cool, then transfer to the fridge for a couple of hours.

To brûlée the crème: Scatter the 2 tablespoons of sugar over the dishes. Use a blowtorch to caramelise the sugar, then put the dishes back into the fridge for at least 30 minutes – or a few hours is fine, too.

WASTE TIPS: Bergamot juice (see Citrus, page 338), Egg whites (page 338)

Venison Osso Buco with Mixed Herb and Citrus Gremolata

This is a rich, hearty, warming, almost decadent dish. Made all the better for the zesty, garlicky, herby hit of the orange and lemon gremolata. Whatever you do, don't be tempted to skip it.

You could follow the same recipe switching the venison for beef oxtail or veal. The important thing is to use pieces of meat of roughly equal size, so they cook at the same rate. If you have some larger, some smaller, when it comes time to return the seared osso buco to the pan just do the larger ones first and then the smaller ones a little after. Serve with potato or other root veg mash to soak up the sauce, and some simply steamed greens.

Serves 4–6

4 tbsp plain (all-purpose) flour

1.5kg (3lb 5oz) venison osso buco

6 tbsp olive oil

70g (2½oz) diced pancetta

2 medium onions

2 medium carrots

2 celery stalks

2 garlic cloves

1 rosemary sprig

¼ tsp mixed spice

1 tbsp sherry vinegar

175ml (6fl oz) white wine

about 750ml (25fl oz) chicken stock

knob of butter

salt and black pepper

For the gremolata

2 garlic cloves

2 unwaxed lemons

1 unwaxed blood or sweet orange

3 bushy sprigs each of tarragon, basil and mint

pinch of salt flakes

Season the flour, spread on a large plate and roll the venison pieces in it so they are covered in a light dusting. Get 2 tablespoons of the oil hot in a large casserole dish over a medium-high heat and, working in batches so as not to crowd the pan, sear the flat edges of each venison piece. As they are done, lift out and set aside. Add more oil to the dish as needed.

Put the pancetta into the dish you just seared the meat in. Turn the heat down. Peel the onions, slice into thin half-moons and add too. As the onions and pancetta gently cook, use that time to trim and wash the carrots (only peel if they really need it) and dice. Trim, wash and dice the celery. Add the carrots and celery to the dish, mix, season with salt and sweat until soft.

recipe continues overleaf...

*WASTE TIPS: Carrot peelings, celery trimmings and onions skins (see Stocks, page 340),
Herb stems (see Stocks, page 340; Soft Herbs, page 341), Citrus juices (page 338)*

Peel and crush the garlic cloves. Add to the pan. Finely chop the rosemary leaves and add those too, along with the mixed spice. Mix well and cook for a few minutes, then pour in the vinegar and wine, and bubble until reduced. Season.

Return the meat to the dish (see note in the recipe introduction about sizes and timing) and pour over enough stock to just about cover. Almost completely cover the dish with a lid and let it very gently simmer for 1½–2 hours, stirring at 30-minute intervals. You want only the gentlest of bubbling on the surface. The meat is done when absolutely tender.

For the gremolata: Peel the garlic cloves and chop as finely as you've ever chopped anything. Put into a bowl and finely grate in the zest of the lemons and orange. Finely chop the leaves of the herbs and add with some salt flakes. Mix.

To serve: Check the seasoning of the osso buco sauce. Dot the knob of butter over so it melts. Give each serving a sprinkling of gremolata, with more on the table to be added to taste.

Venison

In my food memory is an elusive dish I cannot place. Where I had it, who I was with, who cooked it... those things are lost. But as real as if I were able to taste it right now is the memory of having a suet pudding filled with the tenderest, most intensely succulent pieces of venison in a mushroomy, juniper-laced, garlicky, boozy (Marsala maybe?) sauce.

I can tell you it was a cold, cold day. Not only because it would really have to be to tuck into something like that with such relish, but because that is when the venison season traditionally rolls. Wild venison, at any rate. As with the duck over on page 236, I feel there is something of a disconnect between our seasonal understanding – and enjoyment – of venison, and its reality.

The shooting ('stalking') of wild venison has a long-standing place in how deer herds are controlled to minimise the extensive damage they can cause to countryside. The stalkers' focus is on managing herds to manage the land, not to shoot the deer for meat. Consequently not all stalked wild venison ends up for sale at the butchers – the demand (i.e. price) has to be good enough.

I/we emotionally and traditionally connect venison with the winter even when much of the venison available to buy is not wild, it is farmed. Farmed venison can be year-round. And while it may not be as intensively farmed as beef or lamb – the numbers are much, much lower – the practices bear similarity and throw a little shade on the arguments for (farmed) venison as the choice for anyone wanting more environmentally sustainable meat.

All of which brings me back to seeking out wild venison in its winter season as an occasional treat. Or sourcing from farmers who rear what is called 'parkland' venison – herds reared and cultivated where they can enjoy the natural habitat as if in the wild. The difference is they are being purposely bred for their meat. These farms tend to follow the rhythms of the wild venison season and shoot in the autumn/winter.

All venison from all breeds is rich and lean. The steaks should be cooked fast and at high heat to be as tender as they deserve. Joints like shoulder or haunch need low and slow roasting with plenty of juices and fat in the tray to make sure the meat's leanness doesn't become dryness. The offal is even deeper of flavour than its beef equivalents. Diced cuts for stewing or braising are, again, best done with time for them to take on flavour and moisture from whatever they are cooked with. That way they can be wrapped in a suet pastry and never be forgotten.

Rhubarb

Winter – *Spring* – *Summer*

When the days are dank and grey. When the hours of daylight seem to be showing little prospect of lengthening. When winter has lost any romantic allure it once had and you are now just Fed Up with it, a pop of slightly silly colour can be all that is needed to lift the general mood. Handily, that's just the moment that forced rhubarb tartly sashays into the kitchen with its bright pink stalks and, honestly, things feel that little bit cheerier.

Winter's forced rhubarb is pinker, sweeter, tender-er than the maincrop of the summer rhubarb harvest. It is also more welcome, given that when the first forced rhubarb comes there isn't lots else happening on the fruit front. The fact that summer's rhubarb isn't as exciting as winter's barely matters because there is so much else around. That said, if you are reading this in the summer with a bunch of rhubarb in your hand what is to come will set you merrily on your way for using those, too. Just remember: the summer rhubarb is more tartly bitter, will need peeling, and won't give your cooking the bubblegum pink that forced rhubarb does.

In the UK, we have Yorkshire's 'rhubarb triangle' to thank for our forced rhubarb crops. Since Victorian times there have been farms there growing rhubarb in warm, dark sheds. Without the natural light to feed upon the stalks are forced to grow long and thin, with the gorgeous colour I keep mentioning because it never fails to thrill. Harvesting is done by candlelight to limit any danger of sunlight getting into the sheds. (Such caution is impressively zealous given this is Yorkshire in the winter.)

Legend has it that this forcing was discovered in Chelsea Physic Garden in 1817 when a gardener discovered some rhubarb accidentally covered by a pot and growing marvellously. I type with a slightly raised eyebrow. Maybe that's not deserved. Who really knows. It's a nice story. But one swiftly overtaken by those Yorkshire farmers between Wakefield, Morley and Rothwell who embraced the cold of the Pennines and created a rhubarb industry that became so popular it had its own stretch of Victorian railway built to get the rhubarb to its waiting public as quickly as possible. There are fewer farmers doing this now, inevitably. Long may they thrive while protected by PDO status – and also by forced rhubarb's enduring popularity that sees chefs and home cooks alike clamour for it each winter.

Shop

- Look for stalks that are firm along their length, neither drying out, nor going floppy.
- Perky leaves will be a sign the stalks are fresh.

Store

- Keep it in the crisper drawer of the fridge. If it is wrapped up make sure there is some way of letting air in/out, to help keep it crisp.
- Fresh, raw rhubarb doesn't keep terribly well. Use it quickly if you can. And if it starts to look a little sad, try standing it in water as if the stalks were flowers (they are, after all, very nearly as pretty).

Ways to Use

I'm going to mainly focus this on forced rhubarb, but really anything here can apply to summer's crop, too.

Lose the rhubarb's poisonous leaves before you start doing anything. They are good for composting but nothing else.

Rhubarb is, technically and botanically, a vegetable rather than a fruit (it's the lack of seeds that does it), making it less of a surprise than it otherwise might be to find that rhubarb is glorious for savoury dishes.

Quick-pickle it (as on page 252) and you have a punchy, bright partner for meats, fish, or winter salads.

Tagines and khoresh often have fruit in them for that lovely sweet-sour-savoury combination. Rhubarb with its natural tartness is an excellent choice but once that is made you have another: To add the chopped rhubarb early and, in the slow cooking of the dish, the rhubarb will gently give its flavour throughout and almost collapse in the process. Or, cook off the rhubarb pieces separately in a little oil/butter and add towards the end of the cooking time of the main dish. The rhubarb-ness will be punchier, the stalks will hold their shape. Your call.

Sautéing the rhubarb like I just described sets you on your way for other uses: Add in some spices, maybe a little sugar, and you have gently stewed rhubarb to serve as a side. Or you could blitz it up with olive oil and some of the flavour partners to follow, thin it with a little water, and that's a rhubarb dressing for wintry leaves, or some fish. A handy thing to do if you find yourself left with just a little rhubarb.

Poaching rhubarb takes you in both savoury or sweet directions, depending on what you poach with and what you do with it afterwards. Trim and chop the rhubarb, pop it into a pan with some sugar (think 10% weight of sugar to weight of rhubarb – more for summer's tarter stalks), then add your choice of water/stock/wine/vermouth/

orange juice and whatever herbs or spices take your fancy. After barely 6 minutes gently poaching like that, the rhubarb should be cooked through but not mushy, and once drained could turn its hand to being a savoury side; piled on toast, porridge or muesli; or heading towards a crumble, creamy fool or ice cream, or to bake into the middle of a sponge cake for a layer of tartly fruity surprise on slicing. Any otherwise redundant poaching liquor can be bubbled over a high heat and reduced down into a sauce/glaze to serve.

Baked rhubarb brings plenty of the same savoury and sweet possibilities. Follow the basics above in a baking dish rather than a pan, go for a 160°C fan/350°F/gas 4 oven, and let it cook for 20–30 minutes. The less aggressive heat means the rhubarb pieces are more likely to keep their shape, rather than go softly stringy.

Oh, and – if you are brave and like the tarter side of life – then raw rhubarb stalks (never the leaves!) might be for you. Choose thin, pink stalks, dip the end in a little sugar, honey, or maple syrup and have a crunch. Your face will pucker, your taste buds will pop, and you will go back in again.

Flavour Partners

This has to start with one of the truly great flavour partnerships. So iconic and timeless that Fred and Ginger, Posh and Becks, even Kermit and Miss Piggy have got nothing on how well this two-some works: rhubarb and **custard**. A triumph whether we're just talking about custard over a rhubarb crumble or cobbler; custard-y **crème pâtissière** in a sponge with sticks of rhubarb arranged like rays of pink sunshine on top; or getting all fancy with roasted/poached rhubarb and îles flotantes (floating islands of **meringue**). It works because the flavours are so different and offset each other.

That logic means anything else in the sweet, creamy line is going to love being with rhubarb, too. I'm talking **vanilla ice cream**, rich **plain yoghurt**, **crème fraîche** and the rest. Every year on Burns Night I make a rhubarb cranachan, knowing that the poached rhubarb is going to have a fine old time nestling up on a cold night with **whipped cream**, **honey**, **whisky** and **toasted oats**.

I'll make sure there's some **cinnamon** in there, too, because all these lush, rich partnerships benefit from a little edge. Try mixing some **anise** seeds into your crumble topping; add a little **stem ginger** into a rhubarb ice cream; or some **cardamom** or **peppercorns** (black or pink) really any time.

The way rhubarb cuts through rich creamy desserts makes it similarly fabulous with **oily fish**, especially **mackerel**, **salmon**, **trout** and **anchovies**. **Meats: pork** and **lamb**, especially, for the fattiness; **game**, like **venison**, for the richness. Rhubarb will help you along with either.

Cheeses, too. Again, it's the cutting through and why the rhubarb quick-pickle on page 252 is outstanding with the **labneh** that could easily have been some baked **feta** or grilled **halloumi** and often has been.

I like to add a dash of **gin** to my rhubarb poaching/roasting liquor as it is packing **juniper** and plenty of other aromatics that rhubarb will love. Things like **orange**, **lemon**, **rosemary**, **coriander seeds**, **lavender**. For similar reasons I'll reach for the sweet **red vermouth** to poach with, too, and then reduce that right down into the most gorgeous glaze/sauce that is the same colour as the rhubarb, so a double-win.

Just as forced rhubarb is edging out of season, the first great **alphonso mangoes** appear. Let them enjoy a fleeting partnership.

More flavour thoughts: **Apple**; **bay leaves**; **buttermilk**; **coffee**; **demerara sugar**; **mustard seeds**; **nuts**; **orange blossom water**; **oregano**; **pear**; **pomegranate**; **rose** (water or petals); **saffron**; **star anise**; **tahini**; **vanilla**. And if you are here in summer: **Blackberry**; **damson**; **elderflower**; **plum**; **strawberry**.

Preserve

Freeze: For raw rhubarb just give it a wash, dry, chop and freeze in a single layer on a tray before transferring to freezer bags. It will lose some colour but still be lovely. Cooked and cooled rhubarb freezes very well.

Pickle: Try a rhubarb chutney with all the usual pickling spices in there. A red wine vinegar works best. Or a sherry vinegar even.

In alcohol: Choose gin or vodka. Add chopped rhubarb, some sugar, maybe a few of the aromatics mentioned earlier. Give it a week and strain. You will have fruitily, tartly infused, gently pink gin or vodka; and some very boozy rhubarb stalks you could turn into a dessert (or jam).

Cordial: This makes around 1.5 litres (50fl oz). Trim away the ends of 750g (1lb 10oz) rhubarb stalks, then slice into 1cm (½in) pieces. Put into a large pan with 225g (8oz) caster (superfine) sugar, a rosemary sprig and 650ml (22fl oz) water. Cover with a lid, bring to the boil, then turn down to a low simmer for 20 minutes with the lid on. Turn the heat off and (without lifting the lid!) leave for another hour, then push through a fine sieve to get all the juice out of the fruit. (The rhubarb purée by-product can be saved to have with ice cream, granola or porridge.) Once the cordial has cooled, it is ready to store in the fridge or freezer. Use topped up with still, sparkling or soda water; mix into a gin and tonic; add to a glass of sparkling wine - or make the Gimlet on page 257.

Quick-pickled Rhubarb and Labneh Toasts

The kind of day that makes me feel like making and eating this is always one of those very special cold, crisp, bright ones that late winter specialises in. It's a weekday lunch or a weekend brunch of dreams. The punchy flavours of the pickled rhubarb having a gorgeous time with the richness of the labneh.

The labneh needs to be made ahead of time. After that, this is 15 minutes start to finish.

Serves 4 as lunch or brunch;

8 as a sharing plate or starter

For the labneh

450g (1lb) full-fat natural Greek
  yoghurt

½ tsp fine salt

For the quick-pickled rhubarb

2 rhubarb stalks

120ml (4fl oz) red wine vinegar

80g (3oz) light brown sugar

2 tsp fine salt

½ tsp black peppercorns

½ tsp yellow mustard seeds

1 cinnamon stick

To finish

8 slices of bread

1 tsp sumac

flaky salt and black pepper

For the labneh: Stir together the yoghurt and salt in a mixing bowl. Spoon it into a sieve or colander lined with a double layer of muslin (cheesecloth), tying the ends together. Sit it in the sieve over a bowl in the fridge for 6–12 hours to strain. The longer you leave it, the thicker your labneh will be. Transfer to a bowl, cover and store in the fridge until needed.

For the quick-pickled rhubarb: Trim the rhubarb stalks, then cut into thin slices or strips as you prefer, and put into a bowl. Put the vinegar, sugar, salt, peppercorns, mustard seeds and cinnamon stick in a small saucepan with 120ml (4fl oz) water. Heat gently just until the sugar and salt have dissolved. Pour everything over the rhubarb and set aside for 10 minutes.

Toast the bread. Spread each piece of toast with labneh, top with slices of quick-pickled rhubarb, sprinkle over a little sumac and serve with ground pepper and salt flakes over the top.

The rest of the pickling liquor can be kept to use in salad dressings; or top it up with sparkling water for a drink.

WASTE TIP: Labneh juices (page 339)

Rhubarb Sponge with Orange Blossom Crème Fraîche

This is one of my favourite, much-made, easy, cosy and comforting desserts. Imagine a Sunday afternoon curled up on the sofa with a bowl of rhubarb sponge and an old film. That's the general vibe.

It is simply light sponge atop tart rhubarb, whose tartness has had its edge taken off with thyme and honey. It is gorgeous with cream, custard, ice cream... and I think especially with crème fraîche that has some orange blossom water run through to create another gentle flavour partnership with the rhubarb.

With thanks to Margaret Costa, whose recipe in her 1970s *Four Seasons Cookery Book* was the starting point for this.

Serves 4

For the rhubarb sponge
knob of butter
450g (1lb) trimmed rhubarb
leaves picked from 2 thyme sprigs
1½ tsp moscatel vinegar
3 tbsp runny honey
110g (3¾oz) butter, soft at
  room temperature

110g (3¾oz) caster (superfine) sugar
2 eggs
1 tbsp milk
170g (6oz) plain (all-purpose) flour

For the crème fraîche
1 tbsp orange blossom water
500ml (17fl oz) crème fraîche

Preheat the oven to 185°C fan/400°F/gas 6. Grease a baking dish (about 1 litre/ 4-cup capacity) with the knob of butter.

Cut the rhubarb into 3cm (1in) lengths, put into the prepared dish and scatter over the thyme leaves. Pour over the vinegar and the honey.

To make the sponge, use the back of a wooden spoon or an electric beater to cream together the butter and sugar until light and fluffy. Beat in the eggs, the milk, and then fold in the flour. Spoon the sponge mix over the rhubarb. Bake for around 40 minutes until the sponge is risen and a beautiful gold.

Mix the orange blossom water into the crème fraîche and serve alongside the rhubarb sponge (which is best served hot from the oven, or reheated in a microwave).

WASTE TIP: Woody herb stems (see Stocks, page 340)

A few feasting menu ideas

Carrot and Orange Salad with Saffron Aioli and Scallops
(*small plates*)

Mixed Roasted Roots with Black Pudding (or Butter Beans)

Bergamot Crème Brûlée

Cauliflower, Leek and Coconut Soup

Kohlrabi and Sprout Winter Slaw with
Spatchcock Roast Duck

Rhubarb Sponge with Orange Blossom Crème Fraîche

Quick Pickled Rhubarb and Labneh Toasts

One-pot Fragrant Spiced Lamb with Parsnip and Spinach Rice

Shaved Cauliflower, Sultanas, Preserved Lemon and Chilli

Swiss Chard Dumplings, Broth and Crisped Sage Leaves

Fig, Chocolate and Pecan Frangipane Tart (*from Autumn chapter*)

Venison Osso Buco with Mixed Herb and Citrus Gremolata;
celeriac and potato mash; Sautéed Brussels Sprouts and Kale

Blackberry and Cassis Custard Fool (*from Autumn chapter*)

Winter

To drink

For the table

Rhubarb Gimlet

For 1, to scale up
ice
50ml (1¾fl oz) gin
50ml (1¾fl oz) Rhubarb Cordial (page 251)
1 tbsp lime juice
fresh rosemary or orange zest

Put a coupe or other cocktail glass into the fridge ahead of time. Fill a cocktail mixer (or any kind of jug) with ice. Pour over the gin, rhubarb cordial and lime juice and stir rapidly for a minute. Strain into the chilled glass and garnish with rosemary or orange zest.

- Winter's citrus fruits make for beautiful table decorations. Look to blood oranges, bergamot, pomelo, lemons.... Whole or cut into, together in a bowl so the magnificence of their collective beauty can really shine.

- Pick up the brightness of those citrus with small vases of mimosa. Its yellow will brighten any winter's day.

- Lay holly, eucalyptus, thistles or long pieces of fir along the table.

- Hellebores in low vases. Larkspur on each place setting, perhaps bound together with a little rosemary, thyme or sage.

- Float the heads of winter chrysanthemums in shallow bowls.

Spring

Spring is the season of anticipation – fulfilled, and of what's to come.

Its arrival after all the chilly months of us waiting for it, of pretty much willing the ground to offer up those first precious sightings of daffodils and snowdrops, brings produce that's luckily suited to cooking and eating in enough ways for whatever weather a spring day might choose to throw at us. Maybe it's not luck – Mother Nature is pretty smart. After winter's heavier fare there is light relief in the first of the season's purple sprouting broccoli and asparagus, nuggets of new potatoes, hot radishes with cool goats' cheeses....

They all signal a shift in the culinary mood that is perhaps less about courses and more about content. By which I mean embracing the incoming simplicity in their preparation, then putting a selection of dishes together for the more relaxed style of eating that the warmer weather starts to put us in the mood for. There is hope for the summer to come. But the anticipation of its more obvious charms is no excuse to rush the new season along too much. Let's not do that. Let's instead enjoy spring's own produce in its own right and its own moment.

Winter	In Season	Summer
Brussels sprouts, kales and more dark winter greens	Asparagus	Aubergines (eggplants)
Cabbages	Broccoli – purple and white sprouting, and Calabrese	Lamb, hogget, mutton
Carrots, parsnips and salsify	Elderflowers and other spring blossoms	Broad (fava) beans and garden peas
Scallops	Lettuces	Courgettes (zucchini) and other summer squash
Cauliflower	New potatoes	Cucumbers
Celeriac and swede	Radishes	Mackerel
Chard – Swiss, rainbow and ruby	Soft herbs	Summer carrots
Kohlrabi	Goats' and sheep's cheeses	Sweet peppers (capsicums)
Waterfowl – duck and goose	Watercress and baby spinach	Tomatoes
Oranges – Seville, blood, bergamot and mandarins	Trout	Cherries
Venison	Wild garlic	Raspberries and strawberries
Rhubarb	Gooseberries	Stone fruits – peaches, nectarines, apricots, plums

Featured Recipes

Asparagus

Asparagus, Hot-smoked Trout and Pea Shoot Tart

Shaved Asparagus Bucatini

*Roast Chicken with Roasted Asparagus
and Purple Sprouting Broccoli*

Broccoli

Broccoli Tempura with White Miso Mayonnaise

Elderflowers and
Other Spring Blossoms

Elderflower Cordial

*Elderflower Madeleines with
Gin-poached Gooseberries*

Lettuces

Braised Little Gems with Shallots, Pancetta and Peas

Frisée, New Potato and Radish Salad

New Potatoes

The Simple Joy of New Potato Salads

Radishes

Roast New Potatoes and Radishes with Anchovies and Herbs

Smacked Radishes with Sesame, Sumac and Mint

Soft Herbs / Goats' Cheese

Spring Herb and Goats' Cheese Soufflé

Watercress and Baby Spinach / Trout

Trout with Watercress Hollandaise

Wild Garlic

Wild Garlic Farls

Lamb Cutlets, Samphire and Wild Garlic

Gooseberries

Gooseberry and Toasted Coconut Pavlova

Gooseberry Crumble

Spring Feasting

Sherry, Elderflower and Orange Blossom Collins

Asparagus

Spring – *Summer*

In my springtime kitchen – and hopefully yours – it sometimes feels like every day is an asparagus day. That's no bad thing when there are so many ways to have it, and the season so short. In its peak of season, asparagus has unique delicacy and complexity of flavour. Add in the sunshine, longer days and warmer evenings that asparagus usually heralds and the annual furore at its arrival makes a lot of sense.

Much pressure is put on producers to extend the season, and particularly to start it earlier. To literally feed the asparagus anticipation and fill the so-called 'hungry gap' between the last of winter's produce and spring's coming in. I absolutely get the commercial – and kitchen – imperative but, for me, asparagus when it is still cold and blustery feels all wrong. (Purple sprouting broccoli, however, bridges that gap perfectly – head to page 276.)

No, I'll wait for the asparagus, thanks, until spring and its harvest are both properly here. Then I really go for it. Because I know that in barely six weeks' time there'll be a meal when I have to acknowledge with a slightly sad yet asparagus-sated sigh that the spears on our plates are the last of the year. I might fleetingly flirt at extending the season with some imported asparagus. And then I'll wish I hadn't. Asparagus always tastes sweetest when eaten as soon as possible after harvesting.

For me here in the UK that means sourcing the best British asparagus from Suffolk, Kent, Worcestershire and Herefordshire. These green spears grown above ground are distinctly more flavour-forward than the white (more of a bridal cream, really) asparagus that is hugely popular particularly in France, especially in the Loire, and grows under soil so sunlight can't get its chlorophyll going. These have an almost mother-of-pearl lustre to them, a mild flavour and tender texture.

Purple asparagus with its gentle nuttiness has been allowed to grow above ground just long enough to develop colour and flavour. It can happen so quickly that harvested white asparagus becomes purple-tipped after just a few hours in the sun. It'll get more purple along its length as it spends more time exposed to light, and would eventually turn green.

Unless the notes to follow say specifically differently, assume they apply to any colour of asparagus you might have.

Shop

- Look for spears with tight, bright and perky buds.
- Spears will be thin at the start of the season, then get fatter as the season goes on.
- Woody ends mean the spears are drying out from having been out of the ground a while.

Store

- Remove any plastic wrapping and store in the fridge's crisper drawer. Wrapping them in a damp cloth can help prolong their freshness. Don't remove the ends until cooking.
- Rehydrate any slightly tired spears by standing them untrimmed in a jug of water with a damp towel draped over the tips.
- Remember that asparagus is best soon after harvesting: buy, cook, eat.

Ways to Use

The youngest, tenderest, thinnest asparagus – the delicate 'sprue' spears at the beginning of the season – can get away with not being cooked at all. Simply slice them thinly with a mandoline or vegetable peeler and sit them in iced water to keep perky until needed to toss through a salad, or perhaps pasta as on page 272.

As the season progresses, remove the woody parts of the lower stalks, which will defy any attempts to make them tender or tasty. They will snap away easily at the point where the end needs to be taken off. Those ends are still full of asparagus flavour and so not to be wasted. Add them to a freezer bag of veg peelings to use for stock, or let them infuse flavour into spring soups and sauces.

Peeling the rest of the stalk is only worthwhile if they're quite thick and/or it's getting towards the end of the season when things really do tend to toughen up a little. Even then, only go up as high as a couple of inches below the tasty tips.

Steaming – as opposed to boiling – retains as much as possible of the asparagus' flavour. Spears can be tender in as little as 5 minutes. If serving the asparagus cold, refresh them by rinsing in very cold water as soon as they're cooked to prevent them cooking any more. (The steaming water you used will be precious with asparagus flavour for, again, soups and stocks, or for boiling some new-season potatoes in.)

Roasting – in a very hot 220°C fan/475°F/gas 9 oven, for 12 minutes or so – both protects and intensifies the flavour of the asparagus. It also allows you to toss in other flavour partners that can really get in there with the asparagus as they cook (as with the roasting chicken juices in the recipe on page 273). Griddling achieves the same intense heat and charring. Cooking asparagus quickly over fire gives you not only a lovely char but a smokiness that works well.

However you cook them, the aim is for spears that are tender to the point of a knife and holding their shape well.

Flavour Partners

Two basic things to take note of and not forget:
- Somehow asparagus always tastes better when eaten with fingers.
- Really good in-season asparagus is a joy in its own right and its flavours deserve to ring out. You don't need to mess about with it too much.

That said...

Butter or really anything in the buttery, fatty line of things works well. Even if just dipping your spears in melted butter to serve with toast. For a quick sauce, go for barely melted butter (before it gets too thin and oily) with a few fine breadcrumbs stirred through for texture and to help the butter cling to the asparagus.

Eggs all kinds of ways – especially if the yolk is a little runny and able to act as a sort-of impromptu sauce. Use asparagus spears as an alternative soldier. Dunk spears into proper, home-made **mayonnaise** (see page 301, the mayo perhaps lifted with a little **elderflower cordial**); or spoon mayo into a **little gem** leaf and top with roasted asparagus tips.

Go with eggs *and* butter by serving warm asparagus and **hollandaise sauce** (page 318, with or without its watercress) – that's a classic for good reason. Adding redundant woody asparagus ends to hollandaise sauce as it cooks will infuse it with gentle flavour.

Think how to partner asparagus with spring's young **goats' or sheep's cheeses** – in a salad together, or the cheese as the base for a puff-pastry tart, with asparagus spears on top.

Thin slivers of really any **hard cheese** work in an asparagus salad, and then there's **Parmesan**. Try steaming asparagus and laying the spears top-to-tail in a buttered shallow ovenproof dish. Sprinkle grated Parmesan among them as you go, a few knobs of butter on top, and then grill for a couple of minutes.

Tightly wrap a small bundle of spears in a slice of **pancetta** and roast. Drape very thin slices of **lardo** over just-cooked asparagus.

All kinds of **nuts**, but **almonds**, **cashews** or **hazelnuts** are especially good. As a side: For each handful of asparagus pan-fry a large tablespoon of roughly chopped nuts in a big piece of butter for barely a minute, add a squeeze of **lemon**, some **salt** and pour over the cooked spears.

Roasted, griddled or fire-cooked asparagus will benefit from a burst of acidity to lift the flavours. As soon as they come off the heat, give a drizzle of **sherry vinegar** or a squeeze of **lemon**, **lime** or **orange**. Plus – always, always – some good **extra-virgin olive oil**, and plenty of **salt** and **pepper**.

Chopped **mint**, **tarragon**, **dill** or any combination of them are fabulous added to a tumble of roasted asparagus.

As asparagus season nears its end, think about produce whose season is just beginning and feel the flow of the seasons as you cook. Roast the first **wet garlic** bulbs and then scoop out the tender flesh for spooning over roasted asparagus. Early summer **courgettes (zucchini)** make a lovely ribboned salad with late-season asparagus.

More flavour thoughts: **Anchovies**; **bacon**; **black mustard seeds**; **black pepper**; **crab**; **cumin**; **horseradish**; **lavender**; **miso**; **oily fish**; **oysters**; **peas**; **prawns**; **saffron**; **samphire**; **soy sauce**; **sumac**; **tamarind**; **tofu**; *a little* **turmeric** *into asparagus soup*; **wild garlic**.

Preserve

Let's not. I can't think of any way that works sufficiently deliciously for preserving asparagus. It is at its best when fresh, in its own season. And the season is short – so when you get it, eat it.

Asparagus, Hot-smoked Trout and Pea Shoot Tart

This is a springtime joy of a tart. At its best when it's not been out of the oven too long, but also very lovely at room temperature. Serve with new potatoes and perhaps a bowl of dressed leaves.

Serves 6 as a main

250g (9oz) asparagus (typically 1 bundle)

2 tbsp olive oil

2 whole eggs, plus 2 yolks

200ml (7fl oz) double (heavy) cream

100ml (3½fl oz) whole milk

1½ tbsp freshly grated horseradish

300g (10½oz) hot-smoked trout fillets

4 dill sprigs

handful of pea shoots

salt and black pepper

For the pastry case

250g (9oz) plain (all-purpose) flour

150g (5oz) cold butter

1 egg yolk

pinch of salt

1 orange

23cm (9in) loose-bottomed tart tin

For the pastry case: Put the flour into a mixing bowl. Dice the butter and use your fingers to rub it into the flour until it feels like breadcrumbs. Beat the egg yolk and add with a pinch of salt and the zest from the orange. Bring together into a smooth dough. (You might need to add a little cold water to help it come together, but add as little as you can get away with.) Shape into a disc, wrap, and chill for 30 minutes.

Preheat the oven to 170°C fan/375°F/gas 5 with a large baking sheet inside.

Roll out the pastry between 2 pieces of greaseproof paper until about 3mm (⅛in) thick and generously large enough to line the tart tin. Ease the pastry over your rolling pin and carefully lift over the tin, gently pressing it in. Let it overhang the case as the pastry will shrink as it cooks. Prick the base a few times with a fork and chill for 30 minutes.

Sit the tart case on the hot baking sheet, line with a large piece of baking paper and fill with baking beans or rice. Bake for 15 minutes, then remove the paper and beans and return to the oven for another 5 minutes. Take it out of the oven and sit on a wire rack to cool. Up to this point can be done up to a day ahead.

WASTE TIPS: Asparagus ends (see Stocks, page 340), Egg white (page 338), Herb stems (see Stocks, page 340; Soft Herbs, page 341), Horseradish (page 339), Orange juice (see Citrus, page 338)

To make the tart: Snap the woody ends off the asparagus spears. Get a griddle pan very hot, toss the spears in the oil and quickly griddle them to take on some colour. They don't need to be cooked, just charred. Do this under a grill if preferred.

Preheat the oven to 180°C fan/400°F/gas 6 with a baking sheet inside.

Whisk together the whole eggs, yolks, cream and milk in a bowl or jug. Season and stir in the horseradish.

Flake the trout into the pastry case, layering it with the asparagus spears and the dill leaves. Pour over the egg mixture. Just as it gets nearly full, put the tart onto the preheated baking sheet, pour over the last of the egg mixture and then carefully lift the tart into the oven. Bake for 40 minutes until just-about set, rotating it partway through if cooking at all unevenly.

Lift the tart onto a wire rack. Scatter over half of the pea shoots to wilt in the heat of the tart, but don't try to take it out of its tin for about 30 minutes. Serve with the rest of the pea shoots on top for a perky garnish.

Shaved Asparagus Bucatini

What I love most about this pasta dish is that its asparagus spears are shaved so thinly they barely need to cook, they just wilt in the heat of the pasta. The result is a deliciously fresh-tasting dish with pleasing crunch from the toasted breadcrumbs. Speedy, too.

As lovely as it is cooked just like this, I hope you'll also take this recipe as the starting point for whatever you have to hand and are in the mood for. Perhaps skip the lemon breadcrumbs and instead add some slivers of Parmesan. Stir through cream, yoghurt or crème fraîche. Add some chopped anchovies or torn wild garlic leaves at the same time as the shaved asparagus. Swap the mint for basil. Whatever you do, just keep it simple and let the asparagus sing.

Serves 4 as a main

1 tbsp extra-virgin olive oil, plus
   optional extra
40g (1½oz) breadcrumbs
1 unwaxed lemon
pinch of salt flakes

2 mint sprigs
500g (1lb 2 oz) asparagus spears
   (typically 2 bundles)
400g (14oz) bucatini
black pepper

Heat the tablespoon of olive oil in a small frying pan and add the breadcrumbs. Stir round for a minute, or perhaps two – just until the breadcrumbs have browned nicely. Transfer to a cool bowl, grate in the zest of the lemon, and mix with a good pinch of salt flakes. Set aside.

Chop the mint leaves and set aside. Prepare the asparagus by removing the woody ends and using a vegetable peeler or mandoline to shave the spears.

Bring a large pan of well-salted water to the boil. Put the pasta in to cook and turn the heat down so the water is simmering. Check the pasta a minute before the packet instructions' cooking time and, when it is just about tender, remove a mug's worth of the cooking water. Drain the pasta and immediately return it to the pan, quickly adding the shaved asparagus. Stir round over a low heat, adding the pasta cooking water in stages so that it emulsifies but isn't too liquid.

Divide among serving bowls. Sprinkle over the breadcrumbs and mint. Give it a good grinding of black pepper, add a little extra oil if you feel you'd like to, and serve.

WASTE TIPS: Asparagus ends (see Stocks, page 340), Bread (page 338), Herb stems (see Stocks, page 340; Soft Herbs, page 341), Lemon juice (see Citrus, page 338)

Roast Chicken with Roasted Asparagus and Purple Sprouting Broccoli

The best roast chickens always have tender, flavourful flesh beneath skin that is perfectly bronzed and crisp. In my go-to roast chicken recipe those things are achieved by: Using the best high-welfare chicken you can; liberally anointing the skin with a winning combination of dry sherry, olive oil and salt; and stuffing it with aromatics that will release flavour into the meat. As the seasons change I switch up what the chicken is stuffed with. In autumn/winter this fresh, leafy spring stuffing might instead be the end of a leek, onion chunks, a halved orange, garlic cloves, woody herbs like rosemary and thyme....

I also switch up what vegetables I roast in the juices the chicken has released into the tin as it cooks. Those roasting juices are umami-laden gold for autumn/winter's carrots, kale, cauliflower, fennel.... But this is how I do it in spring. Giving seasonal PSB and asparagus gorgeous depth of flavour to accompany the best roast chicken.

Serves 4–6 as a main

1 whole chicken, around 2kg (4lb 8oz)
1 lemon
handful of wild garlic leaves
4 tarragon sprigs
4 oregano sprigs
75ml (2½fl oz) extra-virgin olive oil
100ml (3½fl oz) fino or
   manzanilla sherry

750g (1lb 10oz) purple sprouting
   broccoli
750g (1lb 10oz) asparagus
   (typically 3 bundles)
3 basil sprigs
3 mint sprigs
3 dill sprigs
salt and black pepper

Preheat the oven to 190°C fan/400°F/gas 6.

Sit the chicken in a roasting tin. Halve the lemon and stuff one half inside the chicken along with the wild garlic leaves, tarragon and oregano. Pour the olive oil over the chicken, then the sherry, and finish with lots of salt over the skin. Roast for 1 hour 45 minutes, basting the chicken with its juices twice during the cooking time.

Meanwhile, prepare the veg: Trim away any very woody ends of the purple sprouting broccoli; snap off the woody ends of the asparagus spears.

When the chicken is done, lift it out of its tin onto a serving dish or board. Loosely cover with foil (or I often just put a large stockpot over it) and set aside to rest.

recipe continues overleaf...

WASTE TIPS: *Asparagus ends (see Stocks, page 340), Herb stems (see Stocks, page 340; Soft Herbs, page 241)*

Turn the oven up just a little to 210°C fan/450°F/gas 8. Put the purple sprouting broccoli into the tin the chicken roasted in, toss round and roast for 7–10 minutes depending on how thick their stems are. Next add the asparagus spears, tossing round again. Roast for another 10 minutes or until both the purple sprouting broccoli and asparagus are cooked through.

Transfer the vegetables to a serving dish and squeeze over the remaining lemon half. Chop the basil, mint and dill leaves and mix those through the veg. Give a good grinding of pepper and serve the roasted chicken with its tumble of roasted seasonal vegetables.

Spring Chicken

Chicken as a seasonal food? What a quaint idea. We are not just used to having chicken year-round but our modern food chain demands it. I am not so deluded as to be advocating that this particular food genie is put back into the chicken coop, but: the notion of 'spring chicken' used to be not just a saying but a reality.

When someone says that a person is (or isn't) a spring chicken, we know that means they are (or aren't...) young and sprightly. So that principle obviously once applied to seasonal chickens. A young chicken in spring was prized for its tenderness and flavour. But how we produce chickens now has moved so far away from traditional farming practices that these days it is young chickens where the worries lie. The whole premise of chicken age has been flipped on its head.

Commercial, industrial chicken farming is focused upon them maturing as fast as possible. It's a numbers game. Hatch – grow – slaughter. The quicker the birds can plump up, the quicker they can move through the food chain and fulfil the global demand for cheap chicken meat. Such chickens are typically slaughtered at 5–6 weeks, an age at which they couldn't head outside even if the producer wanted them to – a chicken can't go out until fully feathered, which is also at around 6 weeks.

A free-range, organic bird that has had the opportunity to enjoy some fresh air and pasture will necessarily be older. Often slaughtered at more like 11–12 weeks, but at the same weight as those industrially produced ones. That extra time means less pressure is put upon its body to bulk-up quickly. It will be that much closer to how we all want to think a chicken looks and moves. It will have had the opportunity to use its muscles and move around a bit in the open air. Basically, it will have had a more dignified life, and be tastier. Two goals that I know are not going to sate the wider problems of a food system that relies upon cheap chicken, but they are perhaps things to think about when it comes to the bird you choose to cook at home.

Age is, of course, only one factor in considering chicken welfare – but it is a telling one.

Broccoli – Purple and White Sprouting, and Calabrese

Winter – Spring – Year Round

For the winter-weary cook, the arrival of the first purple sprouting broccoli spears is a sight more heart-warming than all the pink hearts of Valentines put together. They are the first hopeful sign that the days are numbered for my Big Coat, and that Spring will be sprung. Eventually.

It is perhaps unfair on the year-round dense green heads of Calabrese broccoli that it's the seasonality of purple sprouting broccoli (let's agree on PSB from now on) that gives it more elusive allure. That wasn't always the case. Jane Grigson noted in one of her books that for British cooks of the 1970s 'the broccoli we are most used to in this country is the purple flowering kind' and Calabrese was the lesser-known kid on the broccoli block. Maybe then, Jane. Maybe then. But not now.

Calabrese (developed in Calabria, hence the name) has since become somewhat ubiquitous for the same reasons so many other vegetables have taken precedence: It is hardier to grow, package, transport and store. It can also be magnificent. Broccoli's different varieties bring different levels of bitterness and sweetness. I like PSB for its bitter edge – which is, for me, more fun to play with in the kitchen. White sprouting (WSB) is more delicate in its flavour. Sweet Calabrese is what optimistic parents pile up their kids' plates with.

For cooking and enjoying Calabrese it's also worth looking at the notes for cauliflower, its flowering-head brassica cousin, on pages 206–9.

And if you are reading this while clutching some broccoli rabe, the PSB notes here will be helpful for its flowering heads, but rabe – aka rapini or cime de rapa – is not really broccoli, it's a different kind of brassica, and pages 182–3 for cooking its stalks and leaves will be more useful.

Shop

- Check the base and be wary if it's dry or woody. That means it's a little older and will need preparing/cooking accordingly. Avoid limp, bendy stalks.
- Calabrese heads should have dense, compact florets.
- Leaves should be vibrantly perky, and definitely not turning yellow.
- Much of the supermarket Calabrese comes tightly wrapped in cellophane to protect it from the air. That's fine in so far as it will be helping keep the broccoli fresher before it hits your shopping basket, but broccoli wrapped like that is likely to be older (and therefore duller of flavour) than if unwrapped and still looking good.

Store

- Keep broccoli in the crisper drawer of your fridge.

Ways to Use

Purple Sprouting/White Sprouting:
- The very earliest stems will be small and delicate, with stalks that need nothing doing to them bar a possible trim of any very woody ends.
- As the season progresses, these stalks will thicken and toughen. Even so, go gently with how much stalk you trim off. They are packed with flavour and sometimes even the best bit. Only when the stalks get thicker than an asparagus spear will they need more trimming, and perhaps be halved through their length so they cook at the same rate as the heads.
- Leave the leaves on.

Calabrese:
- I regret to admit to many shameful years of lopping off the Calabrese stalk at the base of its head, and then being underwhelmed by the ensuing stubby florets. Now I know to follow the branch lines of the florets down into the stalk and cut long elegant lengths that look far closer to the PSB I love, and which get cooked accordingly.
- Peel the stems if woody and dry.
- Once the florets have been cut away you will have some sweet central stalk left to slice or chop and use exactly as you would the florets.

Steaming broccoli allows its flavours to simply shine. Test attentively with a fork or sharp knife for when the stalks reach their moment of peak tenderness and therefore flavour. For young PSB and WSB, quick steaming is not only all they need but probably all they can bear before becoming over-cooked.

Over-cooked broccoli of any type will smell cabbage-y and not taste good. Unless, that is, you over-cook it intentionally to use in a dish where those factors are compensated for. Like this way for a stellar pasta sauce: Simmer broccoli until just about cooked through, then chop and sauté far beyond al dente with oil, your pick of flavour partners and enough water just to stop the broccoli scorching. Mash with a fork or potato masher, loosen with a little stock or water, and toss through pasta. (Cook the pasta in the same water the broccoli blanched in for a through-line of flavour.)

Roasting brings out broccoli's umami and sweetness, while giving charred bitterness and a gorgeously crunchy texture to the heads and leaves. Roast hot and fast: 220°C fan/475°F/gas 9 for barely 7 minutes in a good slug of oil and plenty of seasoning. The florets will blister and the leaves will crisp up like seaweed.

PSB (or WSB, or even slim Calabrese lengths) make for fabulous pizza toppings as long as you blanch them first and then the very quick, very high heat of the pizza oven is enough to finish them off.

Blanch other times, too, for ensuring anything other than the youngest PSB/WSB spears aren't served with tender heads and tough stalks. Give them a 1–2-minute simmer, drain, refresh in cold water, and then:

- They'll need only a few minutes in a frying pan of oil and other flavour partners.
- When stir frying, dry the blanched spears before they hit the wok otherwise the water will just cool the oil and they'll braise instead.
- Lay the blanched spears in a single layer in a baking dish, give them a little cream/ coconut milk to snuggle up with, add other flavour partners, top with a layer of breadcrumbs, and then bake for a gratin.
- Crush and fritter blanched Calabrese (or broccoli leftovers).
- Deep fry slim raw spears in a tempura batter, as on page 280.

Quick-pickling (as on page 72) is best saved for the thinly sliced stalk of Calabrese. Soups are the saviour of older, tougher, or unintentionally over-cooked broccoli.

Flavour Partners

The inherent sweetness of all the broccolis (to different degrees, see previous page) means they play brilliantly with anything in the salty and umami range of flavours. That is the flavour partner recurring theme.

While a roast **chicken** is resting, cook broccoli spears in its umami-packed roasting tin juices as on page 273.

This for a 15-minute dinner: Add PSB or Calabrese lengths into a pan of simmering **pasta** for the last 5 minutes of its cooking time. Loosely drain, keeping just a little of the cooking water in there. Put it all back into the pan plus **extra-virgin olive oil**, **salt**, **anchovies** and/or grated **Parmesan**, torn **soft herbs**, such as **basil**, **tarragon** and/or **mint,** and serve with plenty of cracked **black pepper**.

Toss nearly tender blanched spears in a frying pan with cooked-down **chorizo** so they can be coated in the fatty, salty, umami, spicy oil. Sticking with the spice theme, reach for the **spice mixes** whenever roasting spears. That could be **panch phoron**, **za'atar**; **baharat**....

Or, go for roasting spears with **chilli flake**s, some grated **root ginger**, and as soon as the tray comes out of the oven stir through **bonito flakes**, a little **honey**, and give it a squeeze of **lemon**, **lime** or **orange** to brighten the flavours. Spoon all that over cooked **rice** or **noodles** (making sure the roasting juices go in there too) and scatter over sliced **spring onions (scallions)**. Now remember each of these flavour partners for using them again individually, or in smaller partnerships.

Broccoli cooked to take on lots of flavour will benefit from a cooling contrast. Spoon a loose **tahini** sauce over roasted spears. Break **burrata** over. Or serve with **labneh** that's been whipped with a **chilli-infused oil** or **harissa** to deliver cool and heat to broccoli with each forkful.

Bring more calm with **nuts**, pounded into a dressing; or toasted to scatter over; or just added to a stir fry. Most usefully **almonds**, **hazelnuts** and **walnuts**. **Nut oils**, too, for dressings.

Like asparagus, broccoli loves anything to do with **butter** or **eggs**. That specifically includes **mayonnaise** and **hollandaise** – the latter especially if it's given a lift with **blood orange** (they should just about still be in season) zest and juice. Serve spears that have roasted to a char with a poached or fried egg on top so its yolk can nestle around the crisped florets. Scramble eggs in a wok with blanched spears, then finish with **soy sauce/tamari**.

Broccoli loves **garlic** nearly as much as it loves anything salty.

More flavour thoughts: **Bacon**; **blue cheese**; **crab**; **cumin**; **dukkah**; **fennel seeds**; **feta**; **horseradish**; **juniper berries**; **mackerel**; **miso**; **mustard** and **mustard seeds**; **'nduja**; **nutmeg**; **pancetta**; **sesame seeds** and **oil**; **shallots**; **sherry vinegar**; **sumac**; **wild garlic**.

Preserve

Broccoli is best when fresh. Maybe make pesto if you have too much. But if wasting is the only alternative then you could:

Freeze: Prepare your broccoli as usual, blanch in boiling water for a few minutes until just-about cooked, then immediately refresh in ice-cold water to stop it cooking further. Drain and dry on kitchen paper. Lay out in a single layer on a tray, freeze, then bag and keep in the freezer. Cook straight from frozen.

Broccoli Tempura with White Miso Mayonnaise

Purple sprouting broccoli would be my preferred choice of broccoli to use here. But, as I really don't want to limit your tempura'ing to spring, the year-round Calabrese is lovely too. The batter is gorgeously light, its crunch the perfect partner for the rich intensity of the miso mayo.

Tempura'ing is a great way to use up odds and ends of veg right through the seasons. Try doing it with slices of courgette (zucchini) or spring onion (scallion), spears of asparagus, cavolo nero leaves, pumpkin slivers....

Serves 4–6 as a sharing plate, starter or side

250g (9oz) purple sprouting broccoli (or Calabrese)

150g (5oz) plain (all-purpose) flour

150g (5oz) cornflour (cornstarch)

½ tsp fine salt

1 tbsp sesame seeds (black, white or a mix) (optional)

1 litre (34fl oz) sunflower oil

2 egg yolks

300ml (10fl oz) chilled sparkling spring water

For the miso mayonnaise

2 large egg yolks, at room temperature

25ml (1 tbsp plus 2 tsp) Japanese brown rice vinegar

2 tsp white miso paste

300ml (10fl oz) rapeseed oil

salt and black pepper

Make the miso mayo first so it is ready and waiting once you have tempura'd. Put the egg yolks into a mixing bowl and whisk with the vinegar and miso paste. Season lightly, then very slowly add the rapeseed oil, whisking after each addition. Whisk until thick and lustrous. Check the seasoning. Set aside in the fridge if making ahead of time, but be sure to return to room temperature before serving.

Prepare your broccoli by trimming off any very woody ends and slicing down through the florets into the stalk to create lengths no more than 1cm (½in) wide. Young, thin PSB spears can be used just as they are.

Sift the flours and salt into a medium bowl. Add the sesame seeds, if using.

Heat the sunflower oil in a deep pan to 185°C/365°F. Only once the oil is hot enough, work quickly to beat the egg yolks and chilled sparkling water into the flour bowl. Still working fast, use a fork to one-by-one dip each piece of broccoli into the batter, then transfer to the hot oil. Fry for a couple of minutes until crisped and only very lightly golden. Take care not to crowd the pan – you will need to do these in stages. Lift the tempura'd pieces out of the oil with a slotted spoon, drain on kitchen paper to remove any excess grease, and serve straight away with the miso mayo on the side.

WASTE TIPS: Deep-frying oil (page 338), Egg whites (page 338)

Elderflowers and Other Spring Blossoms

Spring – *Summer*

In spring I am the embodiment of the cliched Londoner who never leaves home without a long-handled umbrella. It means I'm covered for two very likely seasonal eventualities: rain; or coming across an unexpected patch of elderflower trees whose blossoms are just slightly out of reach and need pulling down. It gives me a literal spring in my step to head out, have a reason to look up and around me, and go see just what kind of elderflower crop the local trees have for me each spring.

One year I kept putting off picking them. For silly, busy reasons. And then one day on my way home I walked past the elderflower trees nearest our flat and noticed that their lacy, ethereal blossoms had become elderflower dust on the pavement. It made me (probably disproportionately) sad to realise I'd missed one of the few chances I had to interact with nature right outside my own front door. It has never happened since.

Less abundant, but coming before the elderflower and therefore being one of the first signs spring is really here, is the hawthorn blossom I also keep my eyes peeled for when out and about. Whether as a tree or a hedge, its heavy, sweet, slightly aniseedy smell gives it away. And if you know of a blackthorn bush to pick sloe berries from in the autumn, then know too that its springtime blossom is a treat.

Forage

– Be sure. Whatever blossoms you are on the hunt for, or stumble upon and get excited about, be sure what they are before you even think about consuming them. Years ago on my first elderflower-picking expedition I nearly made hemlock cordial and would have been on course for my own Shakespearean tragedy right there.
– Be early. Elderflower, hawthorn blossom and blackthorn blossom are all best picked in the morning, early in their season, and on a dry day All those factors mean the flowers will have not given away their flavour to the elements.
– Be generous, and leave some blossoms behind for the bees and butterflies to enjoy. (Your generosity will be rewarded when you go back in the autumn to find elderberries, haws or sloes.)

Store

– Use elderflowers and other blossoms asap after picking. Gently shake to dislodge any insects, but don't wash the heads or flavour will disappear.

Ways to Use

Especially perky heads of elderflower are small and young enough to fritter for accompanying sweet or savoury dishes. For 8 freshly picked small elderflower heads: Mix 80g (3oz) plain (all-purpose) flour with 20g (¾oz) cornflour (cornstarch) (and 1 tbsp caster/superfine sugar if making sweet fritters). Heat 500ml (17fl oz) sunflower oil in a deep saucepan to 190°C/375°F. As soon as it is at temperature, work quickly to whisk 150ml (5fl oz) sparkling water into the flours. Then – one by one – dip each elderflower head into the batter. Shake gently to remove excess, and lower into the hot oil. They'll need just a minute to turn golden and crisp. Lift out with a slotted spoon, sit on kitchen paper to drain, and serve soon. For sweet fritters, dust over more sugar.

Let freshly picked elderflower heads, hawthorn or blackthorn blossoms lounge for a while in still-warm, just-made custard to infuse it with delicate flavour. Then lift/strain the heads out and carry on with whatever that custard is headed for – perhaps ice cream, a fool, crème pâtissière, or being baked into a tart. With more fresh heads or blossoms to be strewn over for the finish.

Elderflowers and hawthorns are too small and fiddly to crystallise for extra special decoration, but it can be done with blackthorn: Paint egg white onto the petals, sprinkle caster (superfine) sugar over, and leave them to thoroughly dry on baking paper on a wire rack before using. Half an hour in a very low temperature oven helps speed that drying process up. Use the cystallised blackthorn blossoms as a garnish that epitomises the transition of seasons in a cocktail made with the last of winter's sloe gin.

Flavour Partners

Elderflower is happiest with its seasonal friends. I'll go as far as saying that everything featured within this spring chapter – whether vegetable, fruit or fish – will enjoy a little elderflower somehow tucked among it to bring musky depth.

That could be elderflower cordial used in a dressing for **lettuces** to go with **trout**; or a few drops of cordial into a rich **mayonnaise** for dunking **asparagus** spears or **radishes**, or for spooning liberally atop steamed **new potatoes**.

Serve savoury frittered heads alongside tempura **purple sprouting broccoli**, or sweet ones with a **gooseberry** compôte. (There's much more on page 328 for partnering elderflower and gooseberry.)

And it's not just the spring produce that elderflower loves. The great thing about preserving elderflower in a cordial is that you have harnessed its flavours to then let it play with summer's produce. Think of it especially for dressing/saucing **courgettes (zucchini)**, **cucumber**, **peas**, **broad (fava) beans**, **cherries**, **peaches**, **apricots** and **mackerel**.

Hawthorn and blackthorn largely emulate elderflower's flavour partners, but both also have a definite **almond** aspect to them. Accentuate that by using with almonds, **walnuts** or **pistachios**.

More flavour thoughts: **Apple**; **basil**; **cauliflower**; **chicken**; **figs**; **honey**; **maple syrup**; **oysters**; **pear**; **raspberry**; **rhubarb**; **shellfish**; **strawberry**; **tomato**; **vanilla**; **white chocolate**.

Preserve

Cordial: Elderflower most often means cordial, and rightly so when the cordial means not just delicious drinks for long after the elderflowers have withered on the trees, but can also be used in so many other seasonal dishes from elderflower mayonnaise to pancakes. See opposite for cordial how-to that includes hawthorn and blackthorn blossom, and uses.

Vinegar: Elderflower, hawthorn and blackthorn blossoms all make for glorious infused vinegars. Choose a light vinegar such as rice, vermouth, muscatel, or any white wine vinegar. Three-quarters fill a 250ml (8½fl oz) sterilised bottle with the vinegar, push in an elderflower head, or a few heads if using the others that are smaller. Seal and set aside for 2–3 weeks, then strain the flowers out, rebottle the now-infused vinegar, and use season-long for salad dressings and more.

Ferment: Elderflower wine or champagne. Fears of bursting corks aside, why not?

Elderflower Cordial

This is what most elderflower ends up as, with good reason when it is so delicious and so useful. Be sure to pick the elderflower heads on a dry day, early in the morning. Do the recipe soon upon getting home and you will be rewarded with a cordial that makes the bought stuff seem flat of flavour in comparison.

Swap the elderflower for similar volumes of hawthorn blossom or blackthorn blossom to make their cordials in the same way, and enjoy the same way too.

Makes about 1 litre (34fl oz)
15 freshly picked elderflower heads
2 lemons

500g (1lb 2oz) caster (superfine) sugar
30g (1oz) citric acid
850ml (28fl oz) water

Shake the elderflower heads to encourage any insects out. Set aside.

Slice the lemons into quarters, then run a thumb between the pith and the fruit to release the flesh. Cut the lemon pieces in half and put into a big pot with the sugar and citric acid. Boil the water, pour over and stir, then gently push in the elderflowers so they are fully immersed in the water. Cover and leave to steep for 24 hours.

The next day, strain through a fine sieve or muslin (cheesecloth). Pour into sterilised bottles. It will keep in the fridge for a couple of weeks or can be frozen for a couple of months (don't fill the bottles right up if you're freezing it as the cordial will expand).

And now, cordial in hand, what are you going to do with it? Here are just a few ideas:

– Drinks first. Elderflower cordial over ice with sparkling water and sprigs of lavender, mint or lemon thyme is a heavenly refresher on a hot day. Try a little in a G&T or a glass of champagne. Martinis are given a light twist with the addition of ½ teaspoon or so of cordial added into the cocktail shaker. Head to page 335 for a Sherry, Elderflower and Orange Blossom Collins.

– Add a little elderflower cordial to a classic salad vinaigrette or other dressing.

– Add to the Hollandaise on page 318 (with or without the watercress); or to page 301's Mayonnaise.

– It makes fabulous ice cream. Add 80ml (3fl oz) cordial to a 3-egg vanilla ice cream recipe when the cream and the custard get mixed together pre-churning. Cherry clafoutis, or gooseberries gently poached in sugar, are crying out for a scoop of it.

– Drizzle a little elderflower cordial over fruits such as peaches or pears before baking them. Or over cold, sliced fruit just before serving.

– And... make Elderflower Madeleines (see overleaf).

Elderflower Madeleines with Gin-poached Gooseberries

I like to kid myself that I'm not a (too) bossy kitchen companion. Here I have to be though: madeleines are not a make-ahead kind of dish. Prepare ahead, yes. But they must *must* be served warm from the oven to be properly experienced.

It's hardly much of a drag when the batter can be done hours before and the madeleines then take just 15 minutes. Just the thing for a lazy afternoon or after dinner. Eating these will make you feel like you're sitting in a garden even if you're not. Serve with the Gin-poached Gooseberries on page 328.

Serves 4, with 3 madeleines each

60g (2¼oz) unsalted butter, plus extra
   for greasing
60g (2¼oz) caster (superfine) sugar
2 eggs
1 unwaxed lemon
a few drops of vanilla extract
60g (2¼oz) plain (all-purpose) flour,
   plus extra for dusting

1 tsp baking powder
pinch of salt
2 tsp elderflower cordial
1 tbsp icing (confectioners') sugar,
   to serve

12-hole 8cm (3in) madeleine tin

Melt the butter in a bowl set over a pan of simmering water (ensure the base of the bowl is not touching the surface of the water). Once melted, remove the bowl from the heat and let the butter come to room temperature but still liquid.

Whisk together the sugar and eggs in a mixing bowl until thickened. Grate in the zest of the lemon and add the vanilla. Sift in the flour, baking powder and salt, and combine thoroughly but gently. Lastly, stir in the melted butter and elderflower cordial. Leave the mixture to rest for at least 2 hours. If your kitchen is warm then put it into the fridge but return to room temperature before using.

To bake: Preheat the oven to 180°C fan/400°F/gas 6.

Melt a small piece of butter in a small pan or in the microwave. Brush each indent in the madeleine tin with the butter, and follow by dusting over 1 tablespoon of flour. Spoon the madeleine mixture among the indents, not quite up to the rims. Sit the tray on a baking sheet to help protect the fluted undersides from getting too done.

Bake for 15 minutes, but check at 12. They're done when the edges are just starting to get nicely browned. Let them sit for a minute out of the oven before lifting the madeleines out of the tin and onto a wire rack. Dust with icing sugar. Serve while still warm with the gin-poached gooseberries in a bowl to spoon on top.

WASTE TIPS: Lemon juice (see Citrus, page 338)

Lettuces

Spring – Summer

Think of the big, beautiful, blousy whole heads of lettuces you might see at a market stall. Those lettuces proudly taking up so much space in the open air, demanding to be admired. Then think of the bags of pre-prepared lettuces, looking so sad in comparison and understandably so, with ripped leaves pushed into a bag that's sealed with nitrogen to stop the lettuce breathing. On an emotional level, there's no contest as to which I'd rather buy and eat. On a practical level, the same holds true. A whole head is likely to be cheaper than a pre-prepared bag (the price we pay for convenience...) and has a world of options far beyond, but definitely including, salad.

The lettuces of spring and summer tend to be the cool, sweet heads that provide a pleasing contrast to winter's more bitter leaves. Some are crisp, some floppy, some a clever hybrid of those as producers look to give us the perfect lettuce. All of these are well worth a look out for:

Romaine/Cos: Two names for the same lettuce type. With long leaves that begin pale and crisp near the lettuce's base and heart, then becoming greener and looser as the leaves grow up and out. The contrast of leaf textures makes them a good choice for salads. Try shredding the floppier leaves into a soup; use the crisper inner leaves for braising.

Iceberg: There was a time where this used to be pretty much the only lettuce variety the UK seemed to have, and it has never quite recovered from the contempt that familiarity bred. A shame, as once the iceberg shakes off its retro vibes this is a gorgeously crisp, clean-tasting lettuce.

Webb's Wonderful: A bit like an iceberg in that it is round and crisp, but with slightly looser and sweeter leaves.

Frisée: aka curly endive, and the most gorgeous tangle of crisp green twirls. The frisée is frizzy. A sharper, more bitter taste than many spring lettuces.

Butterhead: I love these. All loose and floppy and blousy and delicious. Can be delicate so handle with care. A triumph for salads and soups.

Oak leaf: Can be green or tinged with red. Its leaves (astonishingly...) resemble those of an oak tree in shape. Loose-leafed until, as with cos, its crisper centre leaves.

Little gem: A hybrid of the crisp cos and the floppy butterhead, bringing the best texture and flavour characteristics of each. Its size makes it the perfect choice for searing/braising.

Shop

Assuming you are buying whole heads of lettuces:

- Take a look at the base. If it is discolouring that will mean it has been out of the ground and stored for a while, meaning it is less fresh.
- Take a peek into its centre and see how the lettuce is looking. Outer leaves – especially of a loose lettuce – often can't help getting a little damaged, but its inner leaves will be a better indicator of the lettuce's freshness and health.
- Look for leaves that seem vibrant and full of life.

Then for a bag of salad (because sometimes we all have to):

- Look for any sliminess in the leaves at the base of the bag. At any sign of that put the bag down and move on.

Store

- For whole heads: Remove any very dirty or damaged outer leaves, then sit the head on kitchen paper in the salad crisper drawer. Keep the leaves attached to each other for as long as you can.
- For loose leaves from a whole head: Once the leaves are pulled or cut away from the head, and if not using straight away: Wash the leaves in plenty of cold water to remove any soil/grit, pat dry on a tea towel and then, while they are still a little damp, wrap in kitchen paper and put into the fridge.
- For loose leaves in a salad bag: Release the leaves from their oxygen-less bags, wash in cold water, pat dry, wrap in kitchen paper and keep in the fridge.

Ways to Use

Salad, most obviously. Light and easy. It's not a subject to over-complicate so here are just a few hints I find useful:

- Let the leaves spend some time in icy-cold water, to clean them of any soil/grit, and to get them as perky as possible.
- Use a salad spinner. It's the best way of drying leaves well without bruising them.
- Think about balancing different leaf types and textures, using a mix of crisp and loose leaves.
- Remember that an acidic citrus or vinegar dressing will wilt leaves. Crisper styles can take being dressed earlier, looser leaves will benefit from less time in the dressing.
- For loose lettuces such as the glorious butterhead, cut it into wedges (instead of using it as individual leaves) so the dressing can get caught in its folds.

The argument that's often made for bags of leaves is that whole lettuce heads are hard to use up before they fade. With all the many ways that lettuces can be enjoyed there should be little fear of that. Some beyond-salad thoughts for the different lettuce styles:

Crisp lettuces

Individual small, crisp leaves (like ones from a little gem) can be used as boats to hold other ingredients; or use them with your hands as a utensil to scoop things up with.

Shred crisp leaves into a slaw.

Cut down the lettuce, through its base, to create wedges to roast in a hot 200°C fan/ 425°F/gas 7 oven for 10 minutes, with just some oil and salt over. Or do something similar in a frying pan with hot oil/butter, using tongs to turn the wedges so they brown all over. Cook them long enough to be just-about tender through the middle, and nicely charred at the leaves. Add wine, cider or stock to the pan and turn that into braised lettuce (see page 293 for Braised Little Gems with Shallots, Pancetta and Peas).

Pan fry, stir fry or steam shredded crisp leaves – doing any of these ways only very briefly. They're each a very good idea, too, for doing with the central core that many crisp lettuces have.

Arrange torn leaves on the base of a plate for serving freshly cooked vegetables, meat or fish. The leaves will wilt in their heat, and be dressed in their cooking juices.

Floppy lettuces

Looser lettuce leaves lack the strength of structure for many of the cooking styles that suit the crisper types. Their relaxed nature is an asset to stuff and bake like cabbage leaves, as on page 194, but without the need to blanch the lettuce leaves first as they are already plenty soft enough.

A whole head can be stuffed, too: Let it sit in plenty of cold water to release soil/grit, gently separating the leaves to help things along. Drain the lettuce upside down, pat dry, then cut in half without cutting through its base. Season, fill with the stuffing of your choosing, push back together and use string to hold it tight. Sit in a tight-fitting pan with stock or water in the base so things don't dry out, and bake.

All lettuces

Throughout spring and summer I tear lettuce leaves to add in at the end of cooking pretty much anything. Pans of lentils, roasted vegetables, baked chicken thighs, pastas.... The different lettuce styles will take differing times to wilt. Soft leaves take barely seconds; crisper ones a minute or so.

And – lettuce soup! So light and delicious whether served hot or cold, and tasting madly seasonal because really who would want lettuce soup in autumn or winter. Riff on a recipe with this as its base: Cook off chopped spring onions (scallions) or shallots in oil/butter; perhaps add garlic. Chop up and add any crisp leaves, the crisper bases of any soft leaves, and/or the lettuce core if it has one. Add some stock, maybe some herbs. Let that cook for 10 minutes, then add shredded softer leaves. Blitz and season.

Flavour Partners

Where leaves are a simple salad accompaniment (as opposed to the meal's main event) they often need only the merest dressing so as to not overwhelm whatever you are serving the lettuce with. Sometimes just **oil**, sometimes just **vinegar**, sometimes both, always **salt**.

Where the salad is the star you can afford to amp things up. A basic **vinaigrette** is typically two-thirds oil to one-third vinegar. The oil could be just **extra-virgin olive oil**, or perhaps that mixed with **nut oil**, **infused oil** or **sesame oil**. Of the **vinegars**, **sherry**, **white wine**, **red wine** and **cider** are the go-tos. Soft lettuce leaves need a light touch with dressing – maybe leave that basic vinaigrette as it is, or even swap the vinegar for a light drizzle of **orange flower water**. Crisp leaves can stand (and want) heavier dressing. Perhaps add pestled **garlic**, **anchovies**, **walnuts** or **hazelnuts**. Each of those extra elements also working fabulously as 'proper' salad ingredients when left whole, not just as dressing layers.

Fill little gem boats with other salad elements. My favourite combos include a dollop of home-made **mayo** (see page 301) with flaked tinned **tuna** or **hot-smoked trout**, and chopped **capers**. Or sprinkling a little vinegar into the base of each leaf, adding chopped **black olives**, slices of hard-boiled **egg** and then topping with the best tinned anchovies I can find.

The lightness of **white crab** suits soft leaves. Crisp leaves will love that too but are also able to cope with the relative heft of **brown crab**. As salads, or for stuffing leaves, or together in a soup.

You won't go wrong finding all kinds of ways to put lettuces together with pretty much anything across these seasonal pages of spring and summer. Whether that's ribbons of **cucumber**, or the same quick-pickled. **Radish** slivers. **New potato**s carrying their warmth from cooking. A tumble of chopped **soft herbs**. Roasted sweet **young carrots**. Some slices of **stone fruits**. Wedges of little gem will enjoy being roasted/charred with **asparagus**, **purple sprouting broccoli**, **courgettes (zucchini)**, **peppers (capsicums)** and **aubergines (eggplant)**. Braise wedges or leaves with **peas** or **broad (fava) beans**.

Knowing how much lettuce enjoys oil in its dressings, think about letting it wallow in hot fats that bring flavour from cooking other things. Especially the hot oil from cooking **pancetta**, **bacon**, **chorizo** or **black pudding**, poured over shredded leaves to wilt them.

Don't be afraid to give your lettuces a flavour kick. They'll enjoy dressings given some chopped fresh **chilli** or a little **harissa**. Scatter **za'atar** or other spice blends over wedges before roasting or braising. Finish stir-fried leaves with oil that is hot by temperature and flavour. Grate **root ginger** into a salad dressing.

More flavour thoughts: **Chicken**; **cinnamon**; **goats' cheeses**; **juniper**; **mustard**; **raisins**; **rhubarb**; **shallots**; **soy sauce**; **sultanas (golden raisins)**; **tahini**; **dry vermouth**; **white wine**.

Preserve

Ferment: Crisp lettuces can be fermented into kimchi or sauerkraut.

In oil: Try blitzing soft leaves into a pesto.

Braised Little Gems with Shallots, Pancetta and Peas

I make not a single apology for using frozen peas in a seasonal cookbook. But I will say that as spring starts to turn into summer I swap them for freshly podded peas that can be added at the same time as in the recipe here, or for broad (fava) beans. The broad beans would just need to be podded, cooked, refreshed, then have their skins removed before using.

Some bread to mop up the juices is a good idea.

Serves 4 as a side or sharing plate

2 banana shallots	25g (1oz) butter
100g (3½oz) diced pancetta	150ml (5fl oz) chicken stock
1 tbsp olive oil (optional)	1 tbsp sherry vinegar
100ml (3½fl oz) dry vermouth	150g (5oz) frozen peas
2 little gem lettuce	1 tbsp za'atar
	black pepper

Peel and thinly slice the shallots. Set a large frying pan over a medium heat and once it is hot, add the shallot and pancetta. Turn the heat down and cook until the pancetta has crisped and the shallot softened. The pancetta should release enough fat to stop things sticking, but add a little olive oil if you need. Add the vermouth, bubble for a minute for it to reduce, then spoon everything that's in the pan into a bowl. You will need to use the pan again in a moment, so don't wash it up yet.

Remove any outer leaves from the lettuces only if they're very damaged. Cut the lettuces into quarters through the base. Set the pan you just used back over the heat. Add the butter to melt. Lay the little gem wedges into the pan and cook for 3–4 minutes, then carefully turn over and cook for a few minutes more. You want them to gently char. Pour over the stock and vinegar, and cook for 5 minutes. Add the peas and carefully mix them in with the lettuce. Cook for another couple of minutes until the lettuce is just about tender at its core. Spoon over the shallot/pancetta mix.

Finish with lots of cracked black pepper and the za'atar sprinkled over.

WASTE TIPS: Shallot skins (see Stocks, page 340)

Frisée, New Potato and Radish Salad

The slightly bitter twists of frisée leaves are here calmed by the warmth of freshly cooked new potatoes, and then pepped up again with radishes. You could easily switch in any lettuce you have to hand but I do like the frisée here.

Like this it is a simple, hearty side. Add slices of a couple of hard-boiled eggs, and/or some anchovy fillets to turn it into a main.

Serves 4 as a side
400g (14oz) new potatoes
1 frisée lettuce

75ml (2½fl oz) extra-virgin olive oil
8 radishes
salt and black pepper

Wash the potatoes. Put into a pan of well-salted water, bring to the boil, then turn down to a simmer, cover with a partial lid and cook until just about tender, 20 minutes or so. Drain the water away, return the potatoes to the pan, cover, give a smattering of salt and let them finish cooking in their own steam.

Meanwhile, pull the frisée leaves away from the base. Wash well in very cold water and either spin dry in a lettuce spinner, or blot dry in kitchen paper. Put the leaves into a serving dish.

While the potatoes are still warm: Rub off their skins, slice two-thirds of them, and put on top of the leaves. Pour over two-thirds of the oil and add salt. Next, slice the rest of the potatoes and add those too. Trim and thinly slice the radishes, then scatter over. Pour over the rest of the oil, add a little more salt and some freshly ground pepper. Serve straight away.

New Potatoes –
First and Second Earlies

Spring – Summer

Any doubts over nature's ability to rightly connect mood and food should be dispelled by the seasonality of potatoes. The smaller, sweeter, nuttier, new potatoes of spring and summer appear in the nick of time just as winter finally *finally* ebbs away, and as cooks and eaters we are so *so* over the big carby hits of maincrop potato comfort. They bring their vibe of laidback deliciousness, of lunches and dinners eaten outside with bowls of freshly cooked new potatoes that are coated in butter the colour of the sun and lots of salt.

I'll come back to that fabulous simplicity of how to cook and eat them. First up let's clear up that new potatoes are the same as maincrop potatoes, just harvested earlier in their growing cycle. It's why they are often also called 'earlies', with distinctions of first earlies and second earlies depending on when they are taken out of the ground. That might seem pedantic. Why not just call them all new potatoes and be devouringly happy about having them? Because new potatoes change through their season. Spring's first earlies can be barely walnut size, with the most delicate of skins that need only a brush with your thumb to come off. The second earlies of summer have matured to twice the size, or more; with a more substantial skin and different textures.

I am proud even just to say that I have seen the view from the back of a harvester as it drove across a field bringing up the very first of that farm's earlies. The smell of potatoes newly out of the ground is like nothing else. They're as fresh as fresh can be, challenging farmers to get them from the field to our kitchens as fast as possible, with minimal storage time, so as to retain their freshness and optimum flavour.

Good farmers and sellers know that the real joy of earlies is to be found as close as possible to them coming out of the ground. When people complain (as has become a bit

of a spring/summer ritual) that new potatoes 'don't taste like they used to' that is in part nostalgia hangover, but probably also true when many of the potatoes on the shelf are the result of pressure put on farmers to lengthen the selling season at both its ends.

Sometimes the first new-season potatoes to appear in spring are actually ones harvested the previous year and stored for months. It's quite the irony to be piggy-backing onto the anticipation of new potatoes with ones that are actually old. New potato season has become about quantity rather than quality – and of course that impacts on the potatoes' flavour. As cooks and shoppers we'd be naive to think otherwise. New potatoes enjoyed as fresh as possible from the ground and the farm – with as little done to them as possible before selling – are the ones that are going to taste of something rather than nothing.

Their tasting of something has a lot to do with the land and climate they have grown in. It is a telling quirk of new potatoes that we often talk about – and respect – the region they come from more than the variety of potato itself as we would with maincrops. It is an acknowledgement of how much terroir matters to their flavour and texture. Jersey, Cornwall, Pembrokeshire, Ayrshire, Comber (where I was on the harvester...) are all feted for their earlies and it is because these areas' unique combinations of soil and climate can make all the difference.

Not to forget the importance local farming skills also play in turning up new potatoes that not only stand up to nostalgic food lore, but will give us springs and summers of deliciousness to come.

Shop

- Look for potatoes with soil still on them. That means they are the freshest out of the ground, the most newly harvested, the least treated.
- Pre-packed, pre-washed potatoes dominate sales to the detriment of their freshness and therefore flavour. But let's be real, sometimes these are the new potatoes we all have to get. Try if you can to choose ones from regions that specialise in producing top-notch earlies – they will be proud to say on the bag if they're theirs.

Store

- New potatoes will stay freshest with their soil left on. Keep them un-washed in a paper or cloth bag somewhere cool and dark (not the fridge).
- Open up bags of pre-washed new potatoes and store the same way.

Ways to Use

Wash the potatoes and give them just a gentle scrub. Very gentle in the case of the first earlies, which have gossamer-like skin. Even as they develop more of a skin as they mature through the season, cook them with skins on to keep in flavour and nutrients.

The small nuggets of the first potatoes of the season are best steamed to protect their flavour.

Then move onto boiling them. By 'boil' I mean 'simmer', and only until the potatoes are just about starting to become tender. Drain off their water, return the potatoes to the pan, and cover to finish cooking in their own steam. Once cool enough to handle, their skins will slip off.

New potatoes still warm from cooking are best able to take on board salt, butter/oil and any other flavours you want to throw their way. Cut them in half or lightly crush to expose more flesh to the delicious elements. Serve still warm, or let them cool and then chop to turn into a new potato salad (see page 300 for much more on that).

First earlies with their barely there skin can be roasted without parboiling first. Cut a cross into them, toss in oil and salt, roast in a 210°C fan/450°F/gas 8 oven for 20–30 minutes (size depending) and be ready with more salt and the vinegar bottle for as soon as they are tender and crisped.

Second earlies with more of a skin will need 10 minutes or so first in simmering water to achieve roasted new potatoes that are the nirvana of sweetly fudgy flesh and crisp skin. A proper crust can only be achieved with a combination of lots of oil + lots of salt + very hot oven.

The larger second earlies have developed more starch, which means they are that bit more varied and versatile to cook with. Use them for dauphinoises, gratins or tortillas. Thinly slice them and layer into the base of a dish for baking meat or fish on top of – the trout on page 318 would be lovely baked upon sliced second earlies.

All new potato leftovers are to be cherished and can always be turned into something else. Brought back to room temperature and given a dressing freshen-up they will likely be ready to go all over again. Or chop into a frittata; dice and stir fry; or use to thicken a soup of other seasonal veg.

Flavour Partners

Remembering that new potatoes are the same as maincrops, just younger, it stands to obvious reason that the same core flavour partners of the maincrops hold true. Which means: salt, fat, acid, heat, umami. Turn to page 135, take those flavour cues, and use them simply and lightly. The trick is to not overwhelm the new potatoes' flavour.

Butter and/or **extra-virgin olive oil** are hard to beat over steamed or boiled new potatoes that are still warm enough to absorb their fattiness and flavour. A pour of **cream** or spoonfuls of **crème fraîche** or **yoghurt** work better for later dressing once the potatoes are cooled (perhaps with skins slipped off); or for baking slices of second earlies. Dunk earlies in **mayonnaise** and let them lap up **hollandaise**.

Saltiness is the other flavour partner essential. Again, keep it simple and reach for the **salt flakes**. Or look to **anchovies**, **black** or **green olives**, **capers**, **miso**, **dried shrimps** or **samphire** that can wilt in the heat of warm potatoes.

The desire for salt means umami is never far behind. Roast earlies in the fat of a **roasted chicken**; or with a rack of **lamb** roasting on top of them so its juices can get down and dirty with the potatoes. Wherever potatoes are given heavy salty/umami partners, be sure to give some flavour lift back via a spritz of **vinegar**, **lemon juice** or **zest,** or sliced **preserved lemons**.

New potatoes enjoy **spices**, especially for roasting. Once they've been parboiled (if they're larger second earlies), toss in oil and then add **garam masala**, **ground cumin**, **turmeric** and/or **paprika** before they go into the oven.

Partner new potatoes with the produce they are in season at the same time with. Add **asparagus** spears in to cook towards the end of roasting, steaming or boiling earlies. Toss them with **green beans**, quick-pickled **cucumber** or **courgette** (**zucchini**) ribbons, or **radish** slices. Tear **wild garlic** into potatoes as they finish cooking in their own steam; or serve them with the tender roasted flesh from new-season **wet garlic**. Let the warmth of freshly cooked earlies relax **lettuce leaves**. Blitz leftover potatoes into a **pea** or **watercress** soup.

Herbs, too – and plenty of them. Pretty much the only thing that can improve the delicious simplicity of a bowlful of freshly cooked, buttered and salted new potatoes is tossing in plenty of seasonal chopped herbs. Sprigs of **mint** or **tarragon** give a subtle undertone of flavour when added to water the earlies are steaming above or simmering in. Tuck **oregano** into new potato dauphinoises, gratins or whenever baking them. The lemon notes of **sorrel** chime particularly well.

More flavour thoughts: **Almonds**; **bacon**; **basil**; **carrots**; **chervil**; **chilli**; **coconut**; **coriander seeds**; **dill**; **egg**; **ginger**; **horseradish**; **mustard**; **Parmesan**; **pesto**; **smoked fish**; **spring onions** (**scallions**); **tahini**; **tomatoes**; **truffle**; **white fish**.

Preserve

No... just cook, eat and enjoy while you can.

The Simple Joy of New Potato Salads

Simple is often the fastest track to new potato joy. A few basic principles will deliver bowlful upon bowlful of delicious new potato salads all spring and summer long.

Potatoes
Choose ones roughly the same size as each other, so they cook at the same rate. Cutting them to make even-sized pieces allows some flavour to leach out in the cooking – keep them whole if you can. As the season goes along and textures vary, choose waxy new potatoes to hold their shape, or floury varieties if you don't mind them collapsing.

Preparing
Do not peel. Give the potatoes just a gentle wash/scrub depending on how much soil is on there. Treat first earlies especially carefully so as not to scrub away their fine skin.

Cook
Small first earlies are best steamed. Otherwise, put the potatoes into a large pan of cold water, bring to the boil, then reduce the heat to a gentle simmer. Whether steaming or simmering, make sure the water is well salted. Perhaps add a sprig or two of mint, dill or tarragon to the water. Simmer only until the potatoes are just-about tender to the point of a knife – don't take them all the way to cooked through.

Drain and steam
Drain the water away, discard any aromatics, return the potatoes to the pan, put a lid on, and let them finish cooking in their own steam.

Skins and first anointing
Once they are cool enough to handle – but crucially still warm – rub away the skins if you want to, or if they are coming annoyingly loose. Cut to expose more flesh, and/ or gently crush their edges to give what's to come something to cling onto. Then, give them their first burst of fat and flavour while they're warm enough to take those on board. Use butter only if serving the potatoes warm, otherwise extra-virgin olive oil, always plenty of salt, toss well and cover again.

Cut, dress and serve

Optionally cut the potatoes into smaller cubes or slices. They may or may not need more oil – it depends how liberal a dousing they've already had. They will need a second salting as the first will have been absorbed into the potato flesh.

Serve straight away, or keep a while in the fridge. Just be sure to bring back to room temperature before serving.

Flavour boosts

There are as many directions this could go in as there are days in the spring and summer, but some thoughts on how I toss and enjoy them:

– 50/50 ratio of extra-virgin olive oil to sherry vinegar; plus chopped mint, basil and dill; with plenty of flaky salt.
– With roasted asparagus and roasted new-season, small carrots.
– Mix tahini with a little of any type of mustard and some oil; then toss through the potatoes with chopped capers and dill; finish with sliced spring onions (scallions).
– Quick-pickle cucumber and/or courgette (zucchini) ribbons and toss them into the potatoes with a little of the pickling liquor.
– With really good tinned anchovies laid over.
– With white crab meat, mint, dill and preserved lemon.
– Into a big summer salad of leaves, boiled egg, anchovies, cucumber, radishes….
– With a bowl of home-made mayonnaise on the side:
  For 4–6 people and 1kg (2lb 4 oz) potatoes: Whisk 2 large room-temperature egg yolks with 1 tbsp sherry or white wine vinegar and 1 tsp English or Dijon mustard; season; slowly whisk in 200ml (7fl oz) rapeseed oil plus 100ml (3½fl oz) extra-virgin olive oil until the mayo is thick and fabulous; check the seasoning.

Radishes

Spring – Summer

French Breakfast. Cherry Belle. Scarlet Globe. Purple Plum. They're the kind of names you might find on a nail polish bottle or wall paint chart, or – even more happily – on the radishes accompanying a nice glass of something cold on a balmy spring evening.

These small, peppy little buttons of heat that come in a range of gemstone colourways first burst into our kitchens in spring, and last right through the summer. That's at least four, maybe five, months of radish heaven. Given they are primarily enjoyed raw (although not solely – more on that to come), you'd think radish boredom might set in at some point. Yet, somehow, absolutely not.

Shop

- Freshness is key. Radishes should be smooth and firm, with unblemished bright skin. That is when they'll be at their crunchiest and tastiest. As radishes age they lose that brightness and firmness.
- If the leaves are attached make sure they are crisp, and not going slimy.

Store

- Remove any leaves as soon as you can so they don't leach water from the radish. Wash the leaves well in very cold water, wrap in kitchen paper while still damp and put into the fridge. The moisture in the paper will help keep them fresh.
- The radishes themselves should be either similarly wrapped in damp kitchen paper and stored in the fridge; or put them in a bowl of cold water in the fridge. It's all about helping them retain moisture.
- Radishes that have been stored too long and need perking up can be revived by sitting them in a bowl of iced water for a few hours. The water will seep into the radish flesh, rehydrating.

Ways to Use

Let's assume you are here with a lovely bunch of crisp, firm, young radishes. The very best thing you can do with them is hardly anything at all. Wash them in plenty of cold water, shake dry, put onto a plate, and serve with any of the salty, fatty partners to come.

If they still have their leaves on (meaning you've only recently got them, because otherwise I know you would have already taken the leaves off, as opposite...) have another dish to hand that the leaves can be put straight into and then dressed with a light vinaigrette for a radish leaf salad.

Indulge in a little vegetable art: Cut 4 slits as a cross down the length of each radish, but crucially without cutting through its base. Sit the radishes in iced water for a few hours and they will open up into kitschly cool flowers that, once drained and dried, can be filled with a little butter and a smattering of salt.

Whole radishes can be tempura'd as on page 280. Or slice radishes into salads. Their leaves could be torn in too, or the leaves used in a salad without the actual radish being there.

I find I quick-pickle radishes nearly as often as having them just as they are. The same principal of water being easily absorbed by their flesh is just as true if the steeping liquid is a mild vinegar. A very delicious side-benefit to doing this is that the leftover pickling liquid can be saved and used for salad dressings, or diluted into a prettily pink drink that will have just a hint of peppery radishness about it. There's more on quick-pickling radishes in the recipe on page 72.

Grate radishes into a yoghurt and herb raita.

Smack radishes with a rolling pin so they open up, douse with salt and let them drain for an hour. This is, unusually, about drying radishes out before giving them moisture back by way of a dressing – like the one on page 306, or chilli oil amped up into a sauce with sesame oil, light soy sauce and a little caster (superfine) sugar.

As briefly mentioned earlier, radishes may be mainly for enjoying raw but not solely. When they get a little older and less crisp, it's time to start thinking about cooking them. Slice, then quickly sauté or stir fry them, to retain the firm texture and crisp flavour. Or, to mellow out their flavour, roast radishes as in the recipe over on page 305.

Flavour Partners

Some of my happiest radish times have been with nothing more than a drink alongside. Depending on the time of day and the general mood: A cool glass of sharp **lemonade**. A **dry martini**. Cold **beer**. Very crisp **white wine**. Or (if even just the word doesn't give you a headache, as it does for me) a good **rosé**.

Remembering how peppery radishes can be (the occasional one so much so they'll wake your taste buds right up) those radish partnerships get even better with a smattering of **salt** for the radishes. The classic salt and pepper affinity is why **soy sauce** works so well for dousing smashed and salted radishes with. And why I always have extra stocks of tinned **anchovies** in my fridge when there are radishes around. Really good anchovies are drained of their oil and served alongside. They don't have to be quite such top quality if pestling them into a salad dressing where their salty hit will welcome **extra-virgin olive oil**, and perhaps a little **mustard** whisked in too before dressing radishes and/or their leaves.

The fat in the oil helps carry the salt to the radishes and acts as a flavour bridge. Try the same idea with a little **butter** dotted onto a cut radish and then salt sprinkled over. Layer up slices of raw radish with **oily fish**, such as **trout** on a **rye bread** sandwich. Crumble **feta** into a radish salad. Whip **sheep's or goats' curd**, or **cream cheese**, with chopped **soft herbs**, then give that a squeeze of **lemon** juice and serve alongside raw radishes.

Which herbs? Any of the seasonal soft ones of pages 308–10, but I think especially **chervil**, **chives**, **dill**, **tarragon** and **mint**.

Eggs often act as an excellent carrier of the partners radishes will love. Dip crisp radishes into the rich **mayonnaise** on page 301, or the **miso** version on page 280. Serve radishes as a part of a mezze/picnic with hard-boiled eggs topped with anchovies (I know, again) or **capers**.

The oiliness of **walnuts** works very well. Perhaps in a salad, or switch them for **almonds**. Shaved **Parmesan** into that salad would bring salty, fat notes. Add slices of **orange** to take things in a fresher direction – and I rather love the idea of that as a seasonal handover between the last of winter's **blood oranges** and the first of spring's radishes.

That more zesty, punchy direction is amplified by quick-pickling. The best **vinegars** for that will be **vermouth**, **red wine** or **white wine**. Add in some spices such as **coriander seeds**, **cumin** or **caraway**. Any and all of those are also excellent for tossing over radishes before roasting.

More flavour thoughts: **Blackcurrant**; **cherry**; **chilli** flakes; **cucumber**; **horseradish**; **labneh**; **lime**; **nasturtium**; **pomegranate**; **potatoes**; **sesame oil** and **seeds**; **sherry vinegar**; **spring onions (scallions)**; **tahini**; **za'atar**.

Preserve

I'm going to have to repeat the preserving advice for asparagus and say: please don't. Just enjoy any abundance of radishes as quickly and as often as you can – radish season may not be short, but it will somehow still pass in a flash.

Roast New Potatoes and Radishes with Anchovies and Herbs

Radishes are so often eaten raw but take on a lovely, mellower flavour when cooked. This recipe also makes use of their peppery leaves, partners them with new potatoes that are roasted to become meltingly tender inside and crisp on the outside, and then amps the whole lot up with anchovies and seasonal herbs. It is great as a side dish for meat or fish, or make this the main event with just a few lettuce leaves (I'd go for butterhead) to go with it.

Serves 4 as a side

600g (1lb 5oz) new potatoes

5 tbsp extra-virgin olive oil

250g (9oz) French breakfast radishes, with leaves

6 anchovy fillets in oil

1 tbsp sherry vinegar

handful of fresh mint and tarragon

1 unwaxed lemon

flaky salt and black pepper

Preheat the oven to 210°C fan/450°F/gas 8.

Wash the potatoes and rub just enough to remove any loose skin. Parboil only if they are large: Put them into a large saucepan, cover with cold water, add plenty of salt, bring to the boil, simmer for 6 minutes, then drain and cut into chunks.

Put the potatoes into a baking dish. Toss with 4 tablespoons of the olive oil, sprinkle with salt flakes and put into the oven for 20 minutes, or until they're just about tender and taking on colour. Toss the potatoes halfway through the cooking time.

Meanwhile, prep the radishes: Pull off the leaves, sit them in a bowl of very cold water for 5 minutes, then drain and dry with kitchen paper. Trim away the radish tops, wash the radishes, dry them and halve lengthways.

Drain the anchovies of their oil and chop.

Once the potatoes have had 20 minutes roasting, add the radish halves, anchovies and vinegar, and toss together. Roast for another 10 minutes so the radishes can soften.

Chop the herb leaves and tear the radish leaves. Toss them all into the potatoes and radishes. Grate over the zest of the lemon, drizzle with the remaining tablespoon of olive oil, and finish with lots of cracked black pepper. Serve warm or at room temperature.

WASTE TIPS: Anchovies (page 338), Herb stems (see Stocks, page 340; Soft Herbs, page 241), Lemon juice (see Citrus, page 338)

Smacked Radishes with Sesame, Sumac and Mint

By bruising the flesh, and slightly drying it out, radishes can really become immersed in the bright flavours of this dressing. These make the perfect accompaniment to an aperitif, or turn them from a snack to a starter or side by serving on top of yoghurt.

Serves 4 as a snack, starter or side

400g (14oz) radishes, without leaves

1 tbsp salt

1½ tsp coriander seeds

3 tbsp toasted sesame oil

2 tsp sherry vinegar

½ tsp sumac

2 mint sprigs

450g (1lb) thick plain yoghurt
  (optional)

black pepper

Wash and dry the radishes. Wrap in a clean tea towel and smack them with a rolling pin to crack open. Put them into a bowl, toss in the salt and set aside for 1 hour. Toss them a couple of times so that the salt can get into every crevice created by the smacking. Rinse the radishes thoroughly in cold water, then dry in a towel.

Toast the coriander seeds in a frying pan over a medium heat. Transfer them to a pestle and mortar, and crush. Mix together the toasted sesame oil, sherry vinegar and sumac, then add the crushed coriander seeds. Finely chop most of the mint leaves (keeping some back for garnish) and add to the dressing. Toss the radishes in the dressing and set aside for 30 minutes, tossing them occasionally.

Serve as they are, or spread the yoghurt over a serving dish and top with the radishes (making sure to spoon over every drop of dressing). Finish with the reserved mint leaves torn over and some freshly ground black pepper.

WASTE TIP: Herb stems (see Stocks, page 340; Soft Herbs, page 341)

Soft Herbs

Spring – Summer – *Year Round*

Bergamot, lemon verbena, lovage, basil, mint, dill, tarragon.... Those words feel like bursts of spring sunshine for the culinary soul. Even the ones in that bunch we've got accustomed to chopping up and using for year-round garnishing take on extra lustre when put into their rightful season.

These herbs might be soft but they wield considerable power in the springtime kitchen. As well as the ones already mentioned, keep an eye out for chives, lemon balm, fennel (the herb, which is related to, but not the same as, the fronds on a fennel bulb), marjoram or oregano.

Shop

– Look for herbs that are undamaged, not wilting and a vibrant green. Any yellowing means they are old and drying out.

Store

– Cut herbs are best kept in the fridge, wrapped in kitchen paper. Or put 10cm (4in) or so of water into a large sealable jar, sit the herbs in so the stems are in the water, seal and put either into the fridge or onto a cool windowsill. Change the water every few days.
– Use herbs quickly – that's when their flavour will be brightest.

Ways to Use

This isn't about delicate garnishing just to pretty things up. Harness herb power and use them together and liberally – that's how the vibrant glory of spring's soft green herbs will kick the last vestiges of winter right out of your kitchen.

Add whole sprigs of mint, fennel, dill and/or tarragon (or their picked leaves) to a big bowlful of spring salad. Serve dishes of herbs as a mezze. I love the Persian tradition of sabzi khordan where a platter of those herbs I just mentioned, perhaps plus some radish leaves, is on the dining table throughout a meal – the herbs ready to be reached for whenever a burst of freshness is needed.

Mix chopped soft herbs into soft butter and stuff under the skin of a chicken before roasting. Or strew plenty of soft herbs over a lamb joint, add a little oil and water, cover and slow roast.

Toss them with a tumble of just-cooked new-season vegetables. Add chopped soft herbs into a pan of rice just before it has finished cooking – the herbs will cling to the rice when it is drained/left to steam under a cloth.

Whisk soft herbs into an omelette or frittata. Whip them with yoghurt, labneh, ricotta or goats' curd. Make a sauce of very finely chopped herbs with olive oil and some gently spicing. Try making herb pies with lots – and I do mean lots – of chopped soft herbs, mixed through with hard-boiled eggs and spring onions (scallions), and then baked in puff or filo pastry. A lunchbox treat.

Or you could take inspiration from the Bavarian herb soup, krautlsuppe, that I came across in one of food writer Elisabeth Luard's books. She is so good at capturing food traditions and describes bitter spring herbs often being eaten at Easter as a sign of penitence, and this soup as being typically served on the day before Good Friday. The recipe calls for a simple base of onion and stock, herbs of your choosing but letting bitter chervil dominate. Plus sorrel, watercress, spinach, and potato to thicken. If a bowl of that is meant to be a punishment, it's one I'll happily take.

Flavour Partners

Using a mixed bundle is where the herb flavour magic of spring lies. When the drier, more intense heat of summer comes round I'll use soft herbs more simply – one or two herby flavours is more than enough on a hot day. But in the relative cool of spring, reach for two, or three, or more soft herbs and they'll not just find balance with each other, they find harmony with whatever you put them with. Especially if what you are putting them with is fairly neutral. That explains the **egg** ideas for a herby omelette or frittata. Also for whipping into rich dairy such as **yoghurt**, **labneh**, **ricotta** or **goats' curd**. They'll all be platforms for letting the flavours of the herbs show themselves off.

The simplicity of **chicken** and **fish** lends them towards an abundance of mixed herbs, too. One of the best ways to amplify the flavours of **new potatoes** is to toss them in a medley of seasonal herbs, lots of **butter**, and **salt**. Switch the butter for really good **extra-virgin olive oil** and, again, chopped mixed soft herbs are among the best and simplest way to dress roasted **asparagus** spears or young **carrots**.

A mixed herb dressing or sauce that has as its base **olive oil** and **vinegar** (**red wine** or **sherry** would be my choices), can be taken in different flavour directions with your pick of ground **cinnamon**, **mixed spice**, **mustard** or **mustard seeds**, pestled **anchovies**, chopped **capers** or **black olives**.

More herb flavour partnerships that I am especially keen on:
- **Chervil**, **dill**, **fennel** and **tarragon** (the bitter, aniseed-y herbs) partner well with a touch of sweetness. That could be **raisins** or **sultanas (golden raisins)** in a leafy salad; to dress **peas** or young **broad (fava) beans**; with **white fish** or **shellfish**.
- **Sorrel**'s lemon notes work especially gorgeously with **new potatoes**.
- **Mint** and **oregano** are my go-to double act for dressing asparagus, especially if the spears are roasted with a smattering of **za'atar** and a little sherry vinegar.

Preserve

In vinegar: Head to page 284 and see how to make elderflower vinegar, then just switch a couple of herb sprigs for the elderflower head.

Dried: Only dry herbs at their absolute peak of freshness and therefore flavour. A sad, aging herb is not going to have enough flavour life left to give its dried incarnation. Spread the herbs on baking paper on a baking tray, sit that into a 50°C fan/125°F/ gas ¼ oven, with the door slightly open, for up to 6 hours. Strip the leaves from the now brittle stems, and store in an airtight container. Try to use them soon – they'll only deteriorate with age.

In salt: Blitz herbs and salt flakes together in a grinder (twice the weight of herbs to salt), then spread the mixture on baking paper on a baking tray, sit that into a 50°C fan/125°F/gas ¼ oven, with the door slightly open, for up to 12 hours. As the herbs and salt dry together the flavours of both will intensify. Store in an airtight container and use soon.

In butter: Chop herb leaves (choosing a single flavour, or blend), and mix with soft butter. Roll into logs, wrap and freeze.

See also Waste Tips, page 341.

Goats' and Sheep's Cheeses

Goats' cheese is one of spring's true delights. Not least because it was a relatively recent revelation to me that it was seasonal at all.

Unlike cows, goats do not produce milk all year round. Their milk is at its peak – in quantity and flavour – in the spring and then through early summer as the pasture the goats love grazing upon gets lusher and lusher. The impact that has upon the goats' milk is obvious. The milk is rich, it can be floral or grassy, often with almost nutty or citrus notes.... It is entirely dependent upon what the pasture is made up of. There is something undeniably special about this milk – and that translates to the cheeses it makes, too.

Soft young goats' cheeses, made with spring/summer goats' milk, have an incomparable complex delicacy. If that sounds at all like a contradiction I can only say it is somehow true. As those cheeses age and mature they take on a different character. Also delicious, just different. And that right there is surely one of the delights of eating more seasonally: realising and relishing that some of the produce we are attuned to having all year, and to it tasting the same all year, actually needn't.

This all applies just as much to sheep's milks and cheeses as it does to goats'. Meaning spring is *the* time to seek out artisan dairies and cheesemongers who are churning out (pun clearly intended) absolutely cracking seasonal dairy.

You will find their lightness of flavour and texture are easy wins for so much of spring and summer's vegetables and fruits. On a quick review of all the produce featured here across these seasons there is not a single thing that wouldn't love to nestle up on the plate with some raw or baked, sliced or crumbled, seasonal goats' or sheep's cheese.

Spring Herb and Goats' Cheese Soufflé

Small individual soufflés can teeter on being too formal for home cooking. A bit prissy even. A large soufflé is sassy. Holding herself aloft with enough attitude to wow any crowd.

There is nothing to be nervous about in soufflé-making. Just follow the recipe, get the oven hot before it goes in, don't open the door too early, and – most importantly – make sure whoever you are feeding is at the table ready for when the soufflé comes out of the oven and before it deflates. Serve with lightly dressed leaves, a bowl of new potatoes, and dry white wine – which should all also be prepared and waiting.

Serves 4–6 as a main

25g (1oz) Parmesan (or a strong, hard goats' cheese)

55g (2oz) butter

40g (1½oz) plain (all-purpose) flour

400ml (13fl oz) whole milk

200g (7oz) soft goats' cheese

3 egg yolks

4 egg whites

20g (¾oz) soft herb leaves (any mix of tarragon, chives mint, basil, dill)

salt and black pepper

18–20cm (7–8in) soufflé dish

Preheat the oven to 190°C fan/400°F/gas 6 with a baking tray inside.

Finely grate the Parmesan. Melt 15g (½oz) of the butter in a medium saucepan and brush the inside of the soufflé dish with it. Scatter over the grated Parmesan to coat the sides, shake off any excess, and set the prepped dish aside.

Melt the rest of the butter in the same pan over a low–medium heat. Add the flour and whisk for a couple of minutes, then whisk in the milk, adding it slowly at first. Turn the heat up a little and simmer for 3–4 minutes, whisking all the time, until the sauce thickens. Pour into a large mixing bowl. Crumble 125g (4oz) of the goats' cheese into the sauce and mix it in to melt. Whisk in the egg yolks, then season. Up to this point can be done ahead.

Put the egg whites into a separate and very clean mixing bowl. Whisk until they're stiff but not dry. You should be able to just about tip the bowl upside down without them falling. Chop the rest of the goats' cheese into small pieces and crumble into the soufflé mix. Chop the herb leaves and mix those in, then gently fold in the egg whites keeping as much air as possible – a few streaks of white are fine.

Put the dish into the oven immediately, onto the hot baking tray, and bake for 25–30 minutes. It's ready when golden, risen, and with just a gentle wobble when you move the dish. Under no circumstances be tempted to open the oven door to check on it until it's been in for at least 20 minutes. Serve straight away.

WASTE TIPS: Egg yolk (page 338), Herb stems (see Stocks, page 340; Soft Herbs, page 341), Parmesan rind (page 339)

Watercress and Baby Spinach
Spring – Summer

There's a map on a wall in my flat showing the east end of London, where my husband's family are from, in 1720. Anyone who has ever hung out in Bethnal Green or Hackney might be surprised to see that on the map they are mainly swathes of open land. There would have been watercress beds there until nineteenth-century industrialisation drew people to the city from the countryside and London swelled from 1 million to 7 million inhabitants. The city had to spread to cope, and by the mid-1800s the pure air and water essential for growing watercress were not likely to be found in Bethnal Green or Hackney. It was then home to some of London's worst slums and the only evidence of watercress were the slums' courtyards where the young girls who lived there stored the baskets they used for hawking watercress on the streets to the wealthy Victorians who couldn't get enough of it.

Where was all their watercress coming from, if not any longer from London's own beds? From Kent and Hampshire – areas being in turn transformed by the huge popularity of watercress and the new machines that could operate watercress beds on a much larger commercial scale than ever before. Add in the newly established railway network that meant the watercress, which wilts so quickly, could reach the markets in London before it went off, and you see how behind the apparent fragility of these leaves lies a powerful story of the literally changing landscapes of countrysides and cities, and in how we feed ourselves.

In your kitchen, think of watercress much like baby spinach. Hence their pairing together here. Baby spinach is – fairly obviously – simply spinach that has been harvested early. (The larger leaves of mature spinach are closer in how you cook with them to things like cavolo nero and chard, so head there if that is what you've got.)

Shop

- Buy watercress with its roots still attached to help it keep longer and retain flavour.
- Avoid watercress that is wilting or with leaves turning yellow.
- Both watercress and baby spinach should look vibrant with life and colour.
- Really fresh spinach will squeak as you rub it.

Store

- Watercress is best stored in the crisper drawer of the fridge, sealed in a bag or container with as little air in there as possible.
- A more romantic option (but less effective, especially if it's hot) is to stand your bunch of watercress in cold water like a bunch of flowers.
- Store baby spinach in a plastic bag in the crisper drawer of the fridge, with the spinach still slightly damp, but take care not to let water settle at the bottom of the bag or your spinach will turn slimy.

Ways to Use

Only ever wash watercress or baby spinach in ice-cold water. Pat watercress dry in a clean cloth; baby spinach is strong enough to withstand the salad spinner.

Chop watercress stems into a salad with baby spinach and/or other leaves to maximise all their differing flavours and textures. Save watercress' more delicate leaves for the finishing flourish. Dress the salad only just before serving – baby spinach can turn black if dressed too soon, and delicate watercress leaves will over-wilt.

Use raw watercress as a bed for serving cooked meat or fish, letting their heat gently wilt the leaves.

For watercress soups, warm or chilled, the stems work best. That's where most of the flavour is and they'll give it body too. The leaves can, again, give garnish. They are also a delight to use as a herb. Wherever chervil or tarragon might be headed, watercress will tag along happily. Watercress is especially good for chopping into herb-laden sauces such as a salsa verde.

Blitz watercress or baby spinach to add into the batter for waffles or all kinds of pancakes. Or into dips. Or for fruit or vegetable smoothies.

Finely chop raw watercress or baby spinach as a stuffing or filling for pancakes, omelettes, kuku, dumplings, bourek, meat joints or more. Note that baby spinach will release moisture as it cooks. When using as a filling get its moisture out first to avoid things getting too soggy later. Put the leaves into a pan with a splash of hot water, cover with a lid and set over a high heat for the leaves to wilt in the steam. Then drain, refresh in very cold water, dry thoroughly (really squeezing the excess water out), chop and carry on. Another way to extract its moisture is to rub salt through the baby spinach, let it sit for an hour or so, then rinse, dry, chop and proceed.

Cooked watercress will – like spinach – lose its bulk when you cook it. It doesn't release so much water, though.

Flavour Partners

Watercress and baby spinach are both peppery so let your culinary mind run free with all kinds of salt and pepper combos for both sets of leaves. That could mean **anchovy**, **bacon/pancetta**, **soy/tamari**, **capers**, **olives**, **Parmesan**....

There's a clean minerality to both watercress and baby spinach that makes them a great foil for fattier flavours. Rich, salty **blue, goats'** and **feta cheeses** especially. Think about partnering in salads, tarts, soups, rarebit, or simply cheese on toast with raw leaves between the bread and the cheese.

Stuff **whole fish** with watercress leaves before roasting/baking, and then find other ways that the richness of **oily fish** and **shellfish** works well with these leaves. Perhaps as a bed for them once cooked, or the leaves blitzed into their sauces and dressings as with the hollandaise on page 318. Citrus is a welcome bridging flavour – **grapefruit** perhaps first and foremost, then **orange**. **Lemon** or **lime** less so, but still good.

Sweet fruits bring flavour contrast in watercress/baby spinach savoury dishes. Try chopped **mango** in a salad, **tamarind**, **figs**, griddled **peaches** or **pears**. You might want some **nuts** crumbled over for texture – **walnuts** are especially good here.

Try **cinnamon**, **nutmeg** or **fenugreek** in a dressing, or add baby spinach/watercress at the end of a stir fry that is bouncing with **root ginger**, **chillies** and **coriander seeds**. Or to smooth watercress and spinach's sharp edges: Partner either or both leaves with **egg** in omelettes and kuku; or add a softly poached egg to a watercress/baby spinach salad. Wilt watercress in freshly steamed **new potatoes** plus a light vinaigrette; or simply dressed to go with **steak** and chips. Add **coconut milk** to soups of these leaves; and chopped coconut for their pesto or salads. **Cream**, **crème fraîche**, **soured cream**, **labneh**, **yoghurt** – they'll all round out watercress and baby spinach for soups, sauces and more.

The soft herb partners to reach for include **mint**, **basil**, **tarragon**, **chervil**, **chives**.

More flavour thoughts: **Blackcurrant**; **crab**; **date syrup**; **duck**; **Parmesan**; **pork**; **sesame seeds** or **oil**; **shallots**; **vinegar** (especially **sherry** or **red wine**).

Preserve

Preserving does either few favours. If you really do have an abundance of leaves then make soups and freeze those; or blitz into pesto.

Trout – Wild Sea, Rainbow and Brown

Think of the best salmon you've ever had – hopefully Pacific, see page 48 for why – and then know that wild sea trout is exponentially better. It is somehow more muscular yet also lighter; paler in colour; and with a delicate flavour that simply has more about it. It is also bang in season just when its ease of cooking and eating suits the general food mood.

Sea trout is simply river trout that has decided to stretch its fins and go for a swim. Here in the UK it is our native freshwater brown trout that, once mature, leave the river for the sea and then come back again, older, larger, and more delicious. When a rainbow trout does the same thing it's then called a steelhead.

I'm right to feel drawn to it in the lighter-weather months. That is when wild sea trout are in season and available to buy although perhaps not so easily. Their numbers are limited in part because the season of when it can be fished is kept short to protect stocks and allow us to enjoy wild sea trout for generations to come; and in part because the declining quality of water in the sea threatens their survival.

As for brown vs rainbow trout, the question is really one of farming. Most of the trout we see at the fishmongers is farmed rainbow trout simply because it is the most commercially viable for year-round trout availability. It is absolutely possible to come across farmed brown trout, or even wild brown trout, but mostly it is farmed rainbow that you see. While the ethics and impacts of trout farming can, to some degree, mirror those of salmon farming, the scale involved is far smaller. Look, if you can, for farmed trout reared on 'raceways' – that'll mean they've been exposed to a flow of water that mimics the wild and hopefully means more ethical production throughout its lifecycle.

Whichever kind of trout you have, it will perfectly suit so much of spring and summer's produce and cooking. Steam, poach or roast whole fish or fillets. Cook them with a little white wine, spring's soft herbs, or some grated root ginger. Finish with a drizzling of olive oil and/or a light spritzing of light white wine vinegar such as champagne or muscatel. And then serve with asparagus, purple sprouting broccoli, radishes, wild garlic, new potatoes, broad (fava) beans.... You get the idea.

Trout with Watercress Hollandaise

Opposites attract here as the vibrancy of watercress partners brilliantly with the indulgence of hollandaise, taking the edge off the sauce's richness. There will be lots of ways this sauce could work over the spring and summer but I think it's especially good with fish, and perhaps especially trout, which is also somehow light and decadent at the same time. Some new potatoes on the side would love to lap up the sauce.

Serves 4 as a main

4 rainbow trout (about 500–600g/1lb
  2oz–1lb 5oz per fish), scaled and
  gutted, with heads and tails on or off
  as you prefer
50ml (1¾fl oz) olive oil
flaky salt and black pepper

For the watercress hollandaise

150g (5oz) watercress
250g (9oz) unsalted butter
4 large egg yolks
25ml (1 tbsp plus 2 tsp) lemon juice
salt and black pepper

Preheat the oven to 190°C fan/400°F/gas 6.

Slash the skin of each fish three times on both sides, rub with the olive oil, then lay them in a baking dish top-to-tail. Scatter the fish generously with salt flakes and roast for 20–25 minutes until the flesh is starting to flake.

Meanwhile, make the watercress hollandaise. Put most of the watercress into a colander keeping a few of the prettiest springs back for garnish. Pour plenty of boiling water over the watercress, then dry it in a tea towel. It needs to be thoroughly dry. Finely chop and set aside.

Set a heatproof bowl over a pan of gently simmering water. Put the butter into that bowl, let it melt, then lift the bowl off and set aside to cool down.

Set another heatproof bowl over the pan of simmering water. Whisk in it the yolks and lemon juice with 2 tablespoons of warm water and a pinch of salt. Keeping the heat under the pan so low that the water is barely bubbling, whisk into the eggs the (now just warm) butter, adding it slowly and in stages. Once it has become a thick emulsion, taste and season, then stir in the chopped watercress. If the hollandaise is ready before the trout is, keep the sauce in the bowl over the pan of water but off the heat and covered with a cloth. Like that it will be fine for up to an hour, so could even be made ahead.

Serve the fish with watercress hollandaise spooned over, and the reserved watercress sprigs as a finishing touch with lots of freshly ground black pepper.

WASTE TIPS: Egg whites (page 338)

Wild Garlic

Spring

I worry that, what with this and the section on foraging for blossoms (page 282), I'm giving the impression my spring is spent channelling inner urban-hunter-gatherer instincts. That is only partly true. Let me say here now that (as at time of writing, things can change) I have never yet actually picked any actual wild garlic in the actual wild. But I like to think that I could be that person.

I love the idea of getting out into the spring air, feeling some sun on my face, and picking what is surely one of the brightest of seasonal food highlights. It's just that – unlike seemingly everybody else on social media – I don't trip over wild garlic fields as soon as I leave my front door. Happily I don't go short. Wild garlic is, for its short season, easy to buy in local markets, and I can often get it on my weekly supermarket shop.

Wild garlic is, not at all surprisingly, similar in flavour to its relation the garlic bulb. But whereas the cloves of a bulb are typically cooked down into a dish and therefore more subdued, wild garlic leaves can tend to be a bit more front and centre with their garlic flavour. This is a good thing.

All of the wild garlic is edible. I sometimes like the wild garlic flowers that appear as the season progresses even more than the leaves, for the beautiful garlic garnish they give.

Forage

– Shady bits of the garden, by the side of the road, spread across woodland and parks – these are all places where people (not me, but plenty of other people...) seem to encounter wild garlic. Spot it by its strong smell and long leaves. It tends to grow abundantly, but even so try not to strip a patch bare – leave some for others to enjoy.

Shop

- Make sure the leaves are perkily green, and not at all slimy. Any flower on the stems means they are a little older, but that's more than okay when the flowers are a treat in their own right.

Store

- Washed wild garlic can be stored in damp kitchen paper in the fridge, but use soon.

Ways to Use

The longer wild garlic is cooked the more its flavour will mellow, until eventually it is muted completely. Wild garlic leaves will wilt and shrink when cooked, like spinach does.

To keep real vibrancy to how you enjoy your wild garlic, add it towards the end of cooking:
- A handful of torn wild garlic leaves makes a superb end-of-cooking addition to all kinds of pasta dishes.
- Add torn leaves to wilt in a bowl of freshly cooked new potatoes that are finishing off cooking in their own steam, with some butter and salt.
- Chop wild garlic leaves into an omelette, or add into scrambled eggs.
- A large pot of cooked lentils will love having some wild garlic leaves added in at the end. Same for a rice or pearl barley risotto.
- Wilt leaves in at the end of cooking a spring soup.

Then for when you want your wild garlic a little subtler, cook it a little longer:
- Tear into a pie filling of other spring produce for gentle flavour through the pie.
- Bake leaves on top of white fish in the oven, with butter/oil over.
- Chop into the stuffing for a rolled pork loin or lamb leg.
- Knead chopped wild garlic into focaccia dough, then use more to add to its dimples before baking. Try the same with pizza dough.
- Blitz into a pesto, salsa verde or chimichurri.

Small or sliced leaves can be frittered like the elderflower on page 283, or tempura'd as on page 280. Do the same with the elegant wild garlic flowers – or scatter them across spring salads and tarts, where they'll bring both beauty and flavour.

When a recipe calls for using just the leaf, leaving redundant wild garlic stems, use those like you would a garlic clove to chop and cook down into the base of a dish, to stuff the cavity of whole fish or a chicken, or to infuse soups and sauces.

Flavour Partners

Well this is very easy. You already know what garlic goes with: pretty much everything. That said, wild garlic will – like so much of spring's produce – find its happiest flavour affinities with things that are in season at the same time. The **Asparagus, Hot-smoked Trout and Pea Shoot Tart** of page 270 would be lovely with some chopped wild garlic leaves added in. Try roasting asparagus with wild garlic leaves added towards the end of the roasting time and seasonal soft herbs such as **tarragon**, **mint** or **oregano** added, too.

Blanch spears of **purple sprouting broccoli**, then toss them in a hot pan of **olive oil** with **anchovies** and torn wild garlic leaves, before adding **crème fraîche** and **pasta**. Or PSB spears into a hot wok with **sesame oil**, scramble in some beaten **eggs** and wild garlic leaves, then finish with **soy sauce** and **sesame seeds**.

Wrap **plaice** or **trout** fillets in wild garlic leaves before baking, making sure there's plenty of **butter** around to stop things drying out in the oven. Add a few slivers of **spring onion (scallion)** to serve.

Switch wild garlic for some of the **spinach** in a spanakopita (or any other filo) pie. It'll especially enjoy having lots of **preserved lemon** chopped into the filling, too.

My favourite wild garlic sauce comes with thanks to Italian food writer Anna Del Conte: Blitz around 350g (12oz) wild garlic leaves with 200g (7oz) **bread**, 2 tsp **Dijon mustard** and 150ml (5fl oz) **extra-virgin olive oil**. Season, store in the fridge, and reach for it whenever you want to give anything a garlicky lick.

More flavour thoughts: **Bacon**; **broad (fava) beans**; **brown shrimps**; **chicken**; **chorizo**; **duck**; **fennel**; **lamb**; **lime**; **morels**; **mussels**; **new potatoes**; **nutmeg**; **orange**; **pancetta**; **peas**; **pork**; **prawns**; **sherry vinegar**; **sorrel**; **tahini**.

Preserve

Freeze: Freeze washed wild garlic leaves just as they are. They'll wilt, but they were going to do that anyway as soon as you cooked them. Use straight from frozen or quickly blanch in boiling water to defrost.

In oil: Find any favourite pesto recipe that uses the classic basil, and switch that for wild garlic. The pesto will keep in the fridge or you can freeze it.

In butter: Chop wild garlic leaves and mix with soft butter. Roll into logs, wrap and freeze.

Wild Garlic Farls

What's a farl? Try this: They're a bit like a potato cake, flattened, and crossed with a crumpet. If that doesn't send you running to the kitchen....

Spring's new potatoes are not the thing to use here (wild garlic comes into season slightly before they do, anyway). You need instead the floury, mashing qualities of the last of the maincrops. By this point in their cooking cycle I've usually had enough of mash, but am very happy to take it when made into a dough, mixed with wild garlic, and gently fried.

Serve as, or with, breakfast. Or for a lunch/starter with some quick-pickled radishes (see page 72) and soft young goats' cheese.

Farls are also a good way of using up any leftover mash, gauging the quantities of added flour needed to get the dough texture just right.

Serves 4, with 2 farls each
40g (1½oz) wild garlic
500g (1lb 2 oz) floury potatoes
   (maincrop)
50g (2oz) butter, plus extra for cooking
   and serving

50g (2oz) plain (all-purpose) flour,
   plus extra as needed
¼ tsp baking powder
salt and black pepper

Pull the garlic leaves away from their stems, finely chop the leaves and set aside.

Peel the potatoes, cut into equal-sized chunks, and put into a medium saucepan. Cover with cold water, add salt, and simmer for 15 minutes, or until the potatoes are tender. Drain, return the potatoes to the pan and sit uncovered over a low heat for 30 seconds for them to dry. Take off the heat, add the butter and mash with a potato masher/ricer. Make the mash as smooth as you can.

Transfer the mash to a medium mixing bowl and add the flour, baking powder and chopped wild garlic leaves. Season well. Work it into a smooth dough that easily comes away from the sides of the bowl, adding more flour if you need to.

Dust a work surface and rolling pin with flour. Cut the dough in half, then roll one half into a sort-of circle, about 20cm (8in) in diameter and 5mm (¼in) thick. Cut it into quarters.

Set a large frying pan over a medium heat and melt a small piece of butter in it. Carefully lift each farl into the pan and cook for 3 minutes, or until turning golden, then carefully turn over and do the same on the other side. Lift onto a warm plate and serve straight away with butter on top, or keep them in a warm 75°C fan/200°F/ gas ¼ oven while you repeat the cooking for the other half of dough.

WASTE TIPS: Potato peelings (page 341), Wild garlic stems (page 341)

Lamb Cutlets, Samphire and Wild Garlic

There's a lot to love about this recipe: It is fast; it is deeply tasty; and it brings together a winning combination of great meat, punchy seasonal greens and a delicious, lightly creamy, almost broth-like sauce.

Serve with rice, potatoes, or just as it is. The lamb cutlets are definitely best eaten with your fingers to get at every morsel of meat.

Serves 2 as a main

2 tbsp olive oil
2 oregano sprigs
4 lamb cutlets
20g (¾oz) butter
125ml (4fl oz) white wine

80g (3oz) samphire
40g (1½oz) wild garlic
¼ orange
3 tbsp crème fraîche
salt and black pepper

Heat the oil in a large frying pan over a medium heat, then add the oregano sprigs so they can release their flavour into the oil. After about a minute, add the cutlets to the pan – put them in fat-side down to get that crisped up. Cook for 1½ minutes, then lay the cutlets down on their sides and season. Turn after 2 minutes, then season the other sides and cook for 2 minutes more. Lift the cutlets onto a dish, cover, and set aside somewhere warm. Discard the oregano sprigs.

Melt the butter in the same pan. Pour in the wine and let it bubble for a minute, then stir in the samphire and wild garlic. Squeeze over the juice of the orange, cook the greens just long enough for them to wilt, then stir in the crème fraîche.

Divide the samphire, wild garlic and sauce between plates, sit the cutlets on top and finish with plenty of freshly ground black pepper. Serve straight away.

WASTE TIPS: Herb stems (see Stocks, page 340; Soft Herbs, page 241), Orange (see Citrus, page 338)

Gooseberries

Spring – Summer

There's an old photo I came across recently of me aged eight or so, in our garden, standing back as my dad scrabbled around in our gooseberry patch to pick the fruits he'd then put into the bowl I'm clutching. We didn't grow much produce – just rhubarb, apples, gooseberries. The pie and crumble fruits, and I think there is little coincidence there. My dad would have risked any number of gooseberry bush scratches to get at the best fruit for my mum to turn into one of her special puddings.

In that photo it looks like a hot, hot day. Which makes me think the gooseberries would have been at the sweeter edge of their life, benefitting from weeks of warmth bringing out their sugars and softening them up. When they first come in the spring, gooseberries can be mouth-puckeringly tart. In a good way. In a way that (however much my dad might have protested to the contrary) lends them towards sweet and savoury uses alike.

Dessert varieties of gooseberry are becoming increasingly popular. For obvious reasons. So sweet they can be eaten raw, straight off the bush or out of the punnet. You can use them in all the ways you would the tart gooseberries, just knowing they are sweeter.

Don't be fooled into thinking red gooseberries are necessarily sweeter than the green ones. They look like they should be, and they might be, but they also might not be. Try one if you're not sure. You'll know quickly enough.

Shop

- Markets, farm shops and small grocers are your best bet early in the season. As spring turns into summer, supermarkets are more likely to have gooseberries in stock.
- The market/farm shop/grocer options are also where you are more likely to be able to find out how tart or sweet the gooseberries are. Ask – or ask to taste.
- Frozen gooseberries are a more than decent alternative when/where it is hard to buy fresh ones. Their mushier texture is no problem at all for all the ways to come of cooking gooseberries.

Store

– Keep them in the fridge, unwashed and not yet topped-and-tailed (see below...).

Ways to Use

First thing to do is trim off ('top and tail') the gooseberry tufts of flower and stem.
Use a small sharp knife to just nick those away. Then wash the berries.

Sweet

Most of my gooseberries still head for pies and crumbles. Put them in whole
with your choice of flavour partners, and sugar to sweeten. Remember that tart
gooseberries – especially in the early spring – will need more sugar than the dessert
or later-season fruits.

To loosen gooseberries up but retain their shape: Poach the gooseberries for a few
minutes in a pan with a little water and sugar, just long enough so that they soften
and sweeten but don't collapse. Cooked like this they can be added to sweet muffins
or folded into the batter of a pound/madeira cake before baking. Use them to top a
pavlova (see page 331). Call them a compôte and enjoy accordingly.

For a smooth gooseberry purée: Fully poach the fruit until collapsing, then either
blend or push through a sieve. You're then well on your way to making the gooseberry
curd on page 331, or could use the purée in savoury and sweet sauces.

Loosened or fully puréed gooseberries give you texture options for folding into a
whipped cream/custard/Greek yoghurt fool; for sorbets or ice creams.

Savoury

For savoury dishes, gooseberries similarly bring choices of whether to use raw and
whole, loosened, or puréed.

Sit raw gooseberries into the dimples of a focaccia dough before baking.

Chop raw gooseberries into cooked-down onions and garlic, mix with breadcrumbs,
herbs and plenty of seasoning, and use as a stuffing for meat or fish.

Add a handful of gooseberries in at the end of cooking, again, fish or meats. The
gooseberries will loosen in the heat of the pan or dish, taking on board the flavours
they find there and releasing their own to become a loose sauce/side.

Smooth, puréed gooseberry sauces make for handy accompaniments to oily fish,
or most meats. With some vinegar or horseradish added for real punch.

Finally – as if gooseberries weren't quite tart enough on their own, but for some of
us the tarter the better... – give them a quick-pickle. Halve or quarter, follow the basic
principles of page 72, and try in a salad or with rock oysters.

Flavour Partners

Mother Nature nails it once again. Gooseberries come into the season at the exact same time as **elderflower** and together they take on a magical muskiness that is the heady essence of the best days of spring or early summer. A few ways to make the most of their flavour affinity:

– Fritter the elderflower heads as on page 283 to serve with whatever **meat** or **fish** you are having a loose gooseberry sauce with.

– Add a little sugar to that fritter batter (page 283 again) and you have a sweet elderflower fritter to serve with any kind of gooseberry tart, ice cream or sorbet.

– Put a whole elderflower head in the pan as you poach gooseberries.

– Add a little elderflower cordial or liqueur to gooseberries in a crumble or pie, or when poaching gooseberries.

Orange blossom water similarly lends gooseberries a floral note for poaching, etc.

Or, even better, **gin**-poached gooseberries bring all the complex aromatics of the booze to play with the tart fruit: Put 250g (9oz) topped-and-tailed gooseberries into a small pan with 50ml (1¾fl oz) gin and 1 tbsp **caster (superfine) sugar**, cover and cook for 5 minutes, or until the gooseberries just start to burst. These are the best partner to page 286's Elderflower Madeleines, any plain cake or **vanilla ice cream**.

Talking of ice cream.... Make a delightfully grown-up scoop using gooseberries' fondness for rich **dairy**. Or serve gooseberry crumbles and pies with the lushest **cream** you can get your hands on. Same with fools – get the good stuff for whatever combination/ratio of whipped cream, **custard** or **plain yoghurt** you are going for. Gooseberry compôte will enjoy **mascarpone**.

Brown sugars, **honey** and **maple syrup** give gooseberries a toffee-esque profile. Just don't go too heavy with the sweetening – much of the joy of gooseberries is in their sweet-and-sour flavour. For a gooseberry **meringue** pie I wouldn't add any sugar at all to the fruit. Simply scatter whole, raw gooseberries into a sweet pastry case, top with meringue, then bake and let the tart berries take the sweet edge off the meringue.

The French call the gooseberry 'groseille à maquereau'. The '**mackerel** berry'. There's good reason for that name and why for centuries it's been a flavour partnership that crops up again and again in cookbooks and on restaurant menus. It works because the sharp fruit cuts through the rich fatty nature of the fish. For the same reasons I love a simple spring lunch of toasted slices of **dark rye bread**, with loose or puréed gooseberries spooned over, and topped with **trout**, **salmon** or **scallops**.

Tart gooseberries' ability to cut through richness and fattiness means they are great with **lamb**, **goose**, **pork** or **duck**. Those partnerships can even take some extra kick or spicing. Perhaps grated fresh **horseradish**, a little **white wine vinegar**, **mustard seeds** or grated **root ginger**.

More flavour thoughts: **Anise**; **basil**; **bay leaves**; **celery**; **champagne**; **cinnamon**; **coconut**; **coriander seeds**; **fennel**; **mint**; **octopus**; **oysters**; **prawns**; **radish**; **sage**; **sea bass**; **stem ginger**; **sweet vermouth**; **tarragon**; **vanilla**.

Preserve

Jam: Gooseberries are very high in pectin so perfect for jamming. Lovely in its own right with one or two of the flavour partners here added, and very useful to add in when making jams from the season's lower-pectin fruits such as strawberries.

Freeze: Gooseberries freeze brilliantly. (As mentioned earlier, I buy bags of frozen ones as happily as fresh.) Any loss of texture barely matters as they will collapse anyway once defrosted and cooked. Lay them out in a single layer on a tray in the freezer, then transfer to bags once frozen.

Gooseberry and Toasted Coconut Pavlova

Tart gooseberries spare the over-sweet blushes of a pavlova by bringing a little edge to the flavour party. This is a beauty of a seasonal dessert 'wow', with flavours of elderflower, bay and coconut all chiming in.

This recipe makes more curd than is needed for the pavlova. That is an intentional and very good thing, most especially for spreading onto toast.

Serves 6–8

For the curd

350g (12oz) gooseberries

25ml (1 tbsp plus 2 tsp) elderflower
  cordial

1 fresh bay leaf

2 whole eggs, plus 2 egg yolks

75g (2½oz) unsalted butter

200g (7oz) caster (superfine) sugar

For the meringue

5 large egg whites

pinch of salt

350g (12oz) caster (superfine) sugar

1½ tsp white wine vinegar

To finish

50g (2oz) coconut chips or flakes

500ml (17fl oz) double (heavy) cream

30g (1oz) icing (confectioners') sugar

25ml (1 tbsp plus 2 tsp) elderflower
  cordial or elderflower liqueur

fresh elderflowers or other edible
  flowers (optional)

recipe continues overleaf...

WASTE TIP: Egg yolks (page 338)

For the curd: Top and tail the gooseberries. Put them into a medium saucepan with the elderflower cordial, 50ml (1¾fl oz) water and the bay leaf. Gently simmer for about 5 minutes and watch for when the gooseberries are just starting to collapse. At that point use a slotted spoon to lift out around 50g (2oz) of the gooseberries and set those aside. Carry on cooking the rest for about another 5 minutes until fully collapsed. Discard the bay leaf, set aside to cool, then push everything in the pan through a fine sieve, really rubbing at the fruit with a spoon to get as much through as possible.

Next, beat the eggs (whole and yolks) in a bowl, adding to them the gooseberry purée, butter and caster sugar. Sit the bowl over a pan of gently simmering water, making sure the base of the bowl isn't touching the water. Stir continuously until it thickens, about 10–12 minutes, then straight away push the curd through a sieve. Pour into a bowl and chill for an hour or so to thicken up.

For the meringue: Preheat the oven to 170°C fan/375°F/gas 5. Line a baking tray with baking paper and draw a circle about 23cm (9in) in diameter on the paper.

Put the egg whites into a scrupulously clean mixing bowl, add a pinch of salt and whisk to create stiff peaks. Whisk in about a third of the caster sugar; then add the rest a spoonful at a time, whisking after each addition. Keep whisking until the meringue is thick and glossy. Fold in the vinegar, then spoon the meringue into the circle on the paper, banking it up at the sides a little.

Place in the oven and immediately turn it down to 135°C fan/300°F/gas 2. Cook for 1 hour, then turn the oven off and do not be tempted to open the door. Leave the pavlova in the oven to cool. From here it can be kept for up to a day in an air-tight container.

To build the pavlova: Toast the coconut chips or flakes in a dry frying pan. Whip the cream with the icing sugar and elderflower cordial/liqueur until thick but not completely stiff. Sit the meringue base on a serving plate. Spoon over enough curd for a base of a few millimetres thick, then spoon over the whipped cream. Finish by scattering over the reserved poached gooseberries, the coconut, more curd and, if using, the elderflowers or other edible flowers to decorate. Serve soon.

Spoon the rest of the curd into sterilised jars and store in the fridge.

Gooseberry Crumble

I think it is important not to mess around too much with a classic gooseberry crumble. Not only because as simple as this it immediately evokes childhood memories, but because it really is so good it doesn't need embellishment.

Serve with cream or ice cream. The elderflower ice cream on page 285 would be an absolute winner for some extra glamour.

Serves 4–6

700g (1lb 9oz) gooseberries

1½ tablespoons light soft brown sugar

1 tbsp cornflour (cornstarch)

For the crumble topping

150g (5oz) plain (all-purpose) flour

80g (3oz) cold butter, plus extra for
    greasing

50g (2oz) ground almonds

75g (2½oz) demerara sugar

75g (2½oz) rolled oats

1 tbsp anise seeds

pinch of salt

For the crumble topping: Put the flour into a mixing bowl. Dice the butter and use your fingers to rub it into the flour until it feels like breadcrumbs. Mix in the ground almonds, demerara sugar, rolled oats and anise seeds, add a pinch of salt, then set aside.

Preheat the oven to 180°C fan/400°F/gas 6. Grease a 1.5–2 litre (6–8 cup) baking dish with extra butter.

Top and tail the gooseberries and put into the baking dish. Toss with the soft brown sugar and cornflour. Top with the crumble mix and bake for 30–40 minutes until bubbling and browned.

Let it cool down a little before serving. It's also very good cold.

A few feasting menu ideas

Asparagus, Hot-smoked Trout and Pea Shoot Tart;
Frisée, New Potato and Radish Salad

Gooseberry and Toasted Coconut Pavlova

Broccoli Tempura with White Miso Mayonnaise

Lamb Cutlets, Samphire and Wild Garlic

Rhubarb Sponge with Orange Blossom Crème Fraîche
(from Winter chapter)

Smacked Radishes with Sesame, Sumac and Mint

Roast Chicken with Roasted Asparagus
and Purple Sprouting Broccoli;
Braised Little Gems with Shallots, Pancetta and Peas

Elderflower Madeleines with Gin-poached Gooseberries

Wild Garlic Farls with soft young goats' cheese

Trout with Watercress Hollandaise; Roast New Potatoes and
Radishes with Anchovies and Herbs

Smacked Radishes with Sesame, Sumac and Mint

Spring Herb and Goats' Cheese Soufflé

Gooseberry Crumble and sweet frittered elderflowers

To drink

For the table

Sherry, Elderflower and Orange Blossom Collins

For 1, to scale up
100ml (3½fl oz) fino or manzanilla sherry
25ml (1 tbsp plus 2 tsp) Elderflower Cordial
  (see page 285)
1 tsp orange blossom water
ice
75ml (2½fl oz) sparkling or soda water,
  or more to taste
sprig of lemon balm or lemon thyme

Mix together the sherry, elderflower cordial and orange blossom water. Pour into a rocks or highball glass, with ice. Pour over the sparkling water, stir, then taste and add more water if preferred. Garnish with the herb sprig.

- Lay lengths of magnolia along the table. Similarly, lengths of pussy willow, lily of the valley, or Canterbury bells.

- Arrange irises or peonies in low vases. Float the heads of camelias in shallow bowls.

- Tulips that have already bent over will work better than ones standing too tall.

- Arrange spring herbs along the table, or on place settings. Set a platter of herbs on the table (see page 309 for more on that).

- Chive flowers are beautiful, but be a little careful as the stems will smell of onion/garlic and (especially for indoor feasting) that may not be quite the desired effect.

335

Spring

Waste Tips

Anchovies: The oil accompanying preserved anchovies is fabulously flavourful. It may not be the best quality oil, but it is too good to waste. Whenever you reach the end of a jar or tin of anchovies, use the oil in the beginning of whatever you cook next that will benefit from a layer of anchovy flavour (that will be pretty much anything savoury). Make anchovy butter with any last ones in a jar/tin – simply crush them into soft butter. Roll, wrap, and fridge/freeze.

Bread: Keep a bag/container in the freezer to put blitzed breadcrumbs into. Use straight from the freezer for stuffings; into burgers; for the recipes on pages 228 and 272.

Citrus (bergamot; lemon; lime; orange): Once you have zested away the fruit's protective outer layer it will start to dry out. Juice it soon, and if you have no immediate use for the juice you can freeze it. Ice-cube trays are good for these relatively small amounts. Freeze slices of citrus fruits to use in drinks. The section on oranges (pages 237–42) has ideas that can be applied to the other citruses on what you could do with leftover pieces of fruit/peel.

Deep-frying oil: Let it cool before doing anything with it, then strain it through muslin (cheesecloth) or a coffee filter. Store in a sealable jar, labelled with the date and what you used it for. The oil can then be used one more time, within 6 weeks, and for cooking something similar as for its first frying.

Duck: After roasting, pour the duck fat out of the tin and keep to use for roasting other vegetables or perhaps some sausages. (Note that the duck fat in the recipe on page 234 will be infused with the dukkah spicing.) The backbone and giblets of a duck will make great stock (see overleaf).

Egg whites: I like to make mayonnaise; ergo I like to make meringue, mousses and macarons with the many egg whites I have left behind from the mayo. Freeze the whites in an ice-cube tray where each space in the tray equals 1 egg white.

Egg yolks: Use within a day or two for mayonnaises, custards and ice creams. Or to preserve them: Cure in salt. Sit yolks on a bed of fine salt, then fully cover with more fine salt. Put them into the fridge for 8 hours, then wash the salt off, dry them, and sit the yolks on a rack in a 60°C fan/150°C/gas ¼ oven until hard and dry (it'll take a couple of hours). Keep in the fridge for up to 3 months and grate over pastas, salads, vegetables and more, for a significant umami hit.

Feta cheese: Don't throw away the brine from feta. It is salty and creamy with a lactic edge that makes it a lovely addition to salad dressings, as a marinade for meat, or added into the water when boiling rice.

Filo pastry sheets: These freeze (or even re-freeze) well, but if I am left with just a few I often make Sweet Filo Crisps: Preheat the oven to 200°C fan/425°F/gas 7. Line a baking tray with baking paper. Lay on it a piece of filo, brush with melted butter, sift over icing (confectioners') sugar and perhaps a little ground cinnamon, and repeat with two more layers. Give the top layer of pastry a thicker dusting of icing sugar, cut into strips/squares and tease them slightly apart, then bake for 10–15 minutes until golden and crisp. Serve warm, or store in an airtight container for up to 2 days.

Horseradish: I use fresh horseradish a lot, and always seem to end up grating off more of the root than I need for a recipe. The happy outcome of that is stirring it through whatever crème fraîche or full-fat Greek yoghurt I might also have around, giving it a good squeeze of lemon and lots of black pepper, then keeping that in the fridge for a ready-made horseradish sauce. Note also that horseradish – like fresh root **ginger** – will keep brilliantly in the freezer to grate straight from there without any bother to peel first.

Labneh juices: The whey that yoghurt leaves behind in labneh-making (see page 252) can be used in the same ways as feta brine above.

Parmesan rind: Always keep the last bit of Parmesan to add in as a whole piece to soups, stocks, or any dish that in its cooking will love getting every last bit of Parmesan deliciousness out of the rind. Just remember to take the limp, used piece out at the end before serving.

Vegetables

See also the individual produce profiles that are full of ways to use any excess.

For stocks

- Keep in the freezer a bag or container into which you can easily put the (washed if necessary) peelings and trimmings of vegetables or herbs to use as the basis of making stocks. As the seasons roll round what you add to the freezer bag will change, giving the stocks a natural seasonality of flavour.
- Put the trimmings straight from the freezer into a large pan, cover with an equal volume of water, add salt and whatever fresh herbs might be around. (Add poultry bones for a meat stock.) Simmer for about an hour, strain, and that's your stock ready to use/freeze.

Good things to use: **Asparagus** ends; **broad (fava) bean** pods; **carrot** peelings; **cavolo nero** ribs; **celeriac** peelings; **celery** trimmings; **cucumber** peel, seeds and core; **fennel** trimmings; **garden pea** pods; **soft herb** leaves and stems (e.g. **basil, coriander (cilantro), mint, oregano, parsley**); **leek** trimmings; **onion** skins; **parsnip** peelings; **pumpkin and other squash** fibres/skin (not flesh); **shallot** skins; **spring onion (scallion)** trimmings; **sweet pepper** (capsicum) trimmings; **tomato** skins, seeds and vines; **woody herb** leaves and stems (e.g. **rosemary, thyme**).

Beyond stocks

Asparagus ends: The woody ends that get trimmed off can be used to infuse flavour into soups and sauces.

Cauliflower: Its outer leaves can be used for kimchi – if they are very large and/or gnarly, roast them first. The central core is good to grate into a slaw, or cook off in any way you might the florets themselves.

Cavolo nero/Kale ribs: Keep these in the fridge to finely chop and use over the next few days when you're cooking down onion/garlic.

Potato peelings: No good for stock, but great for potato-peel crisps: Preheat the oven to 210°C fan/450°F/gas 8. Lay the peelings in a single layer on a roasting tray. Give them oil, salt and pepper, then bake for 20 minutes or so until crisp.

Pumpkins and other squash: Wash and use the seeds (pepitas) as on page 143. Any excess roasted pumpkin can be turned into a purée, used as a filling for filo tarts, or blitzed into a soup. See pages 141–3 for more ideas.

Soft herbs: The leaves and/or stalks of soft herbs can be blitzed into herb-infused oils. Blanch herb sprigs for barely 10 seconds in very hot water, then run under cold water and delicately dry in a cloth. Put the herbs – stalk and all – into a blender with the oil. Two or three bushy sprigs per 150ml (5fl oz) oil. Blitz, then strain through a fine sieve/muslin (cheesecloth). Pour into a sterilised bottle and store out of direct sunlight. I like to put a fresh (blanched) sprig of the chosen herb in the bottle. For prettiness as much as to remind me what it is. (I seldom remember to label them, but I know that I should and so should you.)

Sprouts: Don't be tempted to keep sprout trimmings for stock – they will add nothing good in terms of taste or smell. Roast, use in a slaw, or head them to the composter.

Wild garlic leaf stems: Use to infuse sauce with garlic flavour, to stuff a chicken, or chop and cook them down like you might a garlic clove.

Bibliography

To research this book I have immersed myself in the work of so many food writers. What a joy and privilege. These are the writings that have inspired these pages.

Modern Cookery for Private Families, Eliza Acton

Strawberry Pre- and Post-Harvest Management Techniques for Higher Fruit Quality, Md Asaduzzaman, Toshiki Asao

delicious magazine, editor Karen Barnes

Jikoni, Ravinder Bhogal

The Scented Kitchen, Frances Bissell

La Vita è Dolce, Letitia Clark

How to make the perfect..., Felicity Cloake *Guardian* columns

The Vinegar Cupboard and *Borough Market: The Knowledge*, Angela Clutton

Four Seasons Cookery Book, Margaret Costa

Success with Poultry, Grant M Curtis

Herb and *Sour,* Mark Diacono

A Book of Mediterranean Food and *Summer Cooking*, Elizabeth David

Amaretto, Apple Cake and Artichokes, Anna Del Conte

Every Grain of Rice, Fuchsia Dunlop

River Cottage A-Z, Hugh Fearnley-Whittingstall, Pam Corbin, Mark Diacono, Nikki Duffy, Nick Fisher, Steven Lamb, Tim Maddams, Gill Meller, John Wright

River Cottage Fish Book, Hugh Fearnley-Whittingstall and Nick Fisher

The Nutmeg Trail, Eleanor Ford

Zaika, Romy Gill

The Whole Vegetable, Sophie Gordon

Jane Grigson's Fruit Book and *Jane Grigson's Vegetable Book*, Jane Grigson

Cooking with Vegetables, Marika Hanbury-Tenison

Food in England, Dorothy Hartley

Nistisima, Georgina Hayden

Eat Green, Melissa Hemsley

The Complete Nose to Tail, A Kind of British Cooking, Fergus Henderson and Justin Piers Gellatly

Salt, Sugar, Smoke, Diana Henry

Summer Kitchens, Olia Hercules

Ken Hom's Chinese Cookery, Ken Hom

A Matter of Taste, Sylvia Windle Humphrey

Eating for Pleasure, People & Planet, Tom Hunt

Sardine, Alex Jackson

Temperate and Subtropical Fruit Production, Edited by David Jackson, Norman Looney, Michael Morley-Bunker and Graham Thiele

One Pot, Pan, Planet and *The Modern Cook's Year*, Anna Jones

Sight, Smell, Touch, Taste, Sound, Sybil Kapoor

Taste Tibet, Julie Kleeman and Yeshi Jampa

Feeding Britain, Tim Lang

Larousse Gastronomique

How to be a Domestic Goddess and *How to Eat*, Nigella Lawson

Cooking, Jeremy Lee

The Almanac, Lia Leendertz

Mother Tongue, Gurdeep Loyal

The Rich Tradition of European Peasant Cookery and *Potting, Preserving and Pickling*, Elisabeth Luard

Ices and Ice Creams, Agnes B Marshall

Quinces: Growing & Cooking, Jane McMorland Hunter and Sue Dunster

The Scots Kitchen, F. Marian McNeill

Gather, Gill Meller

Herring Tales, Donald S Murray

Polpo, Russell Norman

The Hedgerow Handbook, Adele Nozedar

Flavour, Yotam Ottolenghi and Ixta Belfrage

Jerusalem, Yotam Ottolenghi and Sami Tamimi

Citrus and *Leaf*, Catherine Phipps

13 Foods That Shape Our World, Alex Renton

Market Life Borough Market magazine, editor Mark Riddaway

Notes from a Small Kitchen Island, Debora Robertson

Five Quarters, Rachel Roddy

A New Book of Middle Eastern Food ar *Med*, Claudia Roden

Eating to Extinction, Dan Saladino

Handbook of Vegetable Science and Technology, editors D. K. Salunkhe, S. S. Kadam

The Flavour Thesaurus and *Lateral Cooking*, Niki Segnit

Rambutan, Cynthia Shanmugalingam

The Flavor Equation, Nik Sharma

From The Veg Patch, Kathy Slack

Tender – Volumes I and II, Nigel Slater

The Borough Market Cookbook and *Crave*, Ed Smith

Hungry City, Carolyn Steel

Forgotten Fruits, Christopher Stocks

A Platter of Figs and Other Recipes, David Tanis

Falastin, Sami Tamimi and Tara Wigle

Home Cookery Year, Claire Thomson

Salt & Time, Alissa Timoshkina

Good Things in England, Florence Wh*

In Praise of Veg, Alice Zaslavsky

Index

Index

Acknowledgements

The team on this book have been absolutely extraordinary. Led by Céline Hughes, the most creative and collaborative of publishers. Céline, I shall forever think of you when I go past the ducks in Grovelands Park! I could not be more grateful to you – and all at Murdoch Books – for your belief in *Seasoning* from the very beginning.

Georgie Hewitt, our designer, who has put together every aspect of this book's design with such flair and care. It is a beauty, thanks to you - and to Georgina Luck our illustrator, and Patricia Niven our photographer. Georgina, you were the illustrator I had in mind from the start and I am so happy you said yes! Patsy, I think your shots are breathtaking. Those January King cabbages are definitely going up on the wall. (Thanks, too, to photography assistants Sam Reeves and Georgia Quinn.)

The food styling team of Valerie Berry and Hanna Miller made my food look glorious, and I've learnt that the biggest compliment in food writing is Valerie giving her approval to a dish. Every night after the recipe shoots I couldn't sleep for looking at the photos and the magical work of Georgie, Patsy, Valerie, Hanna, and brilliant props stylist Jennifer Kay. You completely nailed the look I wanted.

Thanks to my editor, Emily Preece-Morrison. Your diligence and directness have been hugely appreciated.

I have tried to acknowledge particular recipe inspirations where relevant, and listed in the bibliography are many more of the food writers whose work has inspired and informed mine. Additionally, thanks to Russell Norman who I knew was the guy to go to when I got into an Italian dumpling quandary; to Marian Joyce for some last-minute recipe testing; and Patricia Gutierrez for arranque recipe wrangling.

I am very lucky to have local to me some terrific food suppliers who never let me down when I need things for recipes: especially Pat at Green Lanes Fisheries, and Alex at Peatchey Butchers.

Sabhbh Curran, my lovely agent at Curtis Brown. Thank you for shepherding the development of this book, and always giving me the time to air whatever worry or idea I can't quite shift. Your smart, cool, calm counsel is a joy. Thanks also to Felicity Blunt - for putting Sabhbh and me together, and for coming up with the book title.

And my James. Nobody could be more supportive. This book has been a long time in the dreaming and making, but all the way through you have given me the space to talk about it whenever I wanted to, knew when not to ask how it was going, and always had faith in it and me.

About the Author

Angela Clutton is an award-winning food writer, cook and presenter. Her first book, *The Vinegar Cupboard*, won the Jane Grigson Trust Award, was a double winner at the Guild of Food Writers Awards, and was the Debut Cookery Book of the Year at the Fortnum & Mason Food and Drink Awards.

Angela has worked extensively with Borough Market as presenter of the *Borough Talks* podcast, host of the Borough Market Cookbook Club, and writing recipes. Her second book, *Borough Market: The Knowledge*, was a finalist at the Guild of Food Writers Awards.

Angela is the co-director of the British Library's annual Food Season of events. Broadcast work includes the Channel 5 *Inside...* series.

She lives in London with her husband, James. *Seasoning* is Angela's third book. @angela_clutton

Published in 2024 by Murdoch Books,
an imprint of Allen & Unwin

Murdoch Books UK
Ormond House
26–27 Boswell Street
London WC1N 3JZ
Phone: +44 (0) 20 8785 5995
murdochbooks.co.uk
info@murdochbooks.co.uk

Murdoch Books Australia
Cammeraygal Country
83 Alexander Street
Crows Nest NSW 2065
Phone: +61 (0)2 8425 0100
murdochbooks.com.au
info@murdochbooks.com.au

For corporate orders and custom publishing,
contact our business development team at
salesenquiries@murdochbooks.com.au

Publisher: Céline Hughes
Project Editor: Emily Preece-Morrison
Designer: Georgina Hewitt
Photographer: Patricia Niven
Illustrator: Georgina Luck
Prop Stylist: Jennifer Kay
Food Stylist: Valerie Berry
Production Director, UK: Niccolò De Bianchi
Production Director, Australia: Lou Playfair

ISBN 978 1 922616555

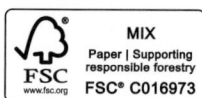 A catalogue record for this
book is available from the
National Library of Australia

Colour reproduction by Born Group, London, UK
Printed by 1010 Printing International Limited, China

OVEN GUIDE: You may find cooking times vary depending on the oven
you are using. The recipes in this book are based on fan-assisted oven
temperatures. For non-fan-assisted ovens, as a general rule, set the oven
temperature to 20°C (35°F) higher than indicated in the recipe.

TABLESPOON MEASURES: We have used 15ml (3 teaspoon)
tablespoon measures.

10 9 8 7 6 5 4 3 2 1

MIX
Paper | Supporting
responsible forestry
FSC® C016973